*How Jews
Became White Folks*

How Jews Became White Folks

and What That Says about Race in America

KAREN BRODKIN

Rutgers University Press
New Brunswick, New Jersey, and London

An earlier version of chapter 1 appeared under the title "How Did Jews
Become White Folks?" in Steven Gregory and Roger Sanjek, eds. *Race*. New
Brunswick, N.J.: Rutgers University Press, 1994.
Some material in chapter 4 was previously published in "Euro-ethnic
Working-class Women's Community Culture," *Frontiers* 13, 4, 1994.

Brodkin, Karen.
    How Jews became white folks and what that says about race in
America / Karen Brodkin.
        p.   cm.
    Includes bibliographical references and index.
    ISBN 0-8135-2589-6 (hardcover : alk. paper). — ISBN 0-8135-2590-X
(pbk.)
    1. Jews—United States—Identity.   2. Jews—United States—Social
conditions.   3. United States—Race relations.   4. United States—
Ethnic relations.   I. Title.
E184.J5B7415   1998
305.892'4073—DC21   98-22606
                                                         CIP

British Cataloging-in-Publication information

For my parents,
Sylvia and Jacob Brodkin

CONTENTS □

ACKNOWLEDGMENTS □

Writing about Jewishness was the last thing I expected to do when I started this project. What began as a rather distant study of the ways that race, ethnicity, class, and gender combine to construct Americans (what we used to call a unified theory of race, class, and gender) turned into an exploration of what the changing places and meanings of Jewishness tell us about Americanness. In the interests of full disclosure, readers should know that my qualifications as a Jew—growing up in a secular Jewish family and spending much of my life in leftist academic and political circles—are a mix best described as Jewish lite, Jewish late, or nouveau Jew. I have spent the better part of the last decade fumbling around in libraries, at conferences, and in conversations trying to make my own Jewishness visible and understandable.

Because this book rests heavily on new scholarship from many fields far from my own, I am indebted to the guidance and kindness of more friends and colleagues than I can name. My greatest debt is to the friends and family whose conversation and daily support nurtured this work through its many iterations. This work first "came out" as Jewish in Eloise Klein Healy's writing group. Emily Abel, Edna Bonacich, Carole Browner, Sondra Hale, Sandra Harding, Carollee Howes, Cindy Murphy, Nancy

Naples, and Miriam Silverberg have all helped me in various ways to sort out my less than clear thoughts, and they read the rawest of drafts, often many times. Over the years, Alice Kessler-Harris has been my guide through the thickets of American labor and women's history and has supportively critiqued more drafts than anyone should ever have to. Emily Abel, Cindy Murphy, and Carollee Howes have told me gently when a new draft does or doesn't yet make sense. My parents, Jack and Sylvia Brodkin, have submitted to endless interviews and still found the energy to read drafts of most of the chapters. Conversations about this project with my brother, Henry Brodkin, my sons Benjamin and Daniel Sacks, and my life partner, Carollee Howes, have also given me lots of new insights.

I have depended as well upon a more far-flung network of friends and colleagues. Eileen Boris, Christine Gailey, Richard Lee, Tom Patterson, Dorothy Remy, Sylvia Rodriguez, Lynn Stephen, Ida Susser, Barrie Thorne, David Trigger, and Soon Young Yoon have all read various chapters and offered encouragement. I am grateful for a Canadian critique of an early version of the manuscript by the University of Toronto "study group": Richard Lee, Bonnie McElhinney, Glynnis George, Claudia Vicencio, Michael Levin, Heike Schimkat, and Krystyna Sieciechowicz.

My guides to Jewishness take many forms and don't really come in a separate compartment. Taken together, they have given this book a considerably bigger slice of Jewishness than it would otherwise have had. I am indebted to Rabbi Haim Beliak for years of supportive conversation and critique, and to Mifgash, the study group that he and Miryam Glazer coordinate, for inviting me to discuss parts of this work. Conversations with Sheila Bernard, Bea DeRusha, Gelya Frank, Abra Grupp, Patricia Gumport, Melanie Kaye/Kantrowitz, Carol Lasser, Vivian Price, Nancy Rose, Bert Silverberg, and Victor Wolfenstein have added to my secular Jewish education. Marlie Wasserman and Leslie Mitchner have salted their professional critique with a liberal amount of Jewish education.

I have benefited on all counts from presentations at the Feminist Research Seminar and the anthropology department at the University of California at Los Angeles as well as from talks at the University of California campuses at Irvine and Berkeley, the University of Toronto, Franklin and Marshall College, the University of Pennsylvania at Millersville, the New School for Social Research, the Graduate Center of City University of New York, Temple University, the Columbia Seminar on Racial and Ethnic Pluralism, New York University, Fordham University at Lincoln Center, the University of Western Australia, Adelaide University, Griffith University, and the University of Sydney. Marlene Arnold, Katya Gibel Azoulay, Carol Counihan, Mike Davis, Jeff Decker, Sandra Harding, Nicholas Harney, Bobby Hill, Max and Estelle Novak, Tom Patterson, Vivian Price, Paul Ritterband, Gail Sansbury, Chaim Seidler-Feller, Nancy Strout, Jim Taggart, Barrie Thorne, and Bonnie Urciuoli all directed me to wonderful sources and provided good conversation. My thanks go also to Ellen Kraut-Hasegawa for suggesting the cover art.

Grants from UCLA's Academic Senate as well as a sabbatical have helped support the research. Final writing was greatly facilitated by a Sir Allen Sewell Fellowship at Griffith University in Brisbane. Over the years, I have benefited from some very able research assistance by Allie Pang, Maria Soldatenko, and Sharon Bays; as well as more recent help from Ellie Zucker, Salorina Motley, and Claudia Dermartirosian.

Finally, but not least, at Rutgers, working with Brigitte Goldstein, my production editor, was pure pleasure; and Arri Sendzimir did a superb copyediting job. And my thanks to my editors, Marlie Wasserman and Leslie Mitchner, at Rutgers University Press go far beyond the usual. They have been a writer's dream, supportive, critical, and nudging at every stage.

*How Jews
Became White Folks*

Introduction □

This book is about the ways our racial-ethnic backgrounds—
American Jewishness in particular—as well as our class and
gender, contribute to the making of social identity in the United
States.[1] We fashion identities in the context of a wider conversation about American nationhood—to whom it belongs and
what belonging means. Race and ethnicity, class, gender, and
sexuality have been staple ingredients of this conversation. They
are salient aspects of social being from which economic practices,
political policies, and popular discourses create "Americans."
Because all these facets of social being have such significant
meanings on a national scale, they also have significant consequences for the life chances of individuals and groups, which is
why they are such important parts of our social and political
identities.

I focus on American Jews partly for personal reasons and
partly because the history of Jews in the United States is a history of racial change that provides useful insights on race in
America. Prevailing classifications at a particular time have
sometimes assigned us to the white race, and at other times have
created an off-white race for Jews to inhabit. Those changes in
our racial assignment have shaped the ways in which American
Jews who grew up in different eras have constructed their
ethnoracial identities. Those changes give us a kind of double

vision that comes from racial middleness: of an experience of marginality vis-à-vis whiteness, and an experience of whiteness and belonging vis-à-vis blackness.[2]

Historical changes in Jews' racial assignment make for different constructions of Jewish political selves within the same family. Consequently, we may experience our racial selves in multiple ways, even within our own families. One of my teenage pranks showed me the differences between my parents' racial experience and mine. As a child, I spent summer vacations at a lake in Vermont in a bungalow colony of Jewish families whose adult members were mostly New York City public school teachers. Late one summer night, a group of us tied up all the rowboats that belonged to our group of families out in the middle of the lake. We looked forward to parental surprise when they woke up, but we weren't prepared for their genuine alarm: This could only be an anti-Semitic act by angry Yankees. What did it portend for our group? We were surprised on two counts: that the adults didn't assume we had done it, since we were always playing practical jokes, and that they thought our Jewishness mattered to Vermont Yankees.

The execution of the Rosenbergs and the Nazi Holocaust had left their indelible mark on our parents. They were all children of immigrants who grew up in New York in the 1920s and 1930s, which was the high tide of American anti-Semitism, a time when Jews were not assigned to the white side of the American racial binary, as we shall see in chapter 1.[3] We, their children, grew up as white, middle-class suburbanites, unaffected by the barriers that kept our parents out of certain jobs and neighborhoods. Their collective alarm connected us in a powerful way to the pervasive anti-Semitic environment that stigmatized them racially, but it was not the world in which we spent most of our time.

In relation to Vermonters and other mainstream white folks, my parents and grandparents lived in a time when Jews were not white. They expected that particular racial assignment to shape their relationship with such people. This was the larger context within which they formed their sense of Jewish ethno-racial identity.

It is important to make a conceptual distinction between ethnoracial assignment and ethnoracial identity. Assignment is about popularly held classifications and their deployment by those with national power to make them matter economically, politically, and socially to the individuals classified. We construct ethnoracial identities ourselves, but we do it within the context of ethnoracial assignment.

However, even though ethnoracial assignment and ethno-racial identity are conceptually distinct, they are also deeply in-terrelated. The Jewish world of my childhood was a product of the community that anti-Semitism produced, and my Jewish identity has its roots there. However, because my racial assign-ment differed from that of my parents, so too did the ethnoracial content of my Jewish identity. Different generations in my fam-ily have different ethnoracial identities. My sons, who did not grow up in a Jewish milieu, tell me they don't really think of themselves as Jewish but rather as generic whites. When I asked my parents, Sylvia and Jack Brodkin, what they thought of that, they both gave me a funny look. "We're Jewish," was my father's answer, to which my mother added that, yes, she supposed that was white, but Jewish was how she saw herself. I see myself as both—white and Jewish.

The "diversity" of ethnoracial identities in my family and the changes in the ethnoracial assignment of American Jews made me curious about the relationship of Jewish political identity to the racial and class positions of American Jewry. On the one hand, as I argue in chapter 1, Jews were granted many institu-tional privileges of white racial assignment after World War II. They were also among the economically most upwardly mobile of the European ethnic groups. On the other hand, and despite being relatively successful in material terms, many American Jews tend to think of themselves as distinctly liberal politically, as invested in social justice and in identification with the un-derdog, and, sometimes, as not white.

What are the roots of that self-construction, and to what extent has it really been preserved in times of Jewish prosperity? How are continuities between generations maintained—indeed, are they maintained?—in the context of a larger American culture that routinely erases history in its pursuit of the new and the novel? These questions emerged from trying to understand my own family's upward mobility in late 1940s and 1950s New York. We moved spatially and socially from a Jewish neighborhood in Brooklyn to a new, white suburb on Long Island.

In retrospect, I see that debates over assimilation, womanhood, and the nature of Jewish identity were part of the fabric of our daily lives. When my mother's mother, Rose Schechter, came to live with us after my grandfather died, her presence brought an older construction of Jewish womanhood into the house and engaged us emotionally with it. What did it mean to be a Jewish woman, and how did that differ from being a white or mainstream one? Why were middle-class Jews Democrats, and some of our equally middle-class Protestant neighbors Republican?

For the last two decades I have interviewed my parents episodically and informally to find answers to these questions. Our conversations and taped interviews shaped my readings and led me to explore the relationship of Jewishness to political identity. Still, one family is less than a full slice of Jewishness, especially for a people who say of themselves, "Two Jews, three opinions." Over a period of several years, almost like a proper anthropologist, I tried out ideas on my "informants," my Jewish friends, then on colleagues when I gave academic talks. I suppose this method is a slightly unorthodox combination of participant observation, insider ethnography, and grounded theory.

My family is exemplary in its ordinariness. Our politics range from classical Jewish liberal to radical, but none of us has ever been a leader or a full-time political activist. My maternal grandfather's activism consisted of reading the Yiddish-language *Freiheit*, a communist newspaper; my parents moved in vaguely progressive circles in the 1930s. My father describes "the milieu you were exposed to was Utopian Democrat with socialist overtones. . . . The Middle European Jew of our class was occupied with climbing out of the ghetto." I knew nothing about progressive or left-wing Jewish institutions like the New York socialist schools or "red diaper" summer camps until I became an adult. My family's political identity consisted of a generalized Jewish commitment to New Deal social justice. My adult identity is not that different, except that I have participated a little more actively than my parents in the mix of civil rights, antiwar, Marxist, union, and feminist movements of my time. My children have been politically active, but only episodically. We don't lead any big movements, and we often are far from the key actions of the year.

But then too, and this is the important point, there are no real movements without a lot of people like us. How did such ordinary people, unconnected to the institutions that sustained a progressive Jewish political identity, nevertheless keep such identities alive in generations whose circumstances are far removed from those that gave them birth? By what means did they convey something of that identity to their children?

More generally, how did the seeds of various radical, progressive traditions in the United States stay alive in depoliticized climates? I do not mean the "big histories" or public records of leftist parties, trade unions, ethnic pride, or civil rights movements but rather the ways that political identities, constructed from family memories and private knowledge, serve as bridges for carrying the larger, community-constructed identities that they embed across the generations.

The operant word is "community." From the vantage point of my eastern European immigrant family, American Jewish political identities—the ethnic and class sense of what it meant to be a Jewish man or woman—were forged in residentially and occupationally ghettoized communities. These communities, as well as the kinds of Jewishnesses constructed within them, which will be discussed in chapter 2, were responses to the racial stigmatization of Jews in the period of the turn of the last century.

My grandparents, my parents, and my brother and I all grew up in Jewish communities, albeit very different ones. I had contact with all of them because the different generations brought their communities' values into the house, where they coexisted, conversed, and clashed.

My view of my grandparents' immigrant, working-class, Jewish communities in New York City comes from stories. Because I remembered the pleasures and the security of my own Jewish childhood community, I filtered the tales through a romantic lens. For example, I had an early sense that married life in the immigrant community departed from 1950s ideals of the womanhood and nuclear family autonomy I lived. When, in the 1900s, some of my maternal grandmother's nine brothers went off to Clarion, Utah, to join an experimental colony of Jewish farmers, my grandmother, who was already married, "made a home," as my mother put it, for her unmarried brothers and a sister who stayed behind. I took away from these stories a positive sense of extended family cooperation. I have similar idyllic direct memories of my summers, perhaps 1944–1946, on a farm in Fitchville, Connecticut, most likely in a *kuchelein*, a working-class institution that dates back to the early twentieth century, where Jewish farmers rented out cabins or rooms to city families.[4] As kids, we swam in a brook, fished, slid down haystacks, milked cows, and took them to pasture.

My parents' memories are more complex. Of the farm, my father says, "We often got in [the farmer's] way in our attempt to relieve our boredom by doing something useful." My mother's view of togetherness in the Jewish community is also less rosy than mine. She recalls life in the house that her grandparents and parents bought together in Coney Island about 1918. They rented out the flats and lived in the basement. In the summertime, they rented lockers to people using the beach on weekends. When she was around eleven, my mother's job was to give out towels and rent out lockers. She also had to sweep the carpets, a job she hated, and take care of her little sister, Evie, because her mother worked in the store. At least she did until Evie got older, at which point Evie had to spend every afternoon and evening of her youth tending the store.

Because the garment industry was seasonal, my grandfather was unemployed for about half the year. My grandmother was in charge of the family finances and always had some kind of little store. As married adults during the Depression, my parents first lived with my mother's parents, and when they got their own apartment it was near both their parents. My grandparents and their brothers and sisters, my great aunts and uncles, were part of their world, and mine as well.

My parents' childhood stories gave me a more nuanced window on the working-class values that pervaded New York's Jewish working-class community in the early twentieth century. Most members of my family were not manual workers, or they were not workers for long. My father's mother ran a pharmacy, and my parents became public school teachers. One of my favorite aunts and my uncle owned a large wholesale business supplying the garment industry. But even this aunt joined my grandmother in mistakenly showing me the Flatiron Building, as the former home of the Triangle Shirtwaist Company. From all of them I heard the story of the Triangle fire and of the deaths of so many women who worked in a shop with locked exit doors, and they told me how important the International Ladies Garment Workers Union (ILGWU) was. To my mother, its president, David Dubinsky, was a hero, someone she pointed out reverentially to me in Lindy's, the famous Jewish restaurant on Broadway.

For me, this immigrant community is a community of memory, lived indirectly through stories and incorporated into my sense of Jewishness, but in a romanticized way. My mother insists correctly that I grew up in a middle-class Jewish community and filtered her working-class community experience through it. As a result, I don't appreciate the downside of working-class life. It was no fun for my mother to be responsible for her baby sister, to have to take her everywhere, to have the boarders tell her how to do the cleaning and ironing, to be a captive of the enforced community, where everybody tells you what to do, feels free to criticize, where you have no privacy as a child or an adult married woman sharing your mother's apartment. She and my father wanted to leave Brooklyn, to have a detached house with a garden, to give their kids their own bedrooms, the privacy they did not have. But they also continued to value the security and support they felt from life in a community of Jewish working people.

When my parents moved to the suburbs in 1949, they moved into, indeed helped create, another kind of Jewish community to sustain them. They reoriented their lives from a family support system to a support network of Jewish workmates and friends who were adjusting to the same changes. That was the community in which I lived most of my childhood, and it too was secure and supportive, although certainly not working class. When I was young, we visited family in Brooklyn a great deal, and family gatherings were my link with the earlier community construction of Jewishness. As I grew older, we all spent more and more social time with friends scattered through Brooklyn and Long Island, and less and less time with family. Consequently, the Brooklyn Jewish community receded for me. My parents continued to take on a wide range of extended family responsibilities, and they still moved between the two community-based cultures more frequently than I did.

Their suburban community was every bit as Jewish in its makeup as the one in which they had grown up. Throughout my adolescence, my parents' workmates and friends were almost all Jews. Even after we moved to the suburbs, like so many Jewish women and quite a few men of their generation, my parents taught at public schools and visited in a Brooklyn Jewish world. We still shopped at Klein's and in Manhattan's Jewish garment district.

I tended to think of the political outlook I learned in this milieu as Jewish. I knew from listening to teachers' shoptalk at my parents' parties that school principals were bosses not so different from garment bosses, as well as jackasses; that the Board of Education was an endless source of trouble and idiocy, and that teachers were what made schools run despite them. I listened to their stories of teacher unions' organizing and learned from childhood that you didn't cross picket lines. I knew that everyone in this dispersed Jewish community was a Democrat and voted for Adlai Stevenson, while my spatial community of Valley Stream went solidly for Eisenhower.

The trial and execution of the Rosenbergs in 1953 heightened our sense of difference. It was a terrifying thing and discussed in the same hushed tones that the Nazi genocide was talked about in our house. Joseph McCarthy was evil incarnate, and we rejoiced at his downfall. My parents talked about these things with their friends, but I do not think they discussed them with our non-Jewish neighbors. I believe this was out of a fear that to do so might evoke an anti-Semitism they suspected our white neighbors harbored but which they didn't want to know about. In one sense then, being a Jew meant being part of a multigenerational community, not really political but Democrat, pro-union, antimanagement, and secular in the way one saw the world. It also meant standing somewhat apart from the white world, being bicultural in a way that Jews shared with other upwardly mobile European ethnics.

We also embraced the white world, especially its middle-class aspects. For both my parents, to have their own house was an exciting opportunity to be seized. It was freedom from parental oversight and offered the promise of making their life as they would like it to be. There was no living culture to learn in the brand-new suburban neighborhoods, no place in the built environment of one-family houses for a socially recognized generation of elders, no duplexes, no flats with married daughters living upstairs from their mothers, as my father's sister Henrietta and her mother had in Coney Island. The generations were separated, connected only by the telephone, the Belt Parkway, and the automobile. Ours was the first generation to inhabit those neighborhoods, and virtually all of our neighbors were fairly young parents, one of each sex, with two young children. At eight, I was part of the big kids on my street and my thirty-five-year-old parents were among the neighborhood elders. The demographics and the sociology of these neighborhoods resonated with a popular culture that celebrated youth and disparaged intergenerational teachings. So my parents, my brother, and I learned suburban living and how to be middle-class whites by the seat of our pants, piecing it together from peers, neighbors, and the increasingly mass media.

Although my parents' Jewishness was formed in a community context organized to cope with times when Jews weren't white, most of my childhood coincided with America's philo-Semitic 1950s, which I discuss in chapter 5, where Jews were a wonderful kind of white folks. We lived where Jews had not been allowed to live a few generations earlier, and we interacted easily with people whose families had been white for a very long time. So, while my parents taught me their Jewishness-as-not-quite-white, they also wanted our family to adjust to Jews' new postwar, racially white place.

This meant we all had to learn the ways of whiteness. Shortly after we moved to Valley Stream, perhaps to help me figure it out, my parents bought me a storybook, *The Happy Family*, where life began in the kitchen and stopped at the borders of the lawn, where Mom, Dad, the kids, and the dog were relentlessly cheerful, and where no one ever raised their voices except to laugh. It was my favorite, and I desperately wanted my family to look like the one in the book. When I became an adolescent, my goal in life became to have a pageboy hairstyle and to own a camel-hair coat, like the pictures in *Seventeen* magazine. I thought of storybook and magazine people as "the blond people," a species for whom life naturally came easily, who inherited happiness as a birthright, and I wanted my family to be like that, to be "normal." Maybe then I'd be normal too. My childhood divide was between everyone I knew and the blond people, between most of the real people I knew, whether in the suburbs or in the city, and the mythical, "normal" America of the then-primitive but still quite effective mass media—radio, magazines, and the new TV.

Still, to be Jewish, to have Jewishness as a central part of my political identity, meant being a little different. At the very least it meant being part of a Jewish social and work world that I shared with my parents. True, this community differed from the Jewish community of my parents' youth, but it also differed from my suburban community of school and neighborhood, not to mention from that of the mythical blond people. Trying to be "normal," that is, white, and Jewish presented a double bind. Neither was satisfactory by itself, and it seemed to me that each commented negatively on the other: to be "normal" meant to reject the Jewishness of my family and our circle, as well as a more congenial kind of girlhood; to be Jewish meant to be a voluntary outsider at school. I wanted to embrace my family *and* to be an insider. At the time, it seemed that I had a choice and that I had to choose; one couldn't be both at the same time and in the same place. This now seems to be part of the condition of at least ethnic whitenesses, as I argue in chapter 5.

In struggles among the women of my family over what it meant to be a Jewish woman, the personal aspect was most intensely political for me. For a woman to be brainy and assertive was fine at home, but it didn't make you popular with the boys at school. I wanted the rewards of femininity, which I understood as popularity, but I couldn't manage the proper feminine submissiveness. The Jewishness I knew supported more assertiveness in daughters than *Seventeen* magazine did, but it demanded more malleability from a wife and mother than it did from a daughter. Intellectually pushy daughterhood was a temporary stage in life, even for Jews.

On a daily basis, my mother, grandmother, and I enacted the dialog between the larger society's constructions of white middle-class womanhood and our different notions of what a Jewish woman should be like. My mother created her version of Middle-class Jewish/White Woman from the images and prescriptions of the mass media and with the support and consensus of her friends. She spent a lot of energy figuring out how to do it. She had no support from her mother, for whom my mother's version of womanhood was a foreign way of being.

I do not think my mother took kindly to suburban domesticity. Even though she swears it was preferable to working, I never believed her. She had been a public school teacher before I was born and, like all the women in her circle of friends, she quit work when I was born. I can attest to her misery at staying home, at feeling idle. With great frequency, she invented Things to Do. I remember a series of craft classes in our first years in Valley Stream. She took up painting on china, painting on glasses, painting on clothing, making rickrack earrings and a little pottery, all of which she disparaged, and the products found their way to the back of the kitchen cabinets. Pushing my brother in the stroller when he got tired, we walked to new construction sites; we walked "downtown" to the commercial center of Valley Stream to get a soda and to teach me how to navigate my way to school. I thought even then that my mother was driven by boredom, but I was glad to be part of the great escape.

This pattern was not quite new. I have vague memories from when we lived in Brooklyn of frequent expeditions by foot and stroller from Sheepshead Bay, where we lived, to Brighton Beach to visit my grandparents while my father was at work. But those excursions were What One Did as opposed to an invention to fill time. A dutiful daughter visits her mother. Having grown up in a household where her mother was always busy running a store or caring for boarders, and whose activity was critical to family income, and where my mother was expected to work in the house and care for her sister from an early age, suburban domesticity must have felt empty. She was trying to be a housewife, to enjoy "freedom" from working, but there was no serious work for an adult to do in the house except to entertain two small children. Without adult company to entertain her too, that was not much fun for very long. I knew from a very early age that full-time domesticity was not for me.

My parents had another community, a Jewish one of teachers and workmates. Teaching gave my mother the respect and affirmation that she was not getting from trying to live up to suburban ideals of mother and wife or from negotiating with her mother's ideas about motherhood. She went back to work when I was about nine. She was an excellent teacher and built a supportive community of teacher friends, among them my father. They taught at the same schools, rode to and from work together every day, and talked shop all the way. They came home, sat down with a cup of tea, and continued the conversation they'd begun in the car. On weekends, they'd attend or give parties for their friends. In the summers of my childhood and teenage years, many of these same families rented neighboring cottages at that Vermont lake where we kids tied up all the boats as a prank. That was the community I wanted when I grew up.

I think that part of the attraction suburbia had for my mother was its emphasis on young families that were starting out—no elders, no in-laws, no parents. Like being your own boss, or in the context of her friends, being accepted as an adult, a competent woman-person. This version of Jewish womanhood was a social position, a political identity, invented by my parents and their circle. It wasn't my grandmother's and it didn't come from the women's magazines. Mothers weren't supposed to be working, certainly not as career women, but my mother and her friends, as well as most other teachers, were doing just that.[5]

Nevertheless, my mother downplayed the importance of teaching in her life. Maybe she felt she wasn't supposed to have those feelings because women weren't supposed to invest themselves in careers. I always thought she undercut herself by refusing to take seriously something that gave her so much pleasure and identity.

However, the way my mother shaped herself as an adult Jewish woman also had continuities with my grandmother's version of womanhood, and I adopted my own version of my mother's. Both of them lived in—they actually had a major hand in creating—the Jewish networks and communities that sustained them. In my grandmother's case, the network was family centered; in my mother's, it comprised family members as well as friend-workmates. Those networks nurtured them and gave me a strong sense of Jewish place and purpose. Both of them accepted the expectations placed upon Jewish women of their times—that they were first of all responsible for their families and households and were either expected or "allowed" to work to the extent that their work did not interfere with those responsibilities.

My parents' circle could not buck the misogyny toward Jewish mothers in the 1950s or the mainstream's devaluation of middle-class white women's motherhood. But they did commiserate among themselves about the problems that institutionalized motherhood caused them. I think they were effective in creating a Jewish community for each other that valued women's place in a professional world made up of women and men. Still, marriage and motherhood were part of being an adult Jewish woman and necessary for participating in this world of peers that mixed work and pleasure, family and community.

When my maternal grandmother, Rose Schechter, came to live with us after my grandfather died in 1952, it became clear that she and my mother did not share the same ideals of Jewish womanhood. They wrestled with each other to sustain their own version. The struggles were usually over mundane things—what to cook, who would cook or clean, how much to eat. But these things were also about whether my grandmother's or my mother's version of Jewish womanhood would prevail in the household. The battles were also about which womanhood I was expected to adopt. We all struggled with what it meant to be mainstream, "normal," or white, and to be a Jewish woman, and what being any kind of woman had to do with being a person at a time and place where, according to the media, a woman wasn't supposed to be a person.

For example, mothering was central to my grandmother's and

my mother's sense of their womanhoods. Grandma's version commanded respect and gave her authority over her children, even when they were adults. No child development experts shook her confidence in the way she mothered, but my mother's efforts to find her own path to mothering shook Grandma's world.

My mother was attracted to the self-confidence and motherly authority that came from Grandma's views. But she also resisted Grandma's notion of mothering because it had no place for the separation, autonomy, and privacy that she wished she had had as a child and that she wanted to give to her children. She was attracted to the views of the newly popular child development experts because they validated her feelings. But she often complained that trying to be the experts' kind of mother was "damned if you do, damned if you don't," that the experts were always giving contradictory advice, and that whatever a mother did wasn't good enough. Whatever good happened was to someone else's credit; all the bad stuff was the mother's fault.

She resented the way motherhood was institutionalized in the postwar middle class. I stress "institutionalized" in the sense that Adrienne Rich used it: of motherhood as a culturally constructed institution whose expectations might or might not be experienced privately.[6] Such expectations are part of the wider social context within which one lives, and they affect the experience: I felt cheated that my mother wasn't home to greet me after school, although I never had any such expectations about my father. I'm not surprised that my mother found motherhood to be a high-risk, low-reward venture. In the 1950s, mother bashing was in vogue among the white mainstream and in the Jewish community. The latter, as in Philip Roth's novels, resonated well beyond a Jewish audience. The distinction between motherhood as institution and as experience is important, but my mother found that the institutionalization affected her experience profoundly, and it must have been heightened by its contrast with Grandma's older, Jewish version of motherhood.

Mom and Grandma also battled over who was in charge of the household and therefore over whose ideas would prevail.

Although my grandmother had endured numerous hardships, she would not have recognized as one of those the compulsory domesticity that I make a living fulminating against as a women's studies teacher. There was a certain kind of domesticity that was central to her sense of self, but it was the community-based domesticity of turn-of-the-century working-class Jewish neighborhoods (which I discuss in chapter 4), very different from the privatized domesticity of my mother's 1950s suburbia. Grandma never worked for wages as far as I know. But her little stores and her household were income-producing workplaces. Work was the center of her domesticity, and work was the way she expressed her love. She worked for her family. This was the Jewish womanhood Grandma modeled.

My grandmother's work identity came out full force in cooking. She took total charge of the kitchen, and meals were high in labor and calories: handmade noodles, rendered chicken fat, matzo balls, split pea soup, blintzes, kugel, potato latkes, gefilte fish. No mixes. No shortcuts. No lean cuisine. Everything from scratch. All the energy Grandma put into cooking went directly into us. There was nothing metaphorical about the process; it was pure calories. She cooked for us, and we ate for her. She gave us love on a plate, and we gave it back by cleaning our plates. My brother and I squabbled over whether Grandma saved the best leftovers for him or for me. As with most of the Jewish and Italian families I knew, love was tied up with food. We acted out rather than discussing. There was not much direct verbal expression of love, pleasure, or happiness. If you showed it, the evil eye might take it away. Love was more safely expressed indirectly. Food was love; work was love.

In our house, the work of making that food was a statement of self-worth among adult women. To cook was to be the woman head-of-household. My grandmother tried to live in our suburban house the way a good Jewish mother in the immigrant working-class community was supposed to live. She felt disempowered when, after her first heart attack, my mother urged her not to clean. I think my mother must also have felt demoted when Grandma took over the kitchen.

There was friction over what to eat and how much to eat, since my mother and I were always dieting. Dieting was about my and my mother's aspirations to blond-people standards of feminine beauty, but it was also about rebellion against my grandmother's control and her version of domesticity. I suspect it was also a mother-daughter struggle over turf and household decision making as well as over the meaning of being a Jewish woman. My grandmother's presence maintained both the older Jewish ideal and my mother's and my engagement with it.

All these struggles over womanhood were contained and shaped by our white racial assignment. As with the wider social construction of motherhood, the Jews' racial assignment affected our racial identities and our identification, which is the argument of chapter 5. Our Jewishness was racially a middle place to experience middle-class womanhood. In relation to "the blond people," mainstream white folks, the women of my family felt different. However, in relation to African Americans, we experienced ourselves as mainstream and white. My grandmother and I manifested our whiteness in different ways.

When my grandmother had a heart attack, my mother hired a Jamaican American household worker, Paula Johnston (not her real name), much to Grandma's distress. The rationale was that my grandmother should not overexert herself. Grandma simply wouldn't let the cleaning wait until the weekend for my mother, helped by my father, but not us kids, for that threatened her sense of her own womanhood.

She related to Johnston a little the way John Henry related to the steam drill. Grandma cleaned up before Johnston came so no one would think she kept a dirty house, and she cooked lunch—but never with the choicest leftovers—for both of them so as to stay in charge. Even as she grew to look forward to and depend on Paula Johnston's company as a break from lonely days in an empty house, Grandma would often refer to her as "the shwartze," a racist term that infuriated my parents and embarrassed me.

Grandma's racism made us uncomfortable because she entered a terrain that we wished to avoid. How was she as a Jewish woman to position herself in it? Her world was no longer one of Jews and non-Jews. Now she had to deal with whether, as an "old-fashioned" Jew, in contrast to her modern daughter and grandchildren, she was on the white or the black side of the American racial divide. Moreover, she had to do this in a context where she was economically dependent upon her daughter and emotionally dependent upon Paula Johnston, who was doing much of the work upon which so much of Grandma's identity and self-respect rested.

The relationship between white and black women around domestic labor, as so many feminists of color have shown, carries deeply racist expectations for white women.[7] Grandma embraced the racial superiority of her position as an employer and a white woman. In this context, to be white is to direct but not perform the dirty work of cleaning, which marks its doers as racially inferior women. Grandma marked her superiority as a white woman by disengaging from the work. However, doing so threatened her identity as a competent adult Jewish woman. This is because a good Jewish woman of her day demonstrated the mental skill of managing a household through physical work. Grandma gave up, albeit under duress, her Jewish womanhood for whiteness, found the latter wanting in a meaningful sense, and seized racial superiority as a consolation prize.

My teenage ideals of womanliness were also formed within the American white-black racial binary (discussed in chapters 2 and 3). My sense of Jewish difference was formed through aspiring to blond-people whiteness, while my sense of belonging, and my uneasiness about the nature of the white womanhood it embedded, came in my relationship with black womanhood (see chapter 5).

The civil rights movement made visible the contradictions between the ideals of white womanhood and of personhood. African American women leaders appeared in heroic form on TV in the 1950s and early 1960s: Daisy Bates, Gloria Richardson, Septima Clark, Ella Baker, and Fannie Lou Hamer. They did not act within the prescripts of white womanhood, and they were not treated with respect, but they were strong, they were people, and they were women. Strong women are without doubt the centers of both generations of my Jewish family. But nowhere in my Jewish community did I hear adult women putting those terms (adult and women) together when talking about the respect to which they were entitled, nor did I hear any direct challenge to notions of womanhood as sacrifice of self for family and children. My first sense of any alternative came from the African American women leaders who were my political tutors in Boston CORE, the Congress of Racial Equality, in the early 1960s. I heard very fine-grained analyses of self and respect among African American women.[8]

Here, and a few years later, while raising children in an African American neighborhood in Detroit, I saw black women sharing a different construction of motherhood among themselves. Most important was the notion that motherhood carried entitlements with it: respect and a recognition of adulthood and its privileges. It differed from the mother-bashing mainstream with which I was most familiar. It was also different from my grandmother's version, where mothering focused on work but where whatever community authority she might have claimed in an earlier milieu was absent by the time I was conscious.

My view of African American women was as romantic as my view of immigrant Jewish communities, a feminist part of the general romanticization of African America by progressive whites of the 1960s, which I discuss in chapter 5. It was also a romantic counterpoint to my grandmother's attempt to be modern "on the backs of blacks," as Toni Morrison put it in describing the lesson that so many immigrants learned—that one could become an American by asserting one's white superiority over African Americans.[9]

Where historical circumstances may have constrained my

mother's generation to live with an unsatisfactory construction of motherhood, Mom still found ways of living her dreams of a fuller existence within the parameters of 1950s womanhood. She and my father also gave me a heritage and a dream of something more. They allowed my generation to challenge some of the institutions that were cramping that dream, even as the prosperity that buoyed the movements of the 1960s has evaporated.

My grandmother grappled, and not always well, with the experience of change, of the continuing break with the known. My mother and I shared the condition of rebelliousness against the shackles of the known and, with my grandmother, the responsibility to construct one's social persona, one's political identity, anew. We all had a sense that each of us was the first generation to make a new world—my grandparents immigrated, my parents moved beyond the small world of the immigrant ghetto and took on the entitlements of middle-class life, and I rebelled against the homogeneity of that life. With each generation, we emphasized our social self-invention, with no continuity from our parents save our rebellions against them.

As we each saw ourselves make our womanhoods differently from our mothers, we each also shared both a deep sense of having lost what we rejected of the older generations and an excitement from creating ourselves in a more fulfilling way. The women in my family encouraged me to make myself new and better, to escape their sadness from having lost something in the process of forming their identities through choices about work and motherhood, where the best choice demanded giving up something they valued. They also passed along a sadness because they were not so sure I could do what they could not.

Alongside a sense of excitement and pride that we could master the mainstream, there was also a feeling that this cost us something. I think we feared the loss of an authentic Jewish self—that we might easily exchange personal connection for a few of the glittering trinkets that were always dangling on the edge of one's vision in those prosperous years. In my house this took different forms. The evil eye could strike you if you were too happy or too successful in worldly achievements. There was also a vague sorrow in my mother and her mother, the sense of having arrived at life's destination only to discover that you have to furnish it yourself, that it comes without any meaningful framework for living.

For my grandmother, Rose Schechter, fulfilling the immigrant dream of suburban prosperity brought no pleasure. The struggle to adjust to one more change did not end well. In Valley Stream, she lost the hard, work-based domesticity she knew and from which she derived her identity and authority. The domesticity of postwar suburbia gave her none of these things. I haven't seen too many stories of immigrant grandmothers in suburbia.[10] There was certainly no place for them in the public iconography of white nuclear family bliss. My grandmother suffered from this social obliteration of her identity as a Jewish woman. Unhappy at feeling like a burden as her health deteriorated, and I suspect her illness was exacerbated by her unhappiness, she committed suicide by taking an overdose of sleeping pills.

☐ I undertook the research for this book not least to make personal sense of my grandmother's death. I came to understand it through the counterpoint between identity and ethnoracial assignment. I use identity in a political sense, to refer to a system of values and meanings shared within a community by which we measure ourselves as social actors. Assignment refers to the ways in which the dominant culture and popular understandings construct different categories of social and political beings in the United States. The meanings and values my grandmother enacted as a Jewish woman found little validation in our white neighborhood or in the Jewish womanhood my mother and her community were struggling to build. I think that this was not from lack of understanding or empathetic attempts to accommodate my grandmother's womanhood, but rather from the fact that my grandmother did not live in a social context or a community that reinforced her sense of self through daily practices. The ways we construct ourselves as social actors are shaped by larger ethnoracial assignments, social contexts over which we have no direct control. Within their constraints we can be quite creative in constructing ourselves as social beings, but there are limits to that creativity both with respect to individual adjustment and with respect to the kinds of political identities one can construct in any given community.

For me "the Jewish question" is to understand that interplay between ethnoracial assignment and ethnoracial identity, to move from the personal to the political. In my youth in the 1950s and 1960s, the phrase "the Jewish question" was an uneasy in-joke in reaction to the genocidal horrors of World War II. It was self-mocking shorthand for our preoccupation with how so many world issues were likely to affect us as Jews. For me today, "the Jewish question" is about the ways we negotiate our political identities as Jews in relation to our ethnoracial assignments in the world.

Chapter 1 explores the roots of my family's "racial diversity." It deals with the larger, national discourse and the institutionalized practices that made Jews a race and that assigned them first to the not-white side of the American racial binary, and then to its white side.

Chapters 2 and 3 step back and look at the historical structure of racial assignment. Where have Jews stood in relation to the larger American racial binary of whiteness and blackness? Where the first chapter details the policies and practices that made my parents not-quite white, and those that whitened my brother and me, these two chapters show why race and race making have mattered so much to American social organization. They suggest that American Jews have been a microcosm of American race-making processes. They introduce class and gender as key elements of race making in American history and discuss the significance of race for American capitalism and for American ideas about nationhood.

These chapters are an interpretive synthesis of many strands of recent scholarship. They draw upon African American, neo-Marxist, and critical race theory for understandings of how law and policy, work, and popular culture each contributed to the construction of the American working class as "of color" and outside the circle of national belonging, while making American citizens white and middle class. Many other strands of multicultural scholarship, from feminism to postcolonial and cultural studies, have joined them to illuminate the ways in which American racial definitions rest solidly on ideas about what it means to be properly (white) male and female. I have tried to weave them together, to show how race, class, and gender reproduce whiteness as a complexly held political identity and as a stable and powerful system of oppressive economic and political practices that are sustained by opposition to all manner of nonwhitenesses.

Chapter 2 asks where American races and ethnicities come from. What aspects of social organization make race a lived reality? Why does it almost define class? Chapter 3 looks at where the womanhood of the "blond people" came from. It focuses on the history of wage and welfare policies to show how race has been "embodied" in the different versions of womanhood and manhood assigned to peoples with and "without" color. It shows how these stereotypes have shaped public policies about work and welfare and also governed American discourses about national belonging.

In chapter 4, I take a historical look at my grandparents' Jewish community and the one in which my parents became adults. I want to understand the nature of their Jewishness, why they responded to our tying up the boats the way they did. To do that, I deal with what it meant to be a Jew in America when Jews were less than white. What kind of Jewishness did Jews create within the context of institutionalized anti-Semitism? How were American Jews' concepts of class and of proper Jewish womanhood and manhood constructed in response to American anti-Semitism and to Jews' places in the American class structure?

Chapter 5 focuses on the post-World War II world in which I grew up as white, Jewish, and a woman. It asks how Jews reconfigured the meanings of Jewishness in general and Jewish womanhood in particular when they became "white." What did it do to Jewish constructions of womanhood and manhood; what did it do to class and to racial identities? These chapters suggest that Jews' racial assignment, as nonwhite and then as white, deeply affected the meanings of American Jewish ethnoracial identity, as well as the class and gender politics of ethnic Jewishness.

In the conclusion, I suggest that this system of racial, gender, and class assignment constitutes a kind of "metaorganization of American capitalism." By this I mean an integrated system of occupational and residential segregation, race- and gender-based public policy, and a public discourse about the racial and gender construction of the American nation. I suggest that this public discourse has been shaped by what I see as an enduring "core constitutive myth" that the American nation is composed of only white men and women. In this myth, the alternatives available to nonwhite and variously alien "others" has been either to whiten themselves or to be consigned to an animal-like, ungendered underclass unfit to exercise the prerogatives of citizenship. The American ethnoracial map—which indicates who is assigned to which of these poles—has changed and is changing again today, but the binary of black and white is not. As a result, the structure within which Americans form their ethnoracial, gender, and class identities is distressingly stable. What does this mean for the ways Americans can construct their political identities, and what does it mean for creating alternatives that will weaken the hold of this myth that governs American political life?

How Did Jews ☐ *CHAPTER 1*
Become White Folks?

*The American nation was founded and devel-
oped by the Nordic race, but if a few more million members of the Alpine, Mediterranean and
Semitic races are poured among us, the result
must inevitably be a hybrid race of people as
worthless and futile as the good-for-nothing
mongrels of Central America and Southeastern
Europe.*
—Kenneth Roberts, "Why Europe Leaves Home"

It is clear that Kenneth Roberts did not think of my ancestors
as white, like him. The late nineteenth century and early
decades of the twentieth saw a steady stream of warnings by scientists, policymakers, and the popular press that "mongreliza-
tion" of the Nordic or Anglo-Saxon race—the real Americans—by
inferior European races (as well as by inferior non-European
ones) was destroying the fabric of the nation.

I continue to be surprised when I read books that indicate
that America once regarded its immigrant European workers as
something other than white, as biologically different. My parents
are not surprised; they expect anti-Semitism to be part of the
fabric of daily life, much as I expect racism to be part of it. They

came of age in the Jewish world of the 1920s and 1930s, at the peak of anti-Semitism in America.[1] They are rightly proud of their upward mobility and think of themselves as pulling themselves up by their own bootstraps. I grew up during the 1950s in the Euro-ethnic New York suburb of Valley Stream, where Jews were simply one kind of white folks and where ethnicity meant little more to my generation than food and family heritage. Part of my ethnic heritage was the belief that Jews were smart and that our success was due to our own efforts and abilities, reinforced by a culture that valued sticking together, hard work, education, and deferred gratification.

I am willing to affirm all those abilities and ideals and their contribution to Jews' upward mobility, but I also argue that they were still far from sufficient to account for Jewish success. I say this because the belief in a Jewish version of Horatio Alger has become a point of entry for some mainstream Jewish organizations to adopt a racist attitude against African Americans especially and to oppose affirmative action for people of color.[2] Instead I want to suggest that Jewish success is a product not only of ability but also of the removal of powerful social barriers to its realization.

It is certainly true that the United States has a history of anti-Semitism and of beliefs that Jews are members of an inferior race. But Jews were hardly alone. American anti-Semitism was part of a broader pattern of late-nineteenth-century racism against all southern and eastern European immigrants, as well as against Asian immigrants, not to mention African Americans, Native Americans, and Mexicans. These views justified all sorts of discriminatory treatment, including closing the doors, between 1882 and 1927, to immigration from Europe and Asia. This picture changed radically after World War II. Suddenly, the same folks who had promoted nativism and xenophobia were eager to believe that the Euro-origin people whom they had deported, reviled as members of inferior races, and prevented from immigrating only a few years earlier, were now model middle-class white suburban citizens.[3]

It was not an educational epiphany that made those in power change their hearts, their minds, and our race. Instead, it was the biggest and best affirmative action program in the history of our nation, and it was for Euromales. That is not how it was billed, but it is the way it worked out in practice. I tell this story to show the institutional nature of racism and the centrality of state policies to creating and changing races. Here, those policies reconfigured the category of whiteness to include European immigrants. There are similarities and differences in the ways each of the European immigrant groups became "whitened." I tell the story in a way that links anti-Semitism to other varieties of anti-European racism because this highlights what Jews shared with other Euro-immigrants.

☐ *Euroraces*

The U.S. "discovery" that Europe was divided into inferior and superior races began with the racialization of the Irish in the mid-nineteenth century and flowered in response to the great waves of immigration from southern and eastern Europe that began in the late nineteenth century. Before that time, European immigrants—including Jews—had been largely assimilated into the white population. However, the 23 million European immigrants who came to work in U.S. cities in the waves of migration after 1880 were too many and too concentrated to absorb. Since immigrants and their children made up more than 70 percent of the population of most of the country's largest cities, by the 1890s urban America had taken on a distinctly southern and eastern European immigrant flavor. Like the Irish in Boston and New York, their urban concentrations in dilapidated neighborhoods put them cheek by jowl next to the rising elites and the middle class with whom they shared public space and to whom their working-class ethnic communities were particularly visible.

The Red Scare of 1919 clearly linked anti-immigrant with anti-working-class sentiment—to the extent that the Seattle general strike by largely native-born workers was blamed on foreign agitators. The Red Scare was fueled by an economic depression, a massive postwar wave of strikes, the Russian Revolution, and another influx of postwar immigration. Strikers in the steel and garment industries in New York and New England were mainly new immigrants. "As part of a fierce counteroffensive, employers inflamed the historic identification of class conflict with immigrant radicalism." Anticommunism and anti-immigrant sentiment came together in the Palmer raids and deportation of immigrant working-class activists. There was real fear of revolution. One of President Wilson's aides feared it was "the first appearance of the soviet in this country."[4]

Not surprisingly, the belief in European races took root most deeply among the wealthy, U.S.-born Protestant elite, who feared a hostile and seemingly inassimilable working class. By the end of the nineteenth century, Senator Henry Cabot Lodge pressed Congress to cut off immigration to the United States; Theodore Roosevelt raised the alarm of "race suicide" and took Anglo-Saxon women to task for allowing "native" stock to be outbred by inferior immigrants. In the early twentieth century, these fears gained a great deal of social legitimacy thanks to the efforts of an influential network of aristocrats and scientists who developed theories of eugenics—breeding for a "better" humanity—and scientific racism.

Key to these efforts was Madison Grant's influential *The Passing of the Great Race*, published in 1916. Grant popularized notions developed by William Z. Ripley and Daniel Brinton that there existed three or four major European races, ranging from the superior Nordics of northwestern Europe to the inferior southern and eastern races of the Alpines, Mediterraneans, and worst of all, Jews, who seemed to be everywhere in his native New York City. Grant's nightmare was race-mixing among Europeans. For him, "the cross between any of the three European races and a Jew is a Jew." He didn't have good things to say about Alpine or Mediterranean "races" either. For Grant, race and class were interwoven: the upper class was racially pure Nordic; the lower classes came from the lower races.[5]

Far from being on the fringe, Grant's views were well within the popular mainstream. Here is the *New York Times* describing the Jewish Lower East Side of a century ago:

> The neighborhood where these people live is absolutely impassable for wheeled vehicles other than their pushcarts. If a truck driver tries to get through where their pushcarts are standing they apply to him all kinds of vile and indecent epithets. The driver is fortunate if he gets out of the street without being hit with a stone or having a putrid fish or piece of meat thrown in his face. This neighborhood, peopled almost entirely by the people who claim to have been driven from Poland and Russia, is the eyesore of New York and perhaps the filthiest place on the western continent. It is impossible for a Christian to live there because he will be driven out, either by blows or the dirt and stench. Cleanliness is an unknown quantity to these people. They cannot be lifted up to a higher plane because they do not want to be. If the cholera should ever get among these people, they would scatter its germs as a sower does grain.[6]

Such views were well within the mainstream of the early-twentieth-century scientific community.[7] Madison Grant and eugenicist Charles B. Davenport organized the Galton Society in 1918 in order to foster research, promote eugenics, and restrict immigration.[8] Lewis Terman, Henry Goddard, and Robert Yerkes, developers of the "intelligence" test, believed firmly that southeastern European immigrants, African Americans, American Indians, and Mexicans were "feebleminded." And indeed, more than 80 percent of the immigrants whom Goddard tested at Ellis Island in 1912 turned out to be just that, as measured by his test. Racism fused with eugenics in scientific circles, and the eugenics circles overlapped with the nativism of white Protestant elites. During World War I, racism shaped the army's development of a mass intelligence test. Psychologist Robert Yerkes, who developed the test, became an even stronger advocate of eugenics after the war. Writing in the *Atlantic Monthly* in 1923, he noted:

If we may safely judge by the army measurements of intelligence, races are quite as significantly different as individuals. . . . [A]lmost as great as the intellectual difference between negro [*sic*] and white in the army are the differences between white racial groups. . . .

For the past ten years or so the intellectual status of immigrants has been disquietingly low. Perhaps this is because of the dominance of the Mediterranean races, as contrasted with the Nordic and Alpine.[9]

By the 1920s, scientific racism sanctified the notion that real Americans were white and that real whites came from northwest Europe. Racism by white workers in the West fueled laws excluding and expelling the Chinese in 1882. Widespread racism led to closing the immigration door to virtually all Asians and most Europeans between 1924 and 1927, and to deportation of Mexicans during the Great Depression.

Racism in general, and anti-Semitism in particular, flourished in higher education. Jews were the first of the Euro-immigrant groups to enter college in significant numbers, so it was not surprising that they faced the brunt of discrimination there. The Protestant elite complained that Jews were unwashed, uncouth, unrefined, loud, and pushy. Harvard University President A. Lawrence Lowell, who was also a vice president of the Immigration Restriction League, was open about his opposition to Jews at Harvard. The Seven Sister schools had a reputation for "flagrant discrimination." M. Carey Thomas, Bryn Mawr president, may have been some kind of feminist, but she was also an admirer of scientific racism and an advocate of immigration restriction. She "blocked both the admission of black students and the promotion of Jewish instructors."[10]

Jews are justifiably proud of the academic skills that gained them access to the most elite schools of the nation despite the prejudices of their gatekeepers. However, it is well to remember that they had no serious competition from their Protestant classmates. This is because college was not about academic pursuits. It was about social connection—through its clubs, sports and other activities, as well as in the friendships one was expected to forge with other children of elites. From this, the real purpose of the college experience, Jews remained largely excluded.

This elite social mission had begun to come under fire and was challenged by a newer professional training mission at about the time Jews began entering college. Pressures for change were beginning to transform the curriculum and to reorient college from a gentleman's bastion to a training ground for the middle-class professionals needed by an industrial economy. "The curriculum was overhauled to prepare students for careers in business, engineering, scientific farming, and the arts, and a variety of new professions such as accounting and pharmacy that were making their appearance in American colleges for the first time."[11] Occupational training was precisely what had drawn Jews to college. In a setting where disparagement of intellectual pursuits and the gentleman C were badges of distinction, it certainly wasn't hard for Jews to excel. Jews took seriously what their affluent Protestant classmates disparaged, and, from the perspective of nativist elites, took unfair advantage of a loophole to get where they were not wanted.

Patterns set by these elite schools to close those "loopholes" influenced the standards of other schools, made anti-Semitism acceptable, and "made the aura of exclusivity a desirable commodity for the college-seeking clientele."[12] Fear that colleges "might soon be overrun by Jews" were publicly expressed at a 1918 meeting of the Association of New England Deans. In 1919 Columbia University took steps to decrease the number of its Jewish students by a set of practices that soon came to be widely adopted. They developed a psychological test based on the World War I army intelligence tests to measure "innate ability—and middle-class home environment"; and they redesigned the admission application to ask for religion, father's name and birthplace, a photo, and personal interview. Other techniques for excluding Jews, like a fixed class size, a chapel requirement, and preference for children of alumni, were less obvious.[13]

Sociologist Jerome Karabel has argued that current criteria

for college admission—which mix grades and test scores with well-roundedness and character, as well as a preference (or affirmative action) for athletes and children of alumni, which allowed schools to select more affluent Protestants—had their origins in these exclusionary efforts. Their proliferation in the 1920s caused the intended drop in the numbers of Jewish law, dental, and medical students as well as the imposition of quotas in engineering, pharmacy, and veterinary schools.[14]

Columbia's quota against Jews was well known in my parents' community. My father is very proud of having beaten it and been admitted to Columbia Dental School on the basis of his skill at carving a soap ball. Although he became a teacher instead because the tuition was too high, he took me to the dentist every week of my childhood and prolonged the agony by discussing the finer points of tooth-filling and dental care. My father also almost failed the speech test required for his teaching license because he didn't speak "standard," i.e., nonimmigrant, nonaccented English. For my parents and most of their friends, English was the language they had learned when they went to school, since their home and neighborhood language was Yiddish. They saw the speech test as designed to keep all ethnics, not just Jews, out of teaching.

There is an ironic twist to this story. My mother always urged me to speak well, like her friend Ruth Saronson, who was a speech teacher. Ruth remained my model for perfect diction until I went away to college. When I talked to her on one of my visits home, I heard the New York accent of my version of "standard English," compared to the Boston academic version.

My parents believe that Jewish success, like their own, was due to hard work and a high value placed on education. They attended Brooklyn College during the Depression. My mother worked days and went to school at night; my father went during the day. Both their families encouraged them. More accurately, their families expected it. Everyone they knew was in the same boat, and their world was made up of Jews who were advancing just as they were. The picture for New York—where most

Jews lived—seems to back them up. In 1920, Jews made up 80 percent of the students at New York's City College, 90 percent of Hunter College, and before World War I, 40 percent of private Columbia University. By 1934, Jews made up almost 24 percent of all law students nationally and 56 percent of those in New York City. Still, more Jews became public school teachers, like my parents and their friends, than doctors or lawyers. Indeed, Ruth Jacknow Markowitz has shown that "my daughter, the teacher" was, for parents, an aspiration equivalent to "my son, the doctor."[15]

How we interpret Jewish social mobility in this milieu depends on whom we compare them to. Compared with other immigrants, Jews were upwardly mobile. But compared with nonimmigrant whites, that mobility was very limited and circumscribed. The existence of anti-immigrant, racist, and anti-Semitic barriers kept the Jewish middle class confined to a small number of occupations. Jews were excluded from mainstream corporate management and corporately employed professions, except in the garment and movie industries, in which they were pioneers. Jews were almost totally excluded from university faculties (the few who made it had powerful patrons). Eastern European Jews were concentrated in small businesses, and in professions where they served a largely Jewish clientele. We shouldn't forget Jewish success in organized crime in the 1920s and 1930s as an aspect of upward mobility. Arnold Rothstein "transformed crime from a haphazard, small-scale activity into a well-organized and well-financed business operation." There were also Detroit's Purple Gang, Murder Incorporated in New York, a whole host of other big-city Jewish gangs in organized crime, and of course Meyer Lansky.[16]

Although Jews, as the Euro-ethnic vanguard in college, became well established in public school teaching—as well as visible in law, medicine, pharmacy, and librarianship before the postwar boom—these professions should be understood in the context of their times. In the 1930s they lacked the corporate context they have today, and Jews in these professions were certainly not corporation-based. Most lawyers, doctors, dentists, and pharmacists were solo practitioners, depended upon other Jews for their clientele, and were considerably less affluent than their counterparts today.[17]

Compared to Jewish progress after World War II, Jews' prewar mobility was also very limited. It was the children of Jewish businessmen, but not those of Jewish workers, who flocked to college. Indeed, in 1905 New York, the children of Jewish workers had as little schooling as the children of other immigrant workers.[18] My family was quite the model in this respect. My grandparents did not go to college, but they did have a modicum of small business success. My father's family owned a pharmacy. Although my mother's father was a skilled garment worker, her mother's family was large and always had one or another grocery or deli in which my grandmother participated. It was the relatively privileged children of upwardly mobile Jewish immigrants like my grandparents who began to push on the doors to higher education even before my parents were born.

Especially in New York City—which had almost one and a quarter million Jews by 1910 and retained the highest concentration of the nation's 4 million Jews in 1924—Jews built a small-business-based middle class and began to develop a second-generation professional class in the interwar years. Still, despite the high percentages of Jews in eastern colleges, most Jews were not middle class, and fewer than 3 percent were professionals—compared to somewhere between two-thirds and three-quarters in the postwar generation.[19]

My parents' generation believed that Jews overcame anti-Semitic barriers because Jews are special. My answer is that the Jews who were upwardly mobile were special among Jews (and were also well placed to write the story). My generation might well respond to our parents' story of pulling themselves up by their own bootstraps with "But think what you might have been without the racism and with some affirmative action!" And that is precisely what the post-World War II boom, the decline of systematic, public, anti-Euro racism and anti-Semitism, and governmental affirmative action extended to white males let us see.

☐ *Whitening Euro-ethnics*

By the time I was an adolescent, Jews were just as white as the next white person. Until I was eight, I was a Jew in a world of Jews. Everyone on Avenue Z in Sheepshead Bay was Jewish. I spent my days playing and going to school on three blocks of Avenue Z, and visiting my grandparents in the nearby Jewish neighborhoods of Brighton Beach and Coney Island. There were plenty of Italians in my neighborhood, but they lived around the corner. They were a kind of Jew, but on the margins of my social horizons. Portuguese were even more distant, at the end of the bus ride, at Sheepshead Bay. The *shul,* or temple, was on Avenue Z, and I begged my father to take me like all the other fathers took their kids, but religion wasn't part of my family's Judaism. Just how Jewish my neighborhood was hit me in first grade, when I was one of two kids to go to school on Rosh Hashanah. My teacher was shocked—she was Jewish too—and I was embarrassed to tears when she sent me home. I was never again sent to school on Jewish holidays. We left that world in 1949 when we moved to Valley Stream, Long Island, which was Protestant and Republican and even had farms until Irish, Italian, and Jewish ex-urbanites like us gave it a more suburban and Democratic flavor.

Neither religion nor ethnicity separated us at school or in the neighborhood. Except temporarily. During my elementary school years, I remember a fair number of dirt-bomb (a good suburban weapon) wars on the block. Periodically, one of the Catholic boys would accuse me or my brother of killing his god, to which we'd reply, "Did not," and start lobbing dirt bombs. Sometimes he'd get his friends from Catholic school and I'd get mine from public school kids on the block, some of whom were Catholic. Hostilities didn't last for more than a couple of hours and punctuated an otherwise friendly relationship. They ended by our junior high years, when other things became more important. Jews, Catholics and Protestants, Italians, Irish, Poles, "English" (I don't remember hearing WASP as a kid), were mixed up on the block and in school. We thought of ourselves as middle class and very enlightened because our ethnic backgrounds seemed so irrelevant to high school culture. We didn't see race (we thought), and racism was not part of our peer consciousness. Nor were the immigrant or working-class histories of our families.

As with most chicken-and-egg problems, it is hard to know which came first. Did Jews and other Euro-ethnics become white because they became middle-class? That is, did money whiten? Or did being incorporated into an expanded version of whiteness open up the economic doors to middle-class status? Clearly, both tendencies were at work.

Some of the changes set in motion during the war against fascism led to a more inclusive version of whiteness. Anti-Semitism and anti-European racism lost respectability. The 1940 Census no longer distinguished native whites of native parentage from those, like my parents, of immigrant parentage, so Euro-immigrants and their children were more securely white by submersion in an expanded notion of whiteness.[20]

Theories of nurture and culture replaced theories of nature and biology. Instead of dirty and dangerous races that would destroy American democracy, immigrants became ethnic groups whose children had successfully assimilated into the mainstream and risen to the middle class. In this new myth, Euro-ethnic suburbs like mine became the measure of American democracy's victory over racism. As we shall see in chapter 5, Jewish mobility became a new Horatio Alger story. In time and with hard work, every ethnic group would get a piece of the pie, and the United States would be a nation with equal opportunity for all its people to become part of a prosperous middle-class majority. And it seemed that Euro-ethnic immigrants and their children were delighted to join middle America.

This is not to say that anti-Semitism disappeared after World

War II, only that it fell from fashion and was driven underground. In the last few years it has begun to surface among some parts of the right-wing militia movement, skinheads, and parts of the religious Right. Micah Sifry's revelation of Richard Nixon's and George Bush's personal anti-Semitism and its prevalence in both their administrations indicates its persistence in the Protestant elite.[21] While elites do not have a monopoly on anti-Semitism, they do have the ability to restrict Jews' access to the top echelons of corporate America. Since the war however, glass ceilings on Jewish mobility have become fewer and higher. Although they may still suppress the number of Jews and other Euro-ethnics in the upper class, it has been a long time since they could keep them out of even the highest reaches of the middle class. Indeed, the presence of Jews among the finance capitalists and corporate criminals of the 1980s may have fueled a resurgence in right-wing circles of the other anti-Semitic stereotype, of Jews as Shylocks.

Although changing views on who was white made it easier for Euro-ethnics to become middle class, economic prosperity also played a very powerful role in the whitening process. The economic mobility of Jews and other Euro-ethnics derived ultimately from America's postwar economic prosperity and its enormously expanded need for professional, technical, and managerial labor, as well as on government assistance in providing it.

The United States emerged from the war with the strongest economy in the world. Real wages rose between 1946 and 1960, increasing buying power a hefty 22 percent and giving most Americans some discretionary income. American manufacturing, banking, and business services were increasingly dominated by large corporations, and these grew into multinational corporations. Their organizational centers lay in big, new urban headquarters that demanded growing numbers of clerical, technical, and managerial workers. The postwar period was a historic moment for real class mobility and for the affluence we have erroneously come to believe was the American norm. It was a time when the old white and the newly white masses became middle class.[22]

The GI Bill of Rights, as the 1944 Serviceman's Readjustment Act was known, is arguably the most massive affirmative action program in American history. It was created to develop needed labor force skills and to provide those who had them with a lifestyle that reflected their value to the economy. The GI benefits that were ultimately extended to 16 million GIs (of the Korean War as well) included priority in jobs—that is, preferential hiring, but no one objected to it then—financial support during the job search, small loans for starting up businesses, and most important, low-interest home loans and educational benefits, which included tuition and living expenses. This legislation was rightly regarded as one of the most revolutionary postwar programs. I call it affirmative action because it was aimed at and disproportionately helped male, Euro-origin GIs.[23]

GI benefits, like the New Deal affirmative action programs before them and the 1960s affirmative action programs after them, were responses to protest. Business executives and the general public believed that the war economy had only temporarily halted the Great Depression. Many feared its return and a return to the labor strife and radicalism of the 1930s. "[M]emories of the Depression remained vivid, and many people suffered from what Davis Ross has aptly called 'depression psychosis'— the fear that the war would inevitably be followed by layoffs and mass unemployment."[24]

It was a reasonable fear. The 11 million military personnel who had been demobilized in the 1940s represented a quarter of the U.S. labor force. In addition, ending war production brought a huge number of layoffs, growing unemployment, and a high rate of inflation. To recoup wartime losses in real wages that had been caused by inflation as well as by the unions' no-strike pledge in support of the war effort, workers staged a massive wave of strikes in 1946. More workers went out on strike that year than ever before. There were strikes in all the heavy industries: railroads, coal mining, auto, steel, and electrical. For a brief moment it looked like class struggle all over again. But government and business leaders had learned from the experience of bitter labor struggles after World War I just how important it was to assist demobilized soldiers. The GI Bill resulted from their determination to avoid those mistakes this time. The biggest benefits of this legislation were college and technical school educations, and very cheap home mortgages.[25]

☐ *Education and Occupation*

It is important to remember that, prior to the war, a college degree was still very much a "mark of the upper class," that colleges were largely finishing schools for Protestant elites. Before the postwar boom, schools could not begin to accommodate the American masses. Even in New York City before the 1930s, neither the public schools nor City College had room for more than a tiny fraction of potential immigrant students.[26]

Not so after the war. The almost 8 million GIs who took advantage of their educational benefits under the GI Bill caused "the greatest wave of college building in American history." White male GIs were able to take advantage of their educational benefits for college and technical training, so they were particularly well positioned to seize the opportunities provided by the new demands for professional, managerial, and technical labor.

> It has been well documented that the GI educational benefits transformed American higher education and raised the educational level of that generation and generations to come. With many provisions for assistance in upgrading their educational attainments, veterans pulled ahead of nonveterans in earning capacity. In the long run it was the nonveterans who had fewer opportunities.[27]

Just how valuable a college education was for white men's occupational mobility can be seen in who benefited from the metamorphosis of California's Santa Clara Valley into Silicon Valley. Formerly an agricultural region, in the 1950s it became the scene of explosive growth in the semiconductor electronics industry. John Keller has argued that this industry epitomized the postwar economy and occupational structure. It owed its existence directly to the military and to the National Aeronautics and Space Administration (NASA), which were its major funders and market. It had an increasingly white-collar workforce. White men, who were the initial production workers in the 1950s, quickly transformed themselves into a technical and professional workforce thanks largely to GI benefits and to

> the implementation of training programs at a half-dozen junior colleges built in the valley since the mid-1950s. Indeed, a study of the local junior college system in its formative years confirmed how this institutional setup systematically facilitated the transformation of a section of the blue-collar workforce in the area into a corps of electronics technicians: 62 percent of enrollees at San Jose Junior College (later renamed San Jose City College) came from blue-collar families, and 55 percent of all job placements were as electronics technicians in the industrial and service sectors of the county economy.

As the industry expanded between 1950 and 1960 and white men left assembly work, they were replaced initially by Latinas and African American women, who were joined after 1970 by new immigrant women. Immigrating men tended to work in the better-paid unionized industries that grew up in the area.[28]

Postwar expansion made college accessible to Euromales in general and to Jews in particular. My generation's "Think what you could have been!" answer to our parents became our reality as quotas and old occupational barriers fell and new fields opened up to Jews. The most striking result was a sharp decline in Jewish small businesses and a skyrocketing increase in Jewish professionals. For example, as quotas in medical schools fell, the numbers of Jewish M.D.'s shot up. If Boston is any indication, just over 1 percent of all Jewish men before the war were doctors, but 16 percent of the postwar generation became M.D.'s. A similar Jewish mass movement took place into college and university faculties, especially in "new and expanding fields in the social and natural sciences."[29]

Although these Jewish college professors tended to be sons of businessmen and professionals, the postwar boom saw the first large-scale class mobility among Jewish men. Sons of working-class Jews now went to college and became professionals themselves—according to the Boston survey, almost two-thirds of them. This compared favorably with three-quarters of the sons of professional fathers.[30]

But if Jews' upward mobility was due to a lowering of racial barriers, then how have the children of other southern and eastern European immigrants fared? Stephen Steinberg provides one comparison—that of college faculties. Although Jews were the first group to go to college in any great numbers, the proportions of faculty comprising southern and eastern European Catholics has grown rapidly since World War II. Thus, Catholic faculty and graduate students have steadily increased, Protestants have decreased, and Jews have reached a plateau, such that Protestants are underrepresented on college faculties while Catholics were approaching parity by 1974.

Steinberg argues that the lag had less to do with values about education than with difficulties that largely rural Catholic immigrants had in translating rural skills into financial success in an urban industrial setting. Once the opportunities were provided by the GI Bill and associated programs, they too took full advantage of education as a route to upward mobility. Where the first cohorts of Jewish faculty came from small-business backgrounds, Catholic faculty came from working-class families who benefited from postwar programs.[31] Steinberg argues that class backgrounds, more specifically the occupational resources of different immigrant streams, are important for shaping their relative mobility. But we need to place his argument in the broader racial perspective of institutional whiteness. That is, Irish, Jews, and southern and eastern European Catholics were all held back until they were granted—willingly or unwillingly—the institutional privileges of socially sanctioned whiteness. This happened most dramatically after World War II (see chapter 2 for a discussion of the Irish).

Even more significantly, the postwar boom transformed America's class structure—or at least its status structure—so that the middle class expanded to encompass most of the population. Before the war, most Jews, like most other Americans, were part of the working class, defined in terms of occupation, education, and income. Already upwardly mobile before the war relative to other immigrants, Jews floated high on this rising economic tide, and most of them entered the middle class. The children of other immigrants did too. Still, even the high tide missed some Jews. As late as 1973, some 15 percent of New York's Jews were poor or near poor, and in the 1960s, almost 25 percent of employed Jewish men remained manual workers.[32]

The reason I refer to educational and occupational GI benefits as affirmative action programs for white males is because they were decidedly not extended to African Americans or to women of any race. Theoretically they were available to all veterans; in practice women and black veterans did not get anywhere near their share. Women's Army and Air Force units were initially organized as auxiliaries, hence not part of the military. When that status was changed, in July 1943, only those who reenlisted in the armed forces were eligible for veterans' benefits. Many women thought they were simply being demobilized and returned home. The majority remained and were ultimately eligible for veterans' benefits. But there was little counseling, and a social climate that discouraged women's careers and independence cut down on women's knowledge and sense of entitlement. The Veterans Administration kept no statistics on the number of women who used their GI benefits.[33]

The barriers that almost completely shut African American GIs out of their benefits were even more formidable. In Neil Wynn's portrait, black GIs anticipated starting new lives, just like their white counterparts. Over 43 percent hoped to return to school, and most expected to relocate, to find better jobs in new lines of work. The exodus from the South toward the North and West was particularly large. So it was not a question of any lack of ambition on the part of African American GIs. White male privilege was shaped against the backdrop of wartime racism and postwar sexism.

During and after the war, there was an upsurge in white racist violence against black servicemen, in public schools, and by the Ku Klux Klan. It spread to California and New York. The number of lynchings rose during the war, and in 1943 there were antiblack race riots in several large northern cities. Although there was a wartime labor shortage, black people were discriminated against when it came to well-paid defense industry jobs and housing. In 1946, white riots against African Americans occurred across the South and in Chicago and Philadelphia.

Gains made as a result of the wartime civil rights movement, especially in defense-related employment, were lost with peacetime conversion, as black workers were the first to be fired, often in violation of seniority. White women were also laid off, ostensibly to make room for jobs for demobilized servicemen, and in the long run women lost most of the gains they had made in wartime. We now know that women did not leave the labor force in any significant numbers but, instead, were forced to find inferior jobs, largely nonunion, part-time, and clerical.[34]

The military, the Veterans Administration, the U.S. Employment Service (USES), and the Federal Housing Administration effectively denied African American GIs access to their benefits and to new educational, occupational, and residential opportunities. Black GIs who served in the thoroughly segregated armed forces during World War II served under white officers. African American soldiers were given a disproportionate share of dishonorable discharges, which denied them veterans' rights under the GI Bill. Between August and November 1946, for example, 21 percent of white soldiers and 39 percent of black soldiers were dishonorably discharged. Those who did get an honorable discharge then faced the Veterans Administration and the USES. The latter, which was responsible for job placements, employed very few African Americans, especially in the South. This meant that black veterans did not receive much employment information and that the offers they did receive were for low-paid and menial jobs. "In one survey of 50 cities, the movement of blacks into peacetime employment was found to be lagging far behind that of white veterans: in Arkansas ninety-five percent of the placements made by the USES for Afro-Americans were in service or unskilled jobs."[35] African Americans were also less likely than whites, regardless of GI status, to gain new jobs commensurate with their wartime jobs. For example, in San Francisco, by 1948, black Americans "had dropped back halfway to their prewar employment status."[36]

Black GIs faced discrimination in the educational system as well. Despite the end of restrictions on Jews and other Euro-ethnics, African Americans were not welcome in white colleges. Black colleges were overcrowded, but the combination of segregation and prejudice made for few alternatives. About 20,000 black veterans attended college by 1947, most in black colleges, but almost as many, 15,000, could not gain entry. Predictably, the disproportionately few African Americans who did gain access to their educational benefits were able, like their white counterparts, to become doctors and engineers, and to enter the black middle class.[37]

☐ *Suburbanization*

In 1949, ensconced in Valley Stream, I watched potato farms turn into Levittown and Idlewild (later Kennedy) airport. This was the major spectator sport in our first years on Long Island. A typical weekend would bring various aunts, uncles, and cousins out from the city. After a huge meal, we'd pile into the car—itself a novelty—to look at the bulldozed acres and comment on the matchbox construction. During the week, my mother and I would look at the houses going up within walking distance.

Bill Levitt built a basic, 900–1,000 square foot, somewhat expandable house for a lower-middle-class and working-class market on Long Island, and later in Pennsylvania and New Jersey. Levittown started out as 2,000 units of rental housing at $60 a month, designed to meet the low-income housing needs of returning war vets, many of whom, like my Aunt Evie and Uncle Julie, were living in Quonset huts. By May 1947, Levitt and Sons had acquired enough land in Hempstead Township on Long Island to build 4,000 houses, and by the next February, he had built 6,000 units and named the development after himself. After 1948, federal financing for the construction of rental housing tightened, and Levitt switched to building houses for sale. By 1951, Levittown was a development of some 15,000 families.[38]

At the beginning of World War II, about one-third of all American families owned their houses. That percentage doubled in twenty years. Most Levittowners looked just like my family. They came from New York City or Long Island; about 17 percent were military, from nearby Mitchell Field; Levittown was their first house, and almost everyone was married. Three-quarters of the 1947 inhabitants were white collar, but by 1950 more blue-collar families had moved in, so that by 1951, "barely half" of the new residents were white collar, and by 1960 their occupational profile was somewhat more working class than for Nassau County as a whole. By this time too, almost one-third of Levittown's people were either foreign-born or, like my parents, first-generation U.S.-born.[39]

The Federal Housing Administration (FHA) was key to buyers and builders alike. Thanks to the FHA, suburbia was open to more than GIs. People like us would never have been in the market for houses without FHA and Veterans Administration (VA) low-down-payment, low-interest, long-term loans to young buyers. Most suburbs were built by "merchant builders," large-scale entrepreneurs like Levitt, who obtained their own direct FHA and VA loans. In the view of one major builder, "[w]ithout FHA and VA loans merchant building would not have happened." A great deal was at stake. FHA and VA had to approve subdivision plans and make the appraisals upon which house buyers' loans were calculated. FHA appraisals effectively set the price a house could sell for, since it established the amount of the mortgage it would insure. The VA was created after the war, and it followed FHA policies. Most of the benefits in both programs went to the suburbs, and half of all suburban housing in the 1950s and 1960s was financed by FHA/VA loans. Federal highway funding was also important to suburbanization. The National Defense Highway Act of 1941 put the government in the business of funding 90 percent of a national highway system (the other 10 percent came from the states), which developed a network of freeways between and around the nation's metropolitan areas, making suburbs and automobile commuting a way of life. State zoning laws and services were also key. "A significant and often crucial portion of the required infrastructure—typically water, sewer, roads, parks, schools—was provided by the existing community, which was in effect subsidizing the builder and indirectly the new buyer or renter."[40]

In residential life, as in jobs and education, federal programs and GI benefits were crucial for mass entry into a middle-class, home-owning suburban lifestyle. Together they raised the American standard of living to a middle-class one.

It was in housing policy that the federal government's racism reached its high point. Begun in 1934, the FHA was a New Deal program whose original intent was to stimulate the construction industry by insuring private loans to buy or build houses. Even before the war, it had stimulated a building boom. The FHA was "largely run by representatives of the real estate and banking industries."[41] It is fair to say that the "FHA exhorted segregation and enshrined it as public policy." As early as 1955, Charles Abrams blasted it:

A government offering such bounty to builders and lenders could have required compliance with a nondiscrimination policy. Or the agency could at least have pursued a course of evasion, or hidden behind the screen of local autonomy. Instead, FHA adopted a racial policy that could well have been culled from the Nuremberg laws. From its inception FHA set itself up as the protector of the all white neighborhood. It sent its agents into the field to keep Negroes and other minorities from buying houses in white neighborhoods.[42]

The FHA believed in racial segregation. Throughout its history, it publicly and actively promoted restrictive covenants. Before the war, these forbade sales to Jews and Catholics as well as to African Americans. The deed to my house in Detroit had such a covenant, which theoretically prevented it from being sold to Jews or African Americans. Even after the Supreme Court outlawed restrictive covenants in 1948, the FHA continued to encourage builders to write them in against African Americans. FHA underwriting manuals openly insisted on racially homogeneous neighborhoods, and their loans were made only in white neighborhoods. I bought my Detroit house in 1972, from Jews who were leaving a largely African American neighborhood. By that time, restrictive covenants were a dead letter, but block busting by realtors was replacing it.

With the federal government behind them, virtually all developers refused to sell to African Americans. Palo Alto and Levittown, like most suburbs as late as 1960, were virtually all white. Out of 15,741 houses and 65,276 people, averaging 4.2 people per house, only 220 Levittowners, or 52 households, were "nonwhite." In 1958, Levitt announced publicly, at a press conference held to open his New Jersey development, that he would not sell to black buyers. This caused a furor because the state of New Jersey (but not the U.S. government) prohibited discrimination in federally subsidized housing. Levitt was sued and fought it. There had been a white riot in his Pennsylvania development when a black family moved in a few years earlier. In New Jersey, he was ultimately persuaded by township ministers to integrate. West Coast builder Joe Eichler had a policy of selling to any African American who could afford to buy. But his son pointed out that his father's clientele in more affluent Palo Alto was less likely to feel threatened. They liked to think of themselves as liberal, which was relatively easy to do because there were relatively few African Americans in the Bay area, and fewer still could afford homes in Palo Alto.[43]

The result of these policies was that African Americans were totally shut out of the suburban boom. An article in *Harper's* described the housing available to black GIs.

On his way to the base each morning, Sergeant Smith passes an attractive air-conditioned, FHA-financed housing project. It was built for service families. Its rents are little more than the Smiths pay for their shack. And there are half-a-dozen vacancies, but none for Negroes.[44]

Where my family felt the seductive pull of suburbia, Marshall Berman's experienced the brutal push of urban renewal. In the Bronx, in the 1950s, Robert Moses's Cross-Bronx Expressway erased "a dozen solid, settled, densely populated neighborhoods like our own. . . . [S]omething like 60,000 working- and lower-middle-class people, mostly Jews, but with many Italians, Irish, and Blacks thrown in, would be thrown out of their homes. . . . For ten years, through the late 1950s and early 1960s, the center of the Bronx was pounded and blasted and smashed."[45]

Urban renewal made postwar cities into bad places to live. At a physical level, urban renewal reshaped them, and federal programs brought private developers and public officials together to create downtown central business districts where there had formerly been a mix of manufacturing, commerce, and working-class neighborhoods. Manufacturing was scattered to the peripheries of the city, which were ringed and bisected by a national system of highways. Some working-class neighborhoods were bulldozed, but others remained. In Los Angeles, as in New York's Bronx, the postwar period saw massive freeway construction right through the heart of old working-class neighborhoods. In East Los Angeles and Santa Monica, Chicana/o and African American communities were divided in half or blasted to smithereens by the highways bringing Angelenos to the new white suburbs, or to make way for civic monuments like Dodger Stadium.[46]

Urban renewal was the other side of the process by which Jewish and other working-class Euro-immigrants became middle class. It was the push to suburbia's seductive pull. The fortunate white survivors of urban renewal headed disproportionately for suburbia, where they could partake of prosperity and the good life. There was a reason for its attraction. It was often cheaper to buy in the suburbs than to rent in the city. Even Euro-ethnics and families who would be considered working class, based on their occupations, were able to buy into the emerging white suburban lifestyle. And as Levittown indicates, they did so in increasing numbers, so that by 1966 half of all workers and 75 percent of those under forty nationwide lived in suburbs. They too were considered middle-class.[47]

If the federal stick of urban renewal joined the FHA carrot of cheap mortgages to send masses of Euro-Americans to the suburbs, the FHA had a different kind of one-two punch for African Americans. Segregation kept them out of the suburbs, and redlining made sure they could not buy or repair their homes in the neighborhoods in which they were allowed to live. The FHA practiced systematic redlining. This was a practice developed by its predecessor, the Home Owners Loan Corporation (HOLC), which in the 1930s developed an elaborate neighborhood rating system that placed the highest (green) value on all-white, middle-class neighborhoods, and the lowest (red) on racially nonwhite or mixed and working-class neighborhoods. High ratings meant high property values. The idea was that low property values in redlined neighborhoods made them bad investments. The FHA was, after all, created by and for banks and the housing industry. Redlining warned banks not to lend there, and the FHA would not insure mortgages in such neighborhoods. Redlining created a self-fulfilling prophesy.

> With the assistance of local realtors and banks, it assigned one of the four ratings to every block in every city. The resulting information was then translated into the appropriate color [green, blue, yellow, or red] and duly recorded on secret "Residential Security Maps" in local HOLC offices. The maps themselves were placed in elaborate "City Survey Files," which consisted of reports, questionnaires, and workpapers relating to current and future values of real estate.[48]

The FHA's and VA's refusal to guarantee loans in redlined neighborhoods made it virtually impossible for African Americans to borrow money for home improvement or purchase. Because these maps and surveys were quite secret, it took the civil rights movement to make these practices and their devastating consequences public. As a result, those who fought urban renewal, or who sought to make a home in the urban ruins, found themselves locked out of the middle class. They also faced an ideological assault that labeled their neighborhoods slums and called them slumdwellers.[49]

☐ *Conclusion*

The record is very clear. Instead of seizing the opportunity to end institutionalized racism, the federal government did its level best to shut and double-seal the postwar window of opportunity in African Americans' faces. It consistently refused to combat segregation in the social institutions that were key to upward mobility in education, housing, and employment. Moreover, federal programs that were themselves designed to assist demobilized GIs and young families systematically discriminated against African Americans. Such programs reinforced white/nonwhite racial distinctions even as intrawhite racialization was falling out of fashion. This other side of the coin, that white men of northwest European ancestry and white men of southeastern European ancestry were treated equally in theory and in practice with regard to the benefits they received, was part of the larger postwar whitening of Jews and other eastern and southern Europeans.

The myth that Jews pulled themselves up by their own bootstraps ignores the fact that it took federal programs to create the conditions whereby the abilities of Jews and other European immigrants could be recognized and rewarded rather than denigrated and denied. The GI Bill and FHA and VA mortgages, even though they were advertised as open to all, functioned as a set of racial privileges. They were privileges because they were extended to white GIs but not to black GIs. Such privileges were forms of affirmative action that allowed Jews and other Euro-

American men to become suburban homeowners and to get the training that allowed them—but much less so women vets or war workers—to become professionals, technicians, salesmen, and managers in a growing economy. Jews and other white ethnics' upward mobility was due to programs that allowed us to float on a rising economic tide. To African Americans, the government offered the cement boots of segregation, redlining, urban renewal, and discrimination.

Those racially skewed gains have been passed across the generations, so that racial inequality seems to maintain itself "naturally," even after legal segregation ended. Today, I own a house in Venice, California, like the one in which I grew up in Valley Stream, and my brother until recently owned a house in Palo Alto much like an Eichler house. Both of us are where we are thanks largely to the postwar benefits our parents received and passed on to us, and to the educational benefits we received in the 1960s as a result of affluence and the social agitation that developed from the black Freedom Movement. I have white, African American, and Asian American colleagues whose parents received fewer or none of America's postwar benefits and who expect never to own a house despite their considerable academic achievements. Some of these colleagues who are a few years younger than I also carry staggering debts for their education, which they expect to have to repay for the rest of their lives.

Conventional wisdom has it that the United States has always been an affluent land of opportunity. But the truth is that affluence has been the exception and that real upward mobility has required massive affirmative action programs. The myth of affluence persists today long after the industrial boom, and the public policies that supported good union contracts and real employment opportunities for (almost) all are gone. It is increasingly clear that the affluent period between 1940 and 1970 or 1975 was an aberrant one for America's white working class. The Jewish ethnic wisdom I grew up with, that we pulled ourselves up by our own bootstraps, by sticking together, by being damned smart, leaves out an important part of the truth: that not all Jews made it, and that those who did had a great deal of help from the federal government.

Today, in a shrinking economy, where downward mobility is the norm, the children and grandchildren of the postwar beneficiaries of the economic boom have some precious advantages. For example, having parents who own their own homes or who have decent retirement benefits can make a real difference in a young person's ability to take on huge college loans or to come up with a down payment for a house. Even this simple inheritance helps perpetuate the gap between whites and people of color. Sure, Jews needed ability, but that was never enough for more than a few to make it. The same applies today. Whatever advantages I bequeath them, my sons will never have their parents' or grandparents' experience of life on a rising economic tide.

Public policies like the anti-immigrant Proposition 187 and anti-affirmative action Proposition 209 in California, the abolition of affirmative action policies at the University of California, and media demonization of African Americans and Central American immigrants as lazy welfare cheats encourage feelings of white entitlement to middle-class privilege. But our children's and grandchildren's realities are that they are downwardly mobile relative to their grandparents, not because people of color are getting the good jobs by affirmative action but because the good jobs and prosperity in general are ceasing to exist.

Race Making ☐ CHAPTER 2

*Our immigrant labor supply has been used by
American industry in much the same way that
American farmers have used our land supply.*
                    —David Montgomery,
                    Workers' Control in America

*The process of keeping blacks from competing
with whites in the labor market is the foundation upon which American racism is built.*
                    —Henry Louis Taylor Jr.,
                    "The Hidden Face of Racism"

*If one adds to [the number of European immi-
grant workers in the early twentieth century]
workers of foreign parentage and of Afro-American descent, the resulting non-native/nonwhite
population clearly encompassed the great majority of America's industrial workforce.*
                    —Leon Fink,
                    In Search of the Working Class

W hat institutional practices turned Jews and other eastern
and southern Europeans into nonwhites in the first place?
Were they the same practices that created African Americans?
Latino/as? Asian Americans? Why has race mattered so much?
This chapter examines the larger system of ethnoracial assignment.

Prior to the early nineteenth century, all Europeans in the

United States were more or less equally white. Some of those early white European immigrants came from southern and central Europe. For example, Italians and Jews immigrated, but they also assimilated, blended, and were treated as whites with a minimum of fuss early in the century.[1] Many European immigrants before the 1880s did not form ethnic communities at all, or did not form them for very long. More perplexing, southern and eastern European immigrants and their children faced intense racism (and the Irish continued to face residues of it) in the industrial East and Midwest of the late nineteenth century; but when they migrated to the West they were usually considered fully white.[2]

The difficulty that southern and eastern European races were said to have in assimilating is sometimes contrasted with the rapid assimilation of earlier waves of northwestern European immigrants and explained as being due to the fact that most of the latter came from the British Isles and from other "more familiar" northwestern European cultures. But when the Irish first immigrated in the early nineteenth century, they were compared, sometimes unfavorably, to African Americans and were most certainly not treated as white.[3] And one might also ask why Germans and Scandinavians were "more like us" on their first immigration than were the English-speaking Irish. What made Scandinavians "more familiar" than Italians or Jews later in the century? Actually, the concept of a "more familiar northwestern European culture" did not really develop until the 1880s, and then only in contrast to a newly "less familiar" southern and eastern European set of cultures.

Part of that divide had to do with religion. As Barbara Fields has pointed out with regard to colonial times, before there were white and black people, there were Christians and heathens. And British Protestants dominated Irish Catholics, as Theodore Allen has argued. In British-occupied Ireland and in the American colonies, the religious and racial systems of domination overlapped and interpenetrated. In time and with slavery (and adoption of Christianity by bondspeople), "inferior" religious cultures became inferior races.[4] In the nineteenth century, anti-Catholicism and anti-Semitism overlapped and fused with racial stigmatization of southern and eastern Europeans.

☐ *Labor and Race*

What were Jews doing when they became nonwhite? What were the circumstances under which largely non-Protestants—Catholic Irish and southern Europeans as well as Jewish eastern Europeans—became racially subordinated? I suggest that work, especially the performance of work that was at once important to the economy of the nation and that was defined as menial and unskilled, was key to their nonwhite racial assignment.

Even before American industry exploded, following the Civil War, the hard physical labor of Irish immigrants laid the foundations upon which it rose. The Irish excavated the Erie and C&O canals that formed the first freight system, dug the coal in rural Pennsylvania, worked in the textile mills of Philadelphia, unloaded and moved cargo up and down the coast, and cleaned the houses and cared for the children of the emerging urban middle class. In Boston, New York, and Philadelphia before the Civil War, Noel Ignatiev tells us, the Irish became the laborers and domestic servants of America's nascent industrial cities.[5]

At the end of the century, southern and eastern European immigrants and their children constituted the great mass of the 23 million immigrants to the United States. Their immigration coincided with the Industrial Revolution in America. They became its factory workers and the bulk of the urban populations in the East and Midwest. As Jeremy Brecher argued long ago, the golden age of industrialization in the United States was also the golden age of class struggle between the captains of the new industrial empires and the masses of manual workers whose labor made them rich. As the majority of mining and manufacturing workers, immigrants were visibly major players in these struggles.[6]

Only when these immigrants took their places as the masses of "unskilled" and residentially ghettoized industrial workers did

Americans come to believe that Europe was made up of a variety of inferior and superior races. At that point, those who formed the mass of immigrant industrial workers found that they were being classified as members of specific and inferior European races, and for almost half a century, they were treated as racially not-quite-white. Where they were less concentrated, as in the West, they tended to be white and worked under less industrial conditions.[7]

European races were visible, seemingly a natural phenomenon, when one looked at where Americans worked. Immigrants were visible not least because they were concentrated in urban industrial centers. In contrast, a staggering 44 percent of all native-born white male workers in 1910 worked in farming, lumbering, and livestock-raising far from the industrial centers.

The labor force that grew up during this period was occupationally segregated by race and gender at every level from industry and region to job and plant. The industrial working class in the East and Midwest was made up mainly of different kinds of European immigrants. By 1910, 58 percent of the industrial workforce in twenty of the main mining and manufacturing industries were European immigrants.[8] In 1910 and 1920, native-born whites were actually a slight minority (47 percent and 49.3 percent, respectively) of the *total* labor force and hence an even smaller percentage of the working-class labor force.[9] In 1880, only 13 percent of the U.S. population was foreign-born. Yet even then, immigrants made up 42 percent of the workers in manufacturing and mining.

Still, U.S.-born white workers were not a negligible part of the working class. In the early twentieth century, most white workers were not skilled craftsmen. White men formed some 38 percent of the industrial "unskilled" workforce and seem to have been the core of the mining industry, along with Mexicans, in the southern part of the Rocky Mountain region.[10] In 1900, over one-third of the nation's "unskilled" laborers were white. Similar proportions existed among iron- and steelworkers and miners and quarrymen.[11]

However, even where aggregated data show a mix of white and nonwhite workers, closer inspection reveals segregation. For example, mining in Arizona was organized with white workers aboveground and Mexican American workers underground, in the dirtiest jobs. Segregated and unequal company housing heightened the racial segregation.

White workers' everyday practices also played a role in keeping their male and female occupational niches separate from those of nonwhite workers. Thus, jobs held by immigrants have often been by definition "socially inappropriate for native workers." David Brody reports a steelworker's shock that a "white" man asked for a blast-furnace job. "Only Hunkies work on those jobs, they're too damn dirty and too damn hot for a 'white' man."[12] In Pennsylvania's steel industry, because African American and eastern and southern European immigrants did dirty jobs, this was often proof enough that they too were dirty.

> There is a . . . crowd of Negroes and Syrians working there. Many of them are filthy in their personal habits, and the idea of working with them is repugnant to any man who wants to retain his self-respect. It is no place for a man with a white man's heart to be. The Negroes and foreigners are coarse, vulgar and brutal in their acts and conversation.[13]

As a result, Brody notes, steel workers "in the same plant, skilled and unskilled men shared little more than a common employer."[14] As we will explore further later, white workers understood the value of whiteness and made their own original contributions to racist patterns of occupational segregation.

Focusing on turn-of-the-last-century male workforces in heavy industry, David Montgomery has observed that a plentiful supply of immigrant workers underlay the rapid expansion of a system where the skills required for industrial jobs came to be embedded in the machinery, in the organization of the labor process, and in forms of supervision, like piecework, designed to outfox workers' resistance to management's control of productivity. Industrial capitalism, Montgomery tells us, was not a system of scientific management but rather one that treated workers as casual and easily replaced factors of production. The captains of industry put their energy into supervising and into piecework schemes to increase workers' output much like the system of slavery that preceded it. For example, at Goodyear Rubber, there was one inspector for every ten workers. The same pattern prevailed in the oil, chemical, and rubber industries, where two-thirds to three-quarters of the workers were European immigrants, as well as in steel, meatpacking, and textiles with similarly large immigrant workforces. In the very construction of industrial work, workers seem to have been conceptualized as more an instrument or "hand" than fully human, more thing-like than citizen-like, and therefore less entitled to the prerogatives of white men and women of the body politic proper.[15] The work was broken down into simple, repetitive tasks under intense supervision that appeared to justify wages so low that households typically depended upon the income of more than one earner. Driven labor became a "natural" way to organize mass production, a function of responding to competition and to demand on the one hand, and to reliance on "inferior" workers on the other. In turn, degraded forms of work confirmed the apparent obviousness of the racial inferiority of the workers who did it.

In contrast to U.S.-born white women, European immigrant women worked as domestic servants and in factories. Irish and Slovak women typically worked as servants, usually on a live-in basis, while Jewish, Polish, and Italian women worked in meatpacking, textile, and garment manufacturing.[16] Most European immigrant women, and Mexican women as well, worked prior to marriage and tried to avoid such work in favor of home-based income-generating enterprises after they married.[17]

National or ethnic-specific job niches complemented residentially segregated ethnic communities to give the appearance of reality to the proliferation of European races. Not only were industrial cities characterized by a multiplicity of immigrant working-class ghettos, but, as Marc Miller showed for Lowell, "[t]o a great extent, a person's ethnic background defined his or her opportunities." As one textile worker described it,

> In the Merrimack [textile mill], the Greeks could work in the dyehouse, the Irish could work in the yard, and the French could maybe work in the card room, but you never went any higher than that. You just didn't even think of—if you could go to night school and learn to better yourself, forget it. Not in the Merrimack Mill.[18]

Writing of workers at Singer Sewing Machine in Elizabeth, New Jersey, a city of Euro-immigrants, Katherine Newman described plant recruitment prior to World War II as "strictly an ethnic affair." Workers' places in the job hierarchy were set by the timing of their group's immigration, and specific stereotypes were attached to workers according to their ethnicity. However, not until the 1930s depression did recruiters hire African American workers, and then only for the worst, foundry jobs.[19]

John Bodnar surveyed local and firm-based patterns of occupational segregation by nationality across the East and Midwest in the second decade of the twentieth century. He found southern Italians and Serbs working primarily as general laborers, Poles in manufacturing and mechanical occupations, and Greeks in personal service. More finely grained studies of the early twentieth century show even sharper patterns of ethnic and gender segregation. For example, where Jews worked in smaller clothing firms with relatively less de-skilling, Italians were concentrated in larger factories with more degraded work. Polish women "dominated" Chicago's restaurant and kitchen jobs. Croatians in Indiana oil refineries were concentrated in only three specific jobs, while New York City Serbs and Croatians worked in freight handling. Barbershops and construction work in Buffalo, Philadelphia, and Pittsburgh were the province of Italians. Detroit's Peninsular Car Company in 1900 hired Polish workers almost exclusively. In 1920, more than two-thirds of all Slovak men were coal miners, and Mexican men were blast-furnace workers.[20]

The Census carved out a special niche for racialized Europeans—they were not part of "Negroes and other races," but neither were they the same as "native" whites. It created a set of off-white categories by distinguishing not only immigrant from "native" whites by country, but also native whites of native white parentage and native whites of immigrant (or mixed) parentage (i.e., children of immigrants). Because the bulk of northwest European immigration was at least a generation earlier, those of northwestern European ancestry would more likely be classified as "natives," or children of native-born parents, while immigrants and children of immigrants would contain mainly more recent immigrants, or those from eastern and southern Europe. Thus, in distinguishing immigrants/children of immigrants (southern and eastern Europeans) from "native" (northwestern Europeans), the Census mirrored the racial distinctions of the social Darwinists, xenophobes, and eugenicists discussed in chapter 1.[21] Eastern and southern European immigrants were thus "seen" by the state and by popular culture as belonging to races that were less than fully white. Phrases like "not-quite-white," "not-bright-white," or perhaps "conditionally white" more accurately describe this range of racialization.

☐ *Why Did Immigrants Get Bad Jobs?*
Although it is clear that European immigrants in the early twentieth century had an inside track on some of America's worst jobs, it is not obvious why this was so. Nor is it obvious how this connection is related to nonwhite racial assignment. One set of arguments holds that it is because Euro-immigrants lacked skills for better jobs, or that they lacked the labor force commitment to develop such skills. Once (or if) they learned those skills, they got better jobs and assimilated into the mainstream.[22] The experience of immigrant Jews challenges this explanation.

Jews, Skill, and Labor Force Commitment

Thanks to scapegoating, pogroms, and the upheavals of early capitalism in eastern Europe, Jews were transformed in the late nineteenth century more completely than other eastern and southern Europeans into an urban, wage-earning people. Stephen Steinberg has argued that because of their urban position in the 1870s and 1880s, a very high proportion of Jewish workers were quite skilled at a variety of industrial trades. By 1897, one-sixth of the Jewish labor force in Russia worked in garment manufacturing alone, and Jews also played a major role in developing this industry. Jews were prominent as workers and as owners in the developing agricultural trade, in flour milling, tobacco production, woodworking, and sawmills, as well as in a wide variety of skilled trades in late-nineteenth-century Russia.[23]

Jews were also among the most permanent of immigrants to the United States. Unlike southern Italians, for example, few Jews returned to Russia, or even dreamed of it, especially after the pogroms in the first decade of the twentieth century. Despite their skill and permanence, the Jewish labor force was concentrated in one of the most de-skilled and low-paid industries in the United States.

Although eastern European Jews made up a quarter of New York City's population, they comprised almost half the city's industrial workforce. Their employer par excellence was the garment industry, which was also the city's biggest. If the industry was important for Jewish men, it was even more important for women, for it was their chief form of waged labor. In 1900, 40 percent of all "Russian-born" women and almost 20 percent of the men worked in the industry. Clara Lemlich, a future union organizer, newly arrived in New York in 1903, found garment work right away, "at a fraction of the wage her father would have earned for the same work," had he been able to find work. This was no aberration. Bosses were able to pay young women less than men and believed they were less likely than men to unionize.[24] Most women garment workers were young and unmarried, daughters contributing to their households. As we shall see, wage work was expected of daughters, although not of married women.[25]

Despite its organization in small shops, the clothing industry was exemplary in its rapid growth and its shift from a craft organization to an intensely industrial organization based on "unskilled" labor. Both shifts took place at the same time that Jews entered the industry.

> [M]easured by number of workers and value of product, [garment industry growth in the 1890s] was two or three times as rapid as the average for all industries. For the women's clothing industry, the years of sharpest growth were during this period, one that coincided with Jewish immigration.[26]

By 1914, with 510,000 workers and 15,000 shops, the annual payroll came to $326 million and the product value to over $1 billion. In women's clothing, New York City alone produced two-thirds of the value of all apparel made in the United States.[27]

The availability of Jewish immigrant labor enabled the industry's explosive growth and made possible the move in the organization of labor away from a reliance on skilled producers of garments to an assembly line where many workers employed fewer skills to produce a large number of identical garments.[28]

The irony of this situation is that Jews were more skilled than other European immigrants, especially in the garment trades. Two-thirds of all Jewish adult workers who immigrated between 1899 and 1910 were classed as skilled, a much higher proportion than among English, Scandinavian, and German immigrants. Jews were a majority of all immigrant skilled cap and hat makers, furriers, tailors and bookbinders, watchmakers and milliners, cigarmakers, and tinsmiths, as well as "first among immigrant printers, bakers, carpenters, cigar-packers, blacksmiths and building trades workmen."[29] The availability of very high skill levels among immigrant Jewish garment workers could have sustained greatly expanded craft production, but manufacturers reorganized for mass production by de-skilling the jobs and intensifying the work.

What was it about a Jewish labor force that allowed manu-facturers to do this? Occupational restriction was the critical fac-tor. Although many Jewish workers were skilled in the printing, carpentry, painting, and building trades, Jews were frozen out of these occupations almost completely, just as they were fro-zen out of the highly unionized transportation and communica-tion trades. Exclusion of Jews was accomplished largely by the craft unions, especially in building trades, which were part of the American Federation of Labor and adamantly the province of white male workers—a "privileged labor class" of Irish (con-siderably whitened by this time), British, and Germans—who often met immigrants with violence.[30] Such practices were ap-parently highly valued in governmental circles. They earned the trade union movement the approval of the U.S. Immigration Commission in 1910 as "bulwarks of Americanism."[31]

Jews went into the garment industry because they could—they had the skills and those jobs were open to them. They did not become printers or transport or construction workers not because they lacked the skills but because they were not allowed into the unions which controlled the right to engage in these occupations. For those unions, whiteness was an important pre-requisite for membership.

This suggests that job degradation and racial darkening were linked. The immigrants who worked in the garment industry saw their jobs divide and their work de-skill as the industry grew. In contrast, although the construction industry also expanded, its jobs underwent no equivalent de-skilling or division. Indeed, the existence of specific trades unions governed the *way* in which labor was organized as well as who could perform it, which has continued until recently. The degraded jobs of the nonwhite workforce in the garment industry stand in sharp contrast to the artisan-like conditions that prevailed in the building trades, where white unions, with explicit approval from the government and tacit consent or enthusiasm from employers, policed both the conditions of labor and who was allowed to work. The "free-dom" of craft autonomy in the construction of work was a prerogative of whiteness. It stood in contrast to the "servility" of the nonwhite assembly line.[32]

Working-class Racism as Economic Competition

Another explanation for why immigrants were concentrated in degraded jobs is presented most persuasively by Edna Bonacich, who suggests that because immigrants were more vulnerable or less knowledgeable about the workforce, they were willing to work for less, and that employers who took advantage of this also recognized that a racially divided labor force could work to their benefit. White workers' exclusion of immigrants stems less from racism than from fear of having their wages cut by competition from immigrant workers. Thus the argument is that economic competition is at the root of an ethnoracially split labor market, and that this underlies working-class white racism.[33]

Noel Ignatiev's discussion of immigrant Irish competition with free African American workers in the early nineteenth century calls this view into question.

> [T]he initial turnover from black to Irish labor does not imply racial discrimination; many of the newly arrived Irish, hungry and desperate, were willing to work for less than free persons of color, and it was no more than good capitalist sense to hire them.[34]

Thus, Irish immigrants replaced free African American workers and came to make up 87 percent of New York's unskilled laborers, with equivalent monopolies on other domestic service jobs. But he continues:

> Now it was the black workers who were hungry and desperate, willing to work for the lowest wage. Why, then, were they not hired to undercut the wages of the Irish, as sound business principles would dictate?

His answer is, "'White men will not work with him'—the magic formula of American trade unionism!"[35] That is, white workers unionized to effectively exclude African Americans (and Jews) from a white occupational niche.

How, Ignatiev asks, did the Irish become white? Acknowledging that the Irish did not whiten themselves unaided, that they had the ultimate (though not willing) acquiescence of the elites and the support of Jacksonian Democrats, he emphasizes the centrality of organized racial violence against African Americans to Irish claims to whiteness.

His key insight is to tease out the complex links between Irish working-class, organized violence against capitalism and Irish violence against African Americans. Although the Irish did not invent unions, they were central to the history of trade unionism in the United States. Secret societies organized at a county level, Irish gangs, and Irish unions were key in winning the fight for a ten-hour day and in creating labor unions in the antebellum nineteenth century.

But those same groups also fought (literally) to distinguish themselves from African Americans, with whom they shared neighborhoods and jobs. The Irish insisted that they did "white man's work." Given that Irish and free African Americans in the North were both initially laborers and servants, this meant an all-out press to exclude African Americans from these jobs. They also rioted fairly systematically—a right of white citizens during this period, as Ignatiev points out—to drive African Americans out of racially unmarked poor neighborhoods and to turn them into self-defined white ones.

The riots and the refusals to work were only *claims* to whiteness. The Irish did not become white until those claims were recognized by the political and economic elites. Then and only then were the Irish incorporated into the city's governing structure.[36]

Why would some men define themselves as white and not work with those defined as black? Ignatiev suggests that split labor market arguments, that ethnoracial antagonism stems from higher-paid white workers' fears of competition from lower-waged workers, is at best circular: absent white racism, white workers would organize workers of color at least as often as they would exclude them. And indeed, the fact that Irish workers managed to develop eventual unity with German workers but never with African American ones suggests that racial assignment shaped economic patterns more than economic patterns shaped racial assignment.

Yet, Bonacich is also right to insist on corporate responsibility for racial segregation and the degradation of work. Nowhere is this more vividly illustrated than in Venus Green's important study of African American women in the Bell Telephone system.[37] Bell refused to hire African Americans until forced to do so. When it did, it restricted black workers to narrow occupational niches and then degraded the jobs. In her analysis of a racial and gendered "up the down escalator," Green shows how Bell's racial ideology about employment shaped its pursuit of technological change and job construction.

Bell has historically practiced a policy of deliberately excluding black women except "in jobs designated undesirable for white workers."[38] As late as 1955, racist themes pervaded company entertainment—from white women in blackface and traveling minstrel groups to racist theme parties and caricatures of African Americans in company publications. Not surprisingly, it was deliberate Bell policy to exclude African American women from the job of operator (and subsequently from central switching systems) until the period 1960–1970. In this time period, the operator job was reorganized into a more intensely controlled, driven, and degraded (still low-paid) function eventually slated for technological obsolescence.

Only when white women began to flee these jobs did the Bell system consider new workers. As one AT&T vice president stated in 1969:

> The kind of people we need are going to be in very short supply.
> . . . Most of our new hires go into entry level jobs which means we
> must have access to an ample supply of people who will work at

comparatively low rates of pay. That means city people more so than suburbanites. That means lots of black people. . . . We need them because we have so many jobs to fill and they will take them.

It is just a plain fact that in today's world telephone company wages are more in line with black expectations—and the tighter the labor market the more this is true.[39]

Green reminds us that there was nothing natural in Bell's decision to structure the operator job this way in the face of white flight. "Instead of raising wages and creating less stressful work environments to attract people of all races, the Bell System segregated black women into departmental ghettos (operators and low-level clerks) where there was little opportunity for advancement."[40] Although the 1973 consent decree with the Equal Employment Opportunity Commission brought some gains to a relatively small number of black and white women and men workers, many of these gains were temporary, and the majority of black women remained concentrated in the operator and lower-clerical ghetto, where they did not share in gains at all. As Sally Hacker noted at the time, "[P]lanned technological change would eliminate more jobs for women than affirmative action would provide."[41] As both Green and Hacker pointed out, Bell was aided by a union to whom "worker" effectively meant white male, for it failed to fight for the preservation of women's jobs.[42]

It is clear that race has mattered a great deal in U.S. history—and continues to matter—in determining where and how one works and lives and how one is regarded in the civic discourse of the American nation. What is not yet clear is where America's black-and-white racially polarized structure came from in the first place. Without it, the preceding examples of occupationally segregated forms of job degradation would make no cultural sense. We certainly would not see occupational segregation by race and sex as "natural" ways to organize labor.

☐ *Where Did Race Come From?*

This question was first answered more than fifty years ago in Eric Williams's Marxist classic, *Capitalism and Slavery*. Since that time, other African diaspora scholars have taken the lead in demonstrating more fully the ways that slavery made race and the ways that race justified a regime of slave labor. New World patterns of race and racism were part of a larger, hemisphere-wide process by which a European planter class consolidated itself as a ruling class whose wealth came from slave labor.[43]

Joining Williams, Lerone Bennett argued that not only is a segregated labor force at the very center of racism, it is at the core of race making itself. Colonial landholders and would-be planters did not control entirely *who* would comprise their labor force; they experimented. They tried to enslave Native Americans and to import European debtors, convicts, and African servants, singly and together. As Bennett showed, planter-controlled state legislatures began early on to create an edifice of segregation and antimiscegenation laws consciously to keep those they subordinated from intermarrying and rebelling en masse. Antimiscegenation laws, passed in most plantation colonies during the seventeenth century, were part of a never-ending effort by planters to prevent the dispossessed from rebelling together by inventing separate social places called "white," "black," and "red" for them to inhabit.[44]

As southern planters refined their attempts to establish the property rights of slave owners and to keep the indentured from making common cause, they also transformed the bondage of diverse Europeans, Americans, and Africans into the enslavement of African peoples exclusively. Africans were enslaved not because they were black but because Europeans and Native Americans were able to run away more easily. Planters found it possible, though not easy, to isolate and contain Africans. As Barbara Fields observed recently, before there were blacks, there was slavery, and it was slavery that made it possible and desirable for planters to create a black "race" out of a diversity of African peoples. In that process, "Christians" became whites, people from diverse African nations became "Negroes," and, silliest of all, Native Americans became "Indians."[45] As Audrey Smedley has argued, the importance of African slavery and the idea of race that it created cannot be underestimated as the enduring principle upon which capitalist labor has continued to be organized.[46]

Like the garment industry, New World slavery was big business, and planters were agrarian capitalists. Cotton was America's major export prior to the Civil War. Its 5 million bales of annual production were important enough for a war and for Great Britain to consider aiding the Confederacy.[47]

Agrarian slavery was arguably a kind of template for the way industrial labor came to be organized. Closely supervised, intensely driven, and never-ending work for women and men alike were characteristics of the organization of slave labor.

> [I]n the 1850s at least 90 percent of all female slaves over sixteen years of age labored more than 261 days per year, eleven to thirteen hours each day. . . . The enforced pace of work more nearly resembled that of a factory than a farm; Kemble referred to female field hands as "human hoeing machines."[48]

The labor of bondspeople was extraordinarily profitable for the planter class. On the eve of the Civil War, when there were about as many slaves as there were wage laborers, profits from slave labor were vastly greater than those produced by free labor. Eric Williams estimates that bondspeople received the equivalent of twenty dollars a year in food and clothing, while free workers required five times that amount for the same necessities.[49]

Slavery as an economic system was utterly dependent upon a legal and social regime backed by organized force, that classified human beings as black, white, or red racially and that assigned very different social places and attributes to each race. Law and public policy defined Indian people as savage noncitizens, to be expropriated and killed at will. The Constitution defined African peoples as private property and marshaled law, violence, and the full power of the state, as Evelyn Brooks

Higginbotham put it, to "sanction white ownership of black bodies and black labor."[50] With slavery, blackness became stigmatized as servile and worse, and whiteness became a privileged
condition made visible by its never-ending efforts to distinguish
itself from blackness.

Red, White, and Black

American society has been triracial—red as well as black and
white—from the time of its founding. By the Jacksonian period,
in the 1830s, Native Americans were seen as lazy aliens, savages to be dispossessed or exterminated as obstacles to America's
inevitable westward expansion. They were not citizens, not part
of the nation; they would be forever strangers in its midst. Proof
of their savagery was offered when they fought for their land and
when they refused to adopt European forms of economy and gender relations. Native Americans joined Africans in representations of the barbaric pole proffered by evolutionary theories that
sprang up in the second half of the nineteenth century and that
explained humanity's rise from a savagery like theirs to a civilization like that of white America and western Europe. Thus
alongside the black/white contrast there was a red/white contrast. Both existed to distinguish racially inferior from racially
superior humanity.

In turn, the black-and-white dichotomous structure of capitalist America was contained by and defended from the dangerous and alien redness around it. Redness became savage,
threatening, and unassailable. Although stereotypes of blackness
differed from those of redness, the salient dichotomies, those that
were elaborated culturally, were between black and white and
red and white. The stereotypic attributes assigned to blackness
and redness came to blur into one another over the course of
the nineteenth century. Slave rebellions in the United States and
the Caribbean made black dangerous to planters, and the con-
quest and destruction of Native American peoples mitigated images of Indian savagery.[51]

Race, Reconstruction, and Immigration

The abolition of slavery did not end racism as a state-enforced system, and it certainly did not end African Americans' agrarian economic bondage to the planter class. As their part in the Great Compromise of 1877, northern industrialists acquiesced to this second servitude by agreeing not to recruit African Americans into the growing industrial workforce.[52]

The subsequent system of Jim Crow segregation not only supported these racialized economic arrangements—which held almost intact until World War I and did not really fall until the civil rights movement of the 1950s and 1960s—but it also sustained the political hegemony of blackness and whiteness for governing economic and civil relationships in an industrial era when all workers were ostensibly free.[53]

One consequence of this agreement was a politically imposed "shortage" of labor in the North that drove industrialists to look overseas for the workers they needed to run their factories. They promoted immigration from Europe and Asia to solve their labor problems—from Ireland even before the Civil War, then from China, Southern and Eastern Europe, the Philippines, and Japan.

Race became a material force in maintaining social segregation and class division. Race did more than divide and conquer—though it certainly did that. Blackness and whiteness separated, segmented, and segregated the ways of *being* working class.

At this point the triracial system of red, white, and black became somewhat conflated with a binary black-and-white one, as Asian, and to a much smaller extent European, immigrants came to be seen as similar to black workers *and* to Native Americans. The confusion was evident in arguments that Asians or Mexicans, and occasionally Europeans, were so foreign, so savage, and such dangerous criminals that they could never be assimilated into American culture. When immigrants were seen as a necessary part of that working class which did the degraded and driven labor, they were constructed with stereotypes of blackness—stupid, shiftless, sexual, unable to defer gratification.

Despite the fact that the United States recognized many races in its postbellum history, these have been incorporated into the dichotomous remains of a triracial system of white, black, and red. As immigration from Asia and Mexico quickened toward the end of the nineteenth century, meaningful legal and social distinctions depended increasingly upon whether one was assigned to the overlapping black-and-red side or to the white side of the racial divide.

As Tomás Almaguer has shown, the ways that California defined the race of Mexican men and women illustrates the reciprocally defining interdependence of racial classification and social class. Initially categorized as white by virtue of the class standing of the Mexican landowning elite, working-class Mexicans were nevertheless subject to laws based on their actual class position. Thus, the 1855 Vagrancy Act, commonly known as the "Greaser Act," fined, jailed, or enforced labor service on Mexican individuals found guilty of vagrancy.[54] Working class, but not upper class, Mexicans were also often classified by the courts as Native Americans, who, in white supremacist California, could not be citizens and had no rights whatsoever.[55] Racial stigmatization of working-class Mexicans, sporadic in California's early decades of statehood, increased as Mexican men and women became the main labor force for the intensive sugar beet, lima bean, and citrus agribusinesses that developed after 1880. By 1930, racial stigmatization of Mexicans underlay the census presumption that Mexicans were to be classified as nonwhite unless a particular individual was known to the enumerator to be white.[56] Writing of California, George Sanchez notes:

> Segregation was, for the most part, de facto until 1935, when Mexicans (identified as part Indian) were included along with "Chinese, Japanese, Mongolians, and Indians" in a long-standing statute in the state educational code which permitted segregation of these racial minorities.[57]

If not-quite-white Europeans produced America's industrial wealth at the turn of the last century, then Asian and African American men and women workers joined Mexican laborers in producing its agricultural wealth in "factories in the field." Chinese farmers were California's first agricultural labor force until whites drove them off the land. Japanese, Chinese, Korean, and Filipino women and men were the backbone of early Hawaiian plantation agriculture.[58] Later, Mexican and Filipino women and men, working in heavily supervised gang labor conditions, produced food across the Southwest for a national market. On the mainland, the majority of the nation's agricultural workers were African Americans, Mexicans, and Asian immigrants. In the South, African American men were also important as forestry and steel workers and coal miners in Alabama, while Mexican men were a large proportion of miners in the West and Southwest.[59]

Multiracialism and Racial Fluidity Today

Since implementation of the 1965 immigration law and new patterns of immigration, the ethnoracial map of the United States is being reconfigured once again as new arrivals are crowded into the growing sectors of the working class.[60] Although the nature of jobs and the racial composition of the labor force has changed along with the industries in the economic core, the mass of the working class is still—or perhaps more accurately, once again—not-white, racially segregated, and occupationally segmented. In the last two decades, Central American and Asian men and women have become concentrated in rapidly growing personal service industries such as hotels, restaurants, health care, and cleaning, and in the manufacture and processing of food, clothing, and, increasingly, shelter (in the form of nonunion construction). All of these industries have been reorganized around "unskilled" labor working on a minimum wage and temporary basis, and along Taylorist lines.

Racial classifications continue to matter to the American government. Soon after the reopening of immigration in 1965, a Federal Interagency Committee on Education was formed to create a race and ethnicity classification system reflecting the nation's new immigration and addressing the need to monitor the progress of affirmative action. The result was the now-familiar four racial groups: American Indian/Alaskan Native, Asian/Pacific Islander, black, and white. Peoples of diverse Asian-ancestry cultural heritages are lumped together as a race. "White" includes people of diverse European, Middle Eastern, and Indian ancestries. The committee determined that the fifth group, Hispanic, was an ethnic group rather than a race. The governmentese term "Hispanic" foregrounds the Euro-origins of Spanish speakers from many nations. These "Hispanics" are not exactly white, which they were in the 1960 census. Rather they are modified not-quite whites, as in Hispanic whites (and distinct from Afro-Latinos). This system has been the official U.S. racial/ethnic classification guideline used since 1977, except that in the final adoption, East Indian's race was changed from white to Asian.[61]

These categories once again officially mark the American working class racially. Thus, in official census categories in the last thirty years, the races of Mexicans, Middle Easterners, and East Indians have been shuttled back and forth between white and nonwhite. Recent discussion about whether or not to adopt a new biracial option on the census for the year 2000 reflects new patterns of interethnic marriage and perceptions of racial fluidity.[62]

However, any new map of a multiracial nation continues to rest solidly on the preservation of the old black-white binary and continuity of institutionalized racism against African Americans. Assaults on African America, especially since 1980—from massive incarceration to discriminatory policies and practices in employment, education, housing, financial access, health, and welfare—are no secret.[63]

Racism and segregation continue to go together. Intermarriage rates, as Roger Sanjek argues, suggest that social segregation of African Americans is much greater than that facing Latino and Asian groups. Intermarriage rates (mainly with whites) among Hispanic/Latino groups nationally ran at 13 percent in 1980; among Asians at 25 percent; among Jews at over 50 percent. In contrast, African American–white marriage rates were

2 percent. This is low even when compared with the 5 percent for last century's immigrant Jews, which was the lowest rate of intermarriage with whites among first-generation European immigrants.[64] In New York, Sanjek found, racial patterns of residential and social segregation parallel those of intermarriage. As the neighborhood expands from white to include African Americans, as well as Latin American, Caribbean, and Asian immigrants, it does so in a residential pattern that mixes whites with all immigrants but segregates African Americans. Church, social, and local political ties followed the same pattern as residence and intermarriage.[65]

☐ *Summary*

Initially invented to justify a brutal but profitable regime of slave labor, race became the way America organized labor and the explanation it used to justify it as natural. Africans, Europeans, Mexicans, and Asians each came to be treated as members of less civilized, less moral, less self-restrained races only when recruited to be the core of America's capitalist labor force. Such race making depended and continues to depend upon occupational and residential segregation. Race making in turn facilitated the degradation of work itself, its organization as "unskilled," intensely driven, mass production work.

Although they worked in jobs that were termed "unskilled," that label cannot be taken at face value. Workers often possessed skills that they were not allowed to exercise. It is also important to distinguish conceptually the skills *actually required to perform* a job from the job's classification as skilled or unskilled. As Patricia Cooper has noted of the racial and gender pattern to occupational segregation generally, it

> seems to have little relationship to anything concrete. It does not relate to the physical difficulty of the job or to the technologies involved. . . . Given the arbitrary and artificial nature of skill definition and its ideological construction, job sorting is not related

to some abstract definition of skill. Women's jobs are often marked as less skilled because it is women who hold them.[66]

The same argument applies to the jobs of nonwhite men. Indeed, race and gender job segregation are interlinked.

In line with Venus Green's findings, others have noted that when women of color replace white women, or when white women replace white men in significant numbers, the result is job degradation, which takes the form of marking the job as less skilled while driving the workers more intensely. Although hostility from male workers presents a barrier to access by women and workers of color to white-male-type jobs, employers are in ultimate control. They may recruit women with an eye to cutting the price of skilled white male labor, or they may transform a requirement to hire women into an opportunity to de-skill and degrade the job. Such actions, not natural processes, reproduce occupational segregation by race and sex.[67]

In sum, the temporary darkening of Jews and other European immigrants during the period when they formed the core of the industrial working class clearly illustrates the linkages between degraded and driven jobs and nonwhite racial status. Similarly, the "Indianness" of Mexicans and Asians, as they became key to capitalist agribusiness, stands as another variant on the earlier constructions of blackness and redness. I am suggesting that this construction of race almost *is* the American construction of class, that capitalism as an economic organization in the United States is racially structured. Just as the United States is a racial state, as Michael Omi and Howard Winant have argued, so too is American capitalism a racial economic system.[68] This does not mean that there are no white workers in degraded jobs. However, it does suggest that such workers may experience their position as somewhat contradictory or as an out-of-placeness in the American racial way of constructing class.

The next chapter explores the ways in which capitalism is also a system of gender. It discusses how notions of maleness and femaleness are at the base of American understandings of race and linked to the organization of waged labor.

Race, Gender, ☐ CHAPTER 3
and Virtue in
Civil Discourse

For here in the United States we have two things which have made the Teuton strong in this earth: the home with the mother never out of caste, and the rule of the folk by "the most ancient ways"—the supremacy of the majority. Other branches of the Aryan race have come into this continent, have established half-caste homes with native wives, and the outlawed woman has dragged these races down to her level. . . . But the Teutonic Aryan brought his home, kept his Teutonic women full caste; the blood has never degenerated, . . . The free woman in the home has made the free school; the free school has preserved the free man; and the free man, still abiding by the most ancient ways—the rule of the majority—is working out free institutions. . . . Our freedom, that comes from a free mother in a free home, partakes of her self-abnegation. And so we alone of the Aryans that have no bondwoman's blood in our veins, we who have no half-caste mothers, have been able to rear the children of democracy, men to whom freedom means sacrifice.

—William Allen White,
The Old Order Changeth

W illiam Allen White, the author of this piece, shared the
white supremacist belief, widespread in the early twentieth century, that the innate characteristics of their men and
women were what made northwestern European white folks superior to everyone else, and that American democracy depended upon white rule. As the quote suggests, a great deal
rested upon the domesticity, purity, and economic dependence
of white womanhood and the patriarchal manliness of white male
citizens. Just as the ideals of feminine virtue were specific to
white women, so too were the ideals of manhood, including those
about work, specific to white men. Writing of white male craftsmen, David Montgomery notes that "[f]ew words enjoyed more
popularity in the nineteenth century than this honorific [man-
liness], with all its connotations of dignity, respectability, defiant egalitarianism, and patriarchal male supremacy."[1]

Feminist scholars of color have shown that American constructions of gender cannot be understood apart from race. That
is, popular and institutional beliefs about the nature of one's
womanhood and manhood have depended on the race to which
one has been assigned. Reciprocally, stereotypes about the nature of the womanhoods and manhoods of different races have
been key to race making and the structures of American racism. Evelyn Nakano Glenn, in an important theoretical synthesis, argues that the United States has two images of womanhood,
one for white women and another for women of color, and that
women of color have been consistently defined as workers but
not as mothers.[2] This chapter builds upon these ideas of a racially dichotomous system of manliness and womanliness in the
United States: one for nonwhite and not-quite-white people, and
another for whites, who are constructed as if they all have
middle-class values, family circumstances, and types of jobs.

The first part of the chapter locates the origin of these constructions in slavery and social Darwinism and traces their development into a civic discourse. The second part examines
historical differences between the participation of women of
color and white women in the labor force. It argues that these

differences are a material circumstance that supports a civic discourse of beliefs that different race-based womanhoods are a natural and necessary condition of social life. The third part sketches the ways in which public policies are shaped by and in turn codify that civic discourse in racially discriminatory ways. Taken together with chapter 2, this chapter argues that race, class, and gender constitute each other in a circular way: that each is composed of the other two in such a way as to produce two very different kinds of Americans with different and unequal entitlements and places in the body politic and civil society.

☐ *Civic Discourse: Slavery, Savagery, and Civilization*

The American idea that white humanity is "civilized" and superior to nonwhite humanity, and that its ideals of manliness and feminine domesticity prove it, come from two intellectual sources: slavery and modernism. As Thomas Patterson has recently shown so well, the most general source for the claim is in the larger modernist or Enlightenment way of thinking about the world, which came to celebrate the robust industrial capitalism and bourgeois culture that developed in Europe and the United States in the nineteenth century. Its particularly American roots, however, lie in slavery.[3]

Slavery: The Gender of Bondspeople

Slavery itself drew on colonial beliefs that people without property were idle and shiftless, lacking in virtue (if they were virtuous, they would have property). For their own good, they needed to be put to work, regardless of gender, because labor was intrinsically virtuous. They were expected to labor for those with property. People without property were also presumed to be unfit parents. Lacking virtue, they could hardly be expected to instill it in their children, so that many colonies had laws for binding out the children of the poor so that they could be taught the virtues of work by those in a better position to teach them.[4] Property owners had fine characters, worked hard for themselves, made good parents, and lived in patriarchal families. Male suffrage and effective citizenship until the nineteenth century were limited to adult white men with property; and women's rights to raise their children without state interference rested upon marriage to such a man.

State policies were central to denying the privileges of white woman- and manhood to bondspeople. Even state constitutions outside the South "explicitly placed African American men in the same category as women, as 'dependents.' Negro males, whether free or slave, were forbidden to exercise 'manhood' rights—forbidden to vote, hold electoral office, serve on juries, or join the military."[5]

As Jennifer Devere Brody pointed out, African American women, since Sojourner Truth and Harriet Jacobs, have been saying that femininity and "true womanhood" are for white women only.[6] Evelyn Brooks Higginbotham has counted the ways that the laws of slave-owning America constructed black womanhood as a dependency different from that of white womanhood. Under no circumstances, she notes, were African American women ever ladies: they were expected to work incessantly; they were never economically dependent; they were never protected, by men, by law, or by custom. Nobody every helped Sojourner Truth into carriages or over mud puddles, or gave her any best place; nor did they prevent her thirteen children from being sold away. Motherhood was not a bondswoman's right; motherhood was her owner's rights to her labor and the fruits thereof.

In this context, Higginbotham took Sojourner Truth's rhetorical question, "Ar'n't I a woman?" at face value. Were bondswomen women? Did they have the rights that law gave to the unmarked category women? Not according to a Missouri case where a bondswoman killed her owner in self-defense after he tried to rape her when she was ill and pregnant. Her defense appealed to legal protections of "any woman" from rape. In denying her that protection, the court denied her womanhood.[7]

As Leith Mullings has argued, stereotypes of African American women revolve around an "underlying theme of defeminization—the African American woman as being without a clearly ascribed gender identity, that is, as being unfeminine in the sense of not possessing those traits, alleged to be biological, that defined, constrained, but also protected women of the time."[8] The gender stereotypes of black women and men emphasized similarities between them. K. Sue Jewell notes that African American women during and after slavery were portrayed "as the antithesis of the American conception of beauty, femininity and womanhood," possessing "physical attributes and emotional qualities traditionally attributed to males," like hypersexuality, strength, and aggressiveness.[9]

Just as white America did not construct African American women as women, so too did it refuse manhood to African men. A corresponding set of racist stereotypes showed black men as "weak and henpecked, dominated by their robust and overbearing wives."[10] Indeed, white speech, even at the turn of the century, shunned combining terms for African American or American Indian with terms for manhood. The common linguistic pairing, Gail Bederman tells us, was "the Negro" or "the Indian" and "the white man."[11]

An alternative construction of bondswomen—as the fully devoted, asexual, and selfless superworker "mammy," according to Deborah Gray White—was as close as American civic discourse has ever gotten to offering assimilation and uplift to African American women. But this stereotype of a black woman devoted to raising the children of white folks at the expense of her own further legitimated the notion of motherhood as an exclusive privilege of white women.[12]

Modernism and Savagery

As science replaced divine authority in Enlightenment thinking, Social Darwinism—the idea that those who prevailed were inherently the fittest—came to be held as scientific proof that

Europeans were innately superior to those they conquered. Evolutionary anthropological theories that traced human progress from savagery to civilization were central to "scientific proof" and to bourgeois constructions of themselves. Such schemes were as consonant with policies of manifest destiny in a settler nation bent on stealing Native American land as they were of nations scrambling to colonize the rest of the globe. The nascent discipline of anthropology, which developed in this context, enumerated the ways in which nonwhite "primitive others" have differed from "us."[13]

Herbert Spencer was arguably the most influential of these evolutionary thinkers, particularly in setting out the importance of gender in distinguishing savage from civilized humanity.

> Perhaps in no way is the moral progress of mankind more clearly shown, than by contrasting the position of women among savages with their position among the most advanced of the civilized. At the one extreme a treatment of them cruel to the utmost degree bearable; and at the other extreme a treatment which, in some directions, gives them precedence over men.[14]

Spencer read widely about the customs of newly conquered and "discovered" people and developed a narrative that constructed them as latter-day representatives of what early humanity looked like.

Gender-blurred, amoral "savages" were stock figures, foils to civilized ladies and gentlemen in these evolutionary schemes. For Spencer, savage men and women were equally amoral and brutish, but each sex had its own form of barbaric temperament based on its relative strength. Men ruled women only because they were stronger. Men developed ownership in women much as carnivores own their prey, and they knew no morality beyond brute force. For women, male dominance meant that they led a life of hard work, sexual abuse, and generally miserable treatment. They survived it only by developing traits of guile, flattery, and attraction to men of power.

Spencer arranged his bits and pieces of information about

non-Western societies into a linear, historical narrative that ended with Victorian civilization's chivalrous patriarchy and feminine domesticity. Even here, though, women were destined to be the inferiors of men when it came to exercising citizenship. Because their evolution had been stunted to reserve "vital power to meet the cost of reproduction," women had not yet developed "the latest products of human evolution—the power of abstract reasoning and the most abstract of the emotions, the sentiment of justice."[15] Spencer is clear: women (and he meant white ones) were the mothers of the nation; men were its citizens. The idea was that biological and temperamental differences between men and women developed only with the evolution of "civilized" races. "Savages" (nonwhites) did not distinguish between men and women, and even white women, though they were ideally suited to be mothers of citizens, were themselves not yet evolved enough for citizenship.

Edward A. Ross, among the less liberal of the early founders of modern sociology, brought these stereotypes to bear in his analysis of the urban, industrial United States. He constructed Italian immigrants in much the same way that Spencer had constructed "savages."[16] Ross believed that "the Mediterranean peoples are morally below the races of northern Europe." He knew that they were congenital liars, lacking in morality and cleanliness. To illustrate his point, Ross contrasted a stereotypic Anglo-Saxon male, William, with his Italian counterpart: "William does not leave as many children as 'Tonio, because he will not huddle his family into one room, eat macaroni off a bare board, work his wife barefoot in the field, and keep his children weeding onions instead of at school."[17] Ross's anti-immigrant racism and nativism took a characteristically gendered form that also served to support an exploitative class order.

Political democrats from Rousseau to Engels to progressive 1960s anthropologists consistently inverted these schemes. That is, by way of criticizing the social injustices of bourgeois society, they showed the "primitives" as superior to the "civilized." Still, they did not challenge the notion of a dichotomous world made up of "us" and an inherently different "other." Nor did they challenge a unilinear view of history in which the "other" evolved (or, in their case, devolved) into an "us."

Social Darwinism and similar forms of scientific racism had their popular counterparts in a turn-of-the-century American civic discourse that also saw white manliness as a product of evolution, a success story of the rise of refined taste, knowledge, intelligence, and "the manly self-restraint which allowed them to become self-made men." Not only were African Americans said to be evolutionarily lacking in such traits, but so too were the European immigrants who made up the bulk of the late-nineteenth-century working class.[18] In this construction, a core element of white manliness was to protect white womanhood. Reciprocally, a dependent white womanhood was an important pillar not only of white manliness but also of the nation.[19]

Stereotypes invented in service of slavery and imperialism have been rediscovered and recycled to support domination over new groups of proletarians. Thus, nonwhite Asian and Jewish men came to be stereotyped as effeminate, more like "their" women than white men, when they joined the bottom of the labor force, while African American and Polish men were labeled hypermasculine and hypersexual, again, more like "their" women than white men.[20]

For example, Barbara Ehrenreich and Deirdre English have shown how medical beliefs lent support to popular notions that assigned different racial constitutions to middle-class white women and to their then not-yet-fully-white Irish immigrant domestic servants.[21] The former, because of their allegedly delicate nature, were regarded as "sick," the latter as "sickening." That is, in the popular imagination and in medical contexts middle-class white women were constructed as physically delicate and unsuited to hard work, conflict, or much stimulation of any sort. As Ehrenreich and English note, the medical profession's ideal white woman was the sickly dependent of an affluent man, a convenient ideal patient for a medical profession in search of clients. In contrast, the stereotype of working-class Irish women was "typhoid Mary," strong as an ox and immune to the endemic diseases raging through the city, especially its working-class slums. She was biologically constituted for hard labor, but she was also a potential carrier of disease and danger to her mistress's household. She was neither virtuous nor feminine.

The stereotype of disease-carrying domestics justified the policing of spatial segregation for the health of the middle-class domestic establishment well into the twentieth century. Speaking of a trip to Puerto Rico, Eleanor Roosevelt said, "Tuberculosis is widespread everywhere just as it is in the Puerto Rican community here in New York. . . . I assume none of you will be hiring any of them in your homes, but however careful we may be in rearing our children, they can still come into contact with one of these sick people in the streets or in the schools."[22]

Phyllis Palmer has suggested that "sex, dirt, housework, and badness in women are linked in Western unconsciousness and that white middle-class women sought to transcend these associations by demonstrating their sexual purity and their pristine domesticity. Their ease required not only service but contrast with a woman who represented the bad in woman, a woman who does housework and also embodies physical and emotional qualities that distinguish her from the housewife."[23]

Embedded in Palmer's argument are two important ideas: the very performance of waged domestic labor contributed to the racial stigmatization of the women who did it and the agents of this racism have been middle-class white women for whom this is a means of asserting their racial and class privileges.

Jews, Puerto Ricans, Irish, and African Americans appeared as different constructions on a rainbow of state-sanctioned not-whitenesses. Although the stereotypes that were applied to them varied in their particulars, the spectrum was still assigned common cultural attributes: men and women alike were characterized as dirty, lascivious, immoral, and either knaves or fools. And the men, whether hypermasculine or effeminate, all lusted after white women.

☐ *Race, Labor, and Gender*

Where did Americans look to affirm the truth of this sort of commonsense racism? One place was in the waged labor force. Here, systematic differences in the respectability of work done by white women and its lack in that available to women of color seemed to confirm racist stereotypes of women of color.

Not surprisingly, as with class, the dominant American cultural pattern for contrasting white and nonwhite gender constructions can be traced back to the organization of work during slavery. Here, Jacqueline Jones comments, "the quest for an 'efficient' agricultural workforce led slave owners to downplay gender differences in assigning adults to field labor," such that the lives of bondswomen and men across the South were dominated by gang labor.[24] Planters also regarded bondswomen as among their "means of reproduction." Rose Williams was told by her owner that it was her duty to "bring forth portly children," and that he had paid "big money" "cause I wants you to raise me childrens."[25] Bondswomen also did most of the domestic labor and child raising in plantation households as well as in their own.[26] Jacqueline Jones reckons that the life of a house slave has painted with too rosy a brush in most writings by whites, and that it consisted of dawn-to-past-dark backbreaking labor.[27]

In sharp contrast, the ideal white woman of land-owning families did neither field nor domestic work, nor did she share with her menfolk plantation management and political rule. Most plantation mistresses, especially the less wealthy, did some work supervising bondswomen, and of course, poor white women did considerable field and domestic work.[28] None of this changed the fact that white women were idealized as economic dependents of their men, even if in practice they were more often directly dependent upon the labor of bondswomen. As Gerda Lerner pointed out long ago, the gender system made a sharp distinction between white women as feminine but asexual nonworkers and African American women as nonfeminine and highly sexual workers.[29]

In the industrial age, women of color and off-white European women differed sharply in the extent to which they worked for wages outside their homes, and in the degree to which their work segregated them from contact with men. All save white women routinely worked in "unskilled" factory and field labor, or in domestic waged labor, for part of their lives, although women's patterns of work varied greatly from group to group. African American women had by far the highest participation of any women in waged labor. Although they were only 10 percent of the nation's women, they constituted 24.9 percent of the female labor force in 1910 and 18.4 percent in 1920. About half of all African American women worked as private domestic workers, which was also the "typical" occupation of Irish, Slovak, and Mexican immigrant women. There were racial/ethnic differences even within this occupation. African American women worked in laundries (as did Chinese men) and did day work for private households. Irish and other European immigrant women tended to be live-in servants. Jewish, Italian, Polish, Mexican, and French Canadian women more typically worked in factories.[30]

All these jobs placed women in close proximity to men. We have seen that Jewish women worked alongside men in the garment industry, even though their wages and jobs differed. The same was true in the textile mills of Lawrence, Passaic, and Paterson, where women were half of the largely southern and eastern European immigrant labor force in an industry that historian David Goldberg calls "the advance guard of the industrial revolution . . . [and] the first industry in which the adoption of power-driven machinery had enabled capitalists to break jobs down into repetitive and routinized tasks" and to impose "rigid work discipline."[31] The key point is that, whether as household domestic workers, as parts of family groups in agricultural labor, or in manufacturing, the jobs available to women of color and not-quite-white European women put them in close proximity to men. This proximity appeared to confirm their stigmatization as loose women.

In contrast, white women worked in far lower percentages

and in segregated work settings. White women were a minority— 38.4 percent in 1910 and 43.7 percent in 1920—of the female labor force.[32] In contrast to white men, white women were not expected to work for wages, even though in fact many did. Going out to work was simply not respectable; it was part of the male public sphere, and until well into the twentieth century a white woman risked her reputation at least a little by so doing.

Nevertheless, the very first factory labor force in the United States consisted of young white farm daughters. Their recruitment raised a debate over whether female virtue was compatible with waged labor. To assure their women employees they would not be dishonored, early millowners at Lowell created an overwhelmingly single-sex, female workforce in the factories and developed a boardinghouse system. House mothers, compulsory church attendance, and educational improvement schemes were consciously designed to reassure young women that their virtue would be protected.

Occupational segregation came to be the most common way of signaling and ostensibly protecting the respectability and femininity of white women wage workers. Unlike their nonwhite counterparts' jobs, those of white working-class women have historically separated them fairly consistently from white men, and even more so from nonwhite women and men. Significantly, white women did not engage in domestic labor in any numbers. Working-class white women entered the workforce in numbers only in the early twentieth century, with the large growth in clerical and sales jobs and their transformation into clean, respectable white women's occupational preserves.[33]

The organization of waged labor gave force to ethnoracially specific gender stereotypes, and those stereotypes in turn governed the civic discourse that is the language of public policy. We now explore the powerful and consistent role such discourses have played in shaping law and political practices governing labor, welfare, and public health, and how the results codify, in turn, the differential treatment of women and men and the racially unequal treatment of women.

☐ *Civic Discourse, Law, and Policy*

An Alabama senator testifying in favor of immigration restriction in the early twentieth century told a tale that could have been lifted from congressional rhetoric on the eve of the twenty-first. He described the murder of "an American boy bearing an honored American name—William Clifford, Jr.," who for no reason was "stabbed in the back" by a twelve-year-old boy named Paul Rapkowskie, who had just stolen a knife (among other things), which he used to stab William Jr. "[W]hen asked why he had murdered young Clifford he replied: 'I just wanted to see how deep I could drive the dirk into his back.'"[34]

That discourse, civic discourse, and the policies that are informed by it play an important role in making race and race-based gender constructions seem like reality. It is the grandfather of today's talk about treating child offenders like adults, about crime waves (even in the face of falling rates of violent crime) and teen superpredators. Law, talk about it, making it, and enforcing it, is about making and enforcing categories and boundaries. From the Constitution itself, and the establishment and maintenance of private property, slavery, and genocidal warfare against Native American, to immigration policies, sexuality and marriage laws, public health, family and welfare law, census categories, labor law, residential segregation, and urban renewal policies, the state has been a central force in defining races and genders and to assigning them their spatial, cultural, and socioeconomic places in this society.[35]

The concept of the family wage and the ideas that govern public welfare are two examples that illuminate the ways that gender lies at the center of constructing race. As they came to be elaborated in policy discourse and practices, the family wage applied to men and social welfare applied to women. Notions of motherhood as an entitlement of white women only, and family wages as an entitlement of white men only, governed employment practices and social welfare policy mainly to explain why it was fair to expect nonwhites to labor with no such entitlements. The implication was that whites were entitled to benefits, even if they did not always get them.

Family Wage

Alice Kessler-Harris has shown with stunning insight that the very conception of waged labor developed in a gender-specific way that the wage was male from the outset. No abstract embodiment of the value produced by labor, a wage represented the place of the wage earner in society and the social expectations laid upon him. A female wage earner was an anomaly, a failure as a woman. Even those social reformers who argued for "decent" wages for women workers urged only enough income to prevent women from starving to death or becoming prostitutes. They feared that higher wages might deter women from their true calling: making a home for a male wage earner. Men earners were expected to support nonworking wives and advanced their claims for wages upon this basis. A man's wage embodied the belief that

> a man was entitled to a wife to serve him and their home. It contained the assumption that a female who did not have a husband had erred. The differential female wage thus carried a moral injunction, a warning to women to follow the natural order.[36]

The idea that a *man's* wage should allow him to support children and a non-wage-earning wife was never meant to apply to nonwhite men. Inducements to patriarchal family and stability, such as company housing, were offered to and reserved for white men. In rural locales like Pennsylvania's steel mill towns and the mill villages of the southern textile industry, such company policies rewarded and bound male employees to the company by making cheap rental housing available or by helping these workers to buy houses. No such benefits were extended to unskilled European immigrant workers or workers of color, whose communities were in the alleys, in the most polluted areas nearest the plant. Their housing rivaled that of the big-city, immigrant, working-class slums and the rural and mining slums of the South and Southwest.[37] This racial distinction not only furthered internal working-class segregation, it underlined employers' support for family life for white workers and their nonsupport for all other workers.

Patriarchal masculinity was most assuredly not built into the wages of men of color. It might be more accurate to term their wages and working conditions "unmanning." For example, in 1910, an immigrant steelworker, even if he "worked twelve hours every day in the year," would not be able to support a family at even the barest level of existence.[38]

In contrast, male craftsmen were not so used and not so conceptualized. Indeed, it was a mark of masculine pride for these men to refuse to work at all if a supervisor were present. Craftsmen marked themselves off as white in part by the ethic of manliness and brotherhood.[39]

The *whiteness* of the wage has implications as strong as its maleness for the kinds of "moral injunctions" built into state policies and the discourse that governs it. Defining civilized manliness and femininity as white, and a savage, ungendered nature as a property of people of color and off-whites, justified home and family as prerogatives of white workers and a family wage as a specifically white and masculine entitlement. It follows, as Kessler-Harris shows, that white women's entitlement to respectability, femininity, and motherhood is contingent upon marrying a white man. It also follows that all other men have no entitlement to patriarchal masculinity. Likewise, nonwhite women have no entitlement to respectability or motherhood since white men are strongly discouraged from marrying them.

Public programs designed to compensate for the loss of male breadwinners' jobs (and which tacitly acknowledged that the capitalist labor market does not always work as it should) were available in practice to white men only. Thus, for much of its history, unemployment insurance excluded from coverage many of the industries, such as agriculture and domestic labor, in which men of color and women have been concentrated.

As Nancy Rose has shown so clearly, New Deal programs were powerfully shaped by the assumption that a family wage was the prerogative of white men. The Works Progress Administration allowed mainly white men to volunteer as heads of household for its reasonably good, government-created jobs during the Depression: white men made up almost three-quarters of the rolls; white women comprised 11 percent; African American men made up 12 percent; and African American women were a mere 2 percent.[40] Worse, New Deal officials caved in to agribusiness opposition to a minimum wage for work relief because it severely undercut the paltry wages that growers paid for agricultural work. During planting and harvest seasons as recently as the 1960s, all relief to African American and Mexican American men and women was routinely suspended, explicitly to ensure southern and southwestern agribusiness a supply of agricultural and domestic labor. Rose notes that African American and Mexican American women were sometimes not allowed to work the full complement of hours covered by work relief, and that there was a whole arsenal of tactics for limiting the income available to them, including forcing them to accept lower-paid jobs than whites.[41] In addition, during the Depression, Mexican Americans also faced deportation and were sometimes forced to break strikes in order to get any work relief at all. Later, during World War II, when the federal government instituted the Fair Employment Practices Commission to insure equal opportunities in wartime employment, African American women lodged complaints that they were denied the kinds of clerical and communications jobs offered to white women.[42]

Discussions about the revision of Social Security coverage in 1939 made explicit the tacit understanding that those really entitled to the wherewithal to support a family were white men. These revisions led to including dependents of white male workers in Social Security coverage while excluding African American and Mexican farm and domestic workers. This did not happen because no one called the attention of legislators to the racial discrepancy. Alice Kessler-Harris has detailed the forceful efforts at inclusion made by African American organizations, and the mere lip service given them by those in charge of revisions. Although the policy was in part the product of economic and political forces—in this case the interests of southern agribusiness—more general racist and gendered values shaped the conduct of public debate and kept it within those bounds.[43] Those values supported the interests of southern planters and legitimated their views that whites were proper national subjects while African Americans and Mexican Americans were not when it came to public assistance.

The evolution of protective labor laws provides another instantiation in civic discourse of the belief that women of color were fit to work but not to mother, while white women were the nation's idea of mothers. Progressive Era social reformers pushed for legislation to protect all workers from the abuses of industrial capitalism. Among the half-victories won was protection of women (but not men) from being forced to work long hours and at night. The rationale behind these decisions, most notably the Supreme Court decision supporting such laws, was that women were too weak to negotiate fair practices on their own. However, because they were mothers of the next generation of the nation, the state had a legitimate interest in protecting them. It acknowledged no such interest in men, who were supposed to be strong enough to negotiate fair conditions on their own. In this way, courts and legislatures reinforced the notion of women as dependent and domestic creatures in need of public protection. As Gwendolyn Mink notes, this also buttressed "the idea that woman's social responsibility for children overrode her political and economic rights of citizenship."[44] However, three key jobs— domestic labor, home work, and agricultural work, jobs done almost exclusively by women of color and not-quite-white European immigrant women—were pointedly excluded from coverage, just as they were excluded from Social Security, unemployment compensation, and minimum wage coverage.[45]

The work ethic became a measure of working-class virtue for women as well as men in emergent public health discourse. Emily Abel has shown how New York City's turn-of-the-century Charity Organization Society's programs to control tuberculosis also "attributed poverty to the moral failings of the poor," a preponderance of whom were working-class European immigrants. Admission to a tuberculosis sanatorium required inmates to work, as the head of New York's Health Department put it, "not only to return its patients in condition to resume an occupation similar in nature to the one previously followed, but also with the disposition and desire to do so." Not surprisingly, patients objected to the unhealthy conditions of the particular work they were assigned and to the idea that they were working for free.[46]

Welfare

The idea that whiteness and middle-class domesticity are requisites for socially sanctioned motherhood has deep roots that go back to colonial notions of republican motherhood.[47] Many feminist scholars have pointed out the remarkably consistent principles that underlie the history of private charity and public welfare programs.

Progressive Era private charities believed that European immigrant women should work, that they were unfit for motherhood. For example, Stephanie Coontz says that Stephen Humphreys Gurteen,

> one of the most prominent of these reformers . . . opposed financial aid to poor mothers because lower-class women, unlike middle-class ones, *ought* to work; besides, he added, they were such unfit mothers that their children would do better in day nurseries than at home. . . . To create the "true home," one charity leader explained in 1888, it was often necessary to "break up the unworthy family."[48]

Working-class European immigrant women were also stigmatized for nonconformity to bourgeois ideals of domesticity. In the aftermath of the 1912 Lawrence "Bread and Roses" strike by textile workers, Ardis Cameron notes, "women from Poland, Lithuania, Russia, southern Italy, and Syria, were increasingly associated with ignorance, backwardness, and low evolutionary development and frequently portrayed as 'loose women, poor housekeepers, and bad mothers.'"[49]

Stephanie Coontz argues that some of this antipathy stemmed from hostility on the part of middle-class reformers to women's dense neighborhood and kin networks for performing their daily labors. Indeed, progressives often advocated "government aid to the poor . . . partly from a desire to discourage social cooperation and economic pooling beyond the family."[50]

This was the milieu in which Teddy Roosevelt raised his infamous alarm about "race suicide." He meant the white race. Roosevelt blamed Anglo-Saxon women for turning away from their sacred duty of motherhood, thus allowing "native" stock to be outbred by inferior immigrants. In castigating white women for their loss of that maternal "self-abnegation" for which William Allen White had praised them, he reflected a more general, white nativist anxiety. This anxiety sustained successful efforts by the eugenics movement to pass compulsory sterilization laws aimed at women of color and off-white European immigrant women in the majority of states in the early twentieth century. These allowed medical authorities to sterilize people for a wide variety of alleged deficiencies ranging from "feeblemindedness" to alcoholism. In so doing, they made clear that the state opposed motherhood for a broad swath of women who were not white and not middle class. Forced sterilization continued well into the 1970s, and women of color continued to be its primary victims.[51]

The idea that real mothers are white and the dependents of family, wage-earning men has shaped public welfare policy as powerfully as it has private charity. Mothers' Pensions were the first publicly funded programs for supporting mothers and their children. Established in most states between 1911 and 1919, they provided support for mainly white, middle-class widows to stay home and raise their children. A constellation of white women's groups led the struggles to develop these programs, which were designed to support women who had lost their breadwinner through misfortune.

As they were ultimately implemented, these programs revealed their advocates' racial notions of motherhood. Many reformers alternated between condemning poor and immigrant
women as unfit mothers and developing very active programs
to uplift them. They often portrayed immigrant women as child-
like and oppressed by Spencerian, hypersexist men who abused
and treated them like servants. Alternatively, they romanticized
immigrant women as poor but happy and hardworking. However,
"sentimental maternalists," as Molly Ladd-Taylor calls them,
were quite consistent in their avoidance of any contact with poor
African American women and in refusing alliances with the National Association of Colored Women when its members sought
their cooperation.

The Mother's Pensions, forerunners of Aid to Families with
Dependent Children (AFDC), which resulted from white reformers' grassroots efforts, foreshadowed the nativism and bourgeois
domesticity that came to govern public welfare programs.

> Despite initial claims that the pension was a recognition of mater-
> nal service to the nation, most states severely limited those eli-
> gible for aid.
>
> Most states had a "suitable home" provision that held recipi-
> ents up to certain behavioral standards. Aid was limited to "de-
> serving" women who did not have illegitimate children or take in
> male boarders, and who were willing to follow "proper" (Anglo-
> American) methods of housekeeping and childcare.[52]

These programs were designed to promote a particular kind
of full-time, nuclear-family motherhood that stood in sharp contrast to working-class women's waged labor and to their neighbor-
hoodbased cooperative domesticity. This state-supported and
state-supporting version of motherhood was a white woman's prerogative. Discrimination against and exclusion of African American and European immigrants was common. Mothers' Pensions
went disproportionately to white, English-speaking widows. Some
localities explicitly set payments for particular nationalities—
like Mexicans, Czechs, and Italians—lower than for white women.

Inadequate as these pensions were, historian Stephanie Coontz notes that they nevertheless "were made contingent on a woman's display of middle-class norms about privacy and domesticity" that barred her from taking in boarders, working outside the house more than three days a week, or living in a "morally questionable neighborhood."[53] In the end, notes Ladd-Taylor, the advocates of Mothers' Pensions came to resemble charity workers.

Discourse surrounding these pensions put women of color and European immigrants in a double bind. Sometimes the alleged inferiority of peoples of color and European immigrants was used to justify excluding them from private and public programs. At other times their cultural strengths were used to justify lower benefits, when they were paid at all.

> Welfare policy was thus predicated on the assumptions that the Mexican family and community would manage somehow to take care of its own. . . . Their ability to survive through mutual support, however, was held against them, as it became one justification for lower funding.

This seems to have been the case for Chinese and Filipinos in San Francisco as well. Their food allocation was between 10 and 20 percent lower than whites' on the grounds that they could survive on less.[54]

Since the 1950s, public discourse about welfare has imposed a biracial construction of good and bad women on a poly-ethnoracial America. African American women have become the favorite targets of racist practices and discourses, consistently stereotyped as sexually promiscuous welfare queens, lacking in maternal qualities, unfeminine, and unworthy of male protection. Sometimes it seems as if the only growth industry today is of a punditocracy that has once again "discovered" that African American women, not racism, have been responsible for the problems of black communities.

Rickie Solinger has shown how utterly race-specific were the "public policies, professional practices, community attitudes, and

family and individual responses" applied to the unmarried preg-
nancies of black and white women in the 1950s and early 1960s.
At a time when racial and gender hierarchies were beginning to
be challenged by the civil rights and feminist movements, public policies and private practices about teen pregnancy shored
them up.[55]

Instead of punishing white single mothers for life as bad
women, Solinger argues, experts in the 1950s came to see them
as neurotic and unhappy, but rehabilitable. In sharp contrast,
the authorities hardened their attitudes toward black women and
came to write them off as inherently unredeemable, products
of a pathological black family, irresponsible breeders contributing to overpopulation, or calculating welfare queens.[56] Pregnant
white teens were constructed as if they were middle class, and
all the black teens as if they were "lower" class. The script for
white women was to hide them—and their parents' shame—in
a maternity home where they learned to accept submissive womanhood, give up their babies for adoption, and return to the world
of respectability as if nothing had happened. "By allying themselves with these agencies, white unwed mothers and their families acknowledged their ties to gender and class codes of
behavior, and systems of redemption mandated by middle-class
status." The success of this strategy was helped by the carrot of
economic mobility available to whites in the 1950s, as well as
by a booming adoption market for white babies.[57]

The image of disreputable black sexuality was the stick with
which experts and popular opinion beat black women and held
them up as the negative example to enforce chastity and middle-
class respectability on white women. The script for African
American single mothers was consistently punitive. Maternity
homes did not admit them; adoption agencies did not serve
them. Abortion, when available, usually came on the condition
of sterilization. Welfare protocols institutionalized the suspicion
that they had children for profit or pathology.

These stereotypes have been recycled in Daniel P. Moynihan's misogynous racism of the 1960s, and more recently in President Clinton's rhetoric regarding welfare as encouraging "dependency," and in current popular and official discourses around teen pregnancy, all of which blame women of color in general and African American women in particular for the effects of institutionalized racism.[58] These notions hark back to colonial laws that treated people without property as unfit parents. They and their children were believed to need to work for others in order to build any moral fiber. Slavery made these distinctions between the worthy propertied and the unworthy propertyless racially specific. They survive in the practices and policies of the 1996 "Personal Responsibility Act." Its name alone, an insult added to the injury of workfare, betrays its ancestry, even absent Republican proposals for a new wave of taking children away from poor parents of color.

One among many awful consequences of demonizing African American women in order to withdraw government assistance to the poor is to obscure the variety of people in need of support. Nancy Naples has shown that recent U.S. Senate hearings on welfare "reform" treated the needs and circumstances of peoples as diverse as the Hmong in California's central valley and all Spanish-speaking immigrants from many nations (not to mention poor whites) as "marginal" to the programs under discussion. They marginalized the needs of all who were not African American by assuming that their poverty was temporary and not caused by the real problem—personal irresponsibility—that welfare "reform" needed to address. Naples concludes, "Since Hmong men and others who do not fit within the racist frame of the 'long-term recipient' are marginalized within the discourse, they also have no legitimate or recognizable position within the 'social contract.'"[59] The result is that women who are not African American get no support allegedly because they do not need it, and that African American women get no support allegedly because they do not deserve it. At best, in the words of Linda Gordon, they may be "pitied but not entitled" to motherhood.[60]

☐ *Conclusion*

The key distinction to emerge from the policy process was once again between good and bad women. Women of color and off-white working-class women were bad women. African American women were the antithesis of ladies in the popular imagination and in discourses driving public welfare policy. In varying degrees, and at various times, so too were Mexican and European immigrant working-class women. Since they were not supported at home by their husbands, they could hardly be respectable women or good mothers. They worked alongside nonwhite men in "unskilled," intensely supervised gang labor in the capitalist sector, took boarders and piecework into their homes in the early days, and conducted much of their household labor beyond their domestic walls, in their neighborhoods.

Such women had no inalienable rights to motherhood. Put most baldly: bad women were not virtuous no matter what they did. Bad women did not have social problems, they were social problems. They were not supposed to be the mothers of the nation's citizens. Indeed, in the prevailing civic discourse then as now, their motherhood was a threat to national integrity.

White women were by presumption good women; they either did not work for wages or they did so in ways that preserved their femininity and respectability—not least, by being separated from their male peers and nonwhites. White women were presumed to be good women and thereby deserving of male protection, but their virtue was contingent on the extent to which they fulfilled the ideals of dependence upon, and domestic service to, men and stayed in their proper place of heterosexual domesticity. If they left "home," they too risked losing their privileges.

Words can hurt when they govern policymaking. Anyone wishing to be heard by those who wield power in the civic arena is more likely to gain the attention of authorities by making arguments that appeal to prevailing racial beliefs about women and men, and by being silent where that discourse is silent. This is one way in which a historically dominant civic discourse helps insure the perpetuation of the deeply unequal protection of women of color and white women, and of women and men.

I have argued that American ideals about womanhood and manhood are racial in nature; that they inform the views of public officialdom and shape their policy-making discourse; and that the resulting public policies make them material realities that all American women have to deal with. This argument parallels that of chapter 2, which shows how American notions about class are also constructed racially.

I am suggesting here that the belief that different races have different kinds of gender is the flesh on the American idea of race. If race marked the working class as nonwhite, it did so through a civic discourse that represented nonwhite women and men as lacking the manly and feminine temperaments that were requisites for full membership in the body politic and social. If degraded labor was used to stigmatize its doers, then nonwhite women were stigmatized alongside nonwhite men. The American cultural construction—of virtuous mothers as white and of unfit mothers as nonwhite (whose only possible redemption lay through work), of chivalrous citizens as white men and of alien or criminal "hands" as men and women of color—has rested on associating female virtue with heterosexual domestic dependency on a man. Beliefs about who is entitled to such patriarchal domesticity, to a family wage, and to motherhood have been racial. Such beliefs have dominated the civic discourse that effectively shapes the laws and policies governing employment, immigration, public health, and welfare. Although public policy and its practice have been consistently racial, they have had a soft side that sometimes offered the carrot of assimilation to not-quite-white immigrant European women. Rather than undermine beliefs in two dichotomous racial "classes" (one of gender-blurred animal-like beings, the other of chivalrous men and domestic women), assimilationist notions have reinforced them.

Law, state-sanctioned violence, bureaucracy, daily practices, and the dominant civic discourse that governs them, all over-determine this dichotomous race, class, and gender system of domination. Today's political discourse on workfare "reform" evokes stereotypes of African American welfare cheats—women whose breeding produces male criminals and threatens the nation. It also evokes stereotypes of illegal Mexican and Central American immigrant women who cross the border just to have babies and get on welfare. This is an old and dreary discourse whose recycling has not diminished its power. Instead, it functions as a core constitutive myth of the American nation, a story told by people as diverse as William Allen White, William Jefferson Clinton, Daniel Patrick Moynihan, and Herbert Spencer about how the United States came to be what it is, about the people who made it that way and those who threaten it. Its resonance, especially with whites, comes from its familiarity as a civic discourse about who is to be numbered among the nation's real citizens, who is to be included in the circle of recognition, representation, and assistance. The other half of this discourse, about who is to be excluded and policed as a dangerous outsider to civil society, depends on evoking the danger of people out of place, of alien savages poised to invade the nation.

The next two chapters move from ethnoracial assignment to the issue of ethnoracial identity among American Jews. In the last century, Jews in the United States have spent about equal amounts of time on both sides—the not-white and the white— of the American ethnoracial binary. The question to which we now turn is how their ethnoracial assignment has affected the ways that Jews have constructed Jewish identity.

Not Quite White: ☐ CHAPTER 4
Gender and
Jewish Identity

For my father, as for many Jews, my insistence on seeing a relationship between Jewishness and race is a puzzling and not entirely welcome endeavor. What my father finds "most troubling is the inability to understand your basic premise, especially your use of the term 'race' and the Jewish question. Are Jews a race?—a black race if not accepted and white if they are?"

With respect to ethnoracial assignment (the institutionalized practices and discourses of the dominant society), the answer is yes. As the institutional framework of race and ethnicity, assignment is not something an individual has much choice about. However, my father has a point with respect to ethnoracial identities. Groups fashion their identities for themselves, even though they do so in response to ethnoracial assignments. Individuals also construct their ethnoracial identities in the same context, often with a great deal of self-consciousness and emotional investment.[1]

This chapter explores the meaning of Jewish ethnic identity in a period when Jews were assigned to the not-fully-white side of the racial spectrum. The first part argues that one of several coexisting forms of Jewish identity, namely Jewish socialism, was hegemonic in New York City's turn-of-the-century immigrant Jewish communities. The second part homes in on those communities' constructions of Jewish women of my grandmothers' generation, especially about the ways they differed from dominant white ideals. How were my fairly apolitical grandmothers connected as women and as Jews to a progressive, Jewish working-class culture? What was my political inheritance from this culture?

☐ *Jewish Socialism as Hegemonic Jewishness*

The Lower East Side of New York City, like eastern European Jewish neighborhoods in other industrial American cities, was a community of workers and bosses, shopkeepers and socialists, radicals and rabbis who were tied together in a mixture of forced and voluntary interdependence. There was no shortage of conflict over economics and politics. Interminable contests over meaning in general, and the meaning of Jewishness in particular, all took place within a context of intense interdependence where Jews were exploited and ghettoized by the larger society.

In this context, ethnic identity meant identification with a community that was coping with anti-Semitism and inventing dreams of something better. People in these communities used their Jewish heritage on a daily basis to institutionalize and negotiate the meanings, values, and acceptable variants of American ethnic Jewishness. Through Jewishness and *Yiddishkeit,* they found ways of dealing with cross-class relationships. They developed moralities and values that linked religious and secular, progressive and conservative, boss and worker, men and women, within the Jewish community and within a single system of meaning. In short, they found ways to support conflicting interpretations and interests and to contain the inevitable clashes.

They had to invent ways of valorizing the different versions of Jewish identity and practice so that they could coexist in one community and within one shared moral universe at a time when they had nowhere else to go. The edifice of racial assignment forced differences and conflicts to be contained—spatially, discursively, and politically—by a kind of "us-ness," a negotiated, overlapping, and familiar range of practices, meanings, and values that were locally hegemonic.

What Arthur Liebman has called Jewish socialism in his classic *Jews and the Left* became the dominant form of Jewish identity for this community for much of the period between the 1880s and World War II. This does not mean that all Jews were socialists, or even that Jewish socialism was the only recognized way of identifying oneself as a Jew within these communities. It does mean that part of being Jewish was being familiar with a working-class and anticapitalist outlook on the world and understanding this outlook as being particularly Jewish. It also meant that other versions of Jewish identity maintained a respectful dialogue with Jewish socialism. It served as a cultural platform for progressive political activity in part because many of its values were shared even by those who did not share its specific politics.[2]

Paula Hyman's wonderful book *Gender and Assimilation in Modern Jewish History* speaks to the genesis of various forms of Jewish identities. She argues that nineteenth-century western and eastern European Jews built very different forms of Jewishnesses in response to their different circumstances, and that it was the eastern European Jews who gave rise to this particular form of hegemonic American Jewishness. In Western Europe, modernism and the spread of capitalism brought a liberalization of politics and a greater acceptance of Jews as citizens. German Jews, in particular, saw their opportunity to gain civil rights and entry into German society. Whether or how to allow this was "the Jewish question" debated among Christian Germans in the 1840s, in Karl Marx's youth. Nevertheless, assimilation became, for the first time, a possibility, and the relatively middle-class, middleman Jewish minority in Germany, as in France and England, adopted the lifestyle of modern bourgeois society. Marx's equating of Jews with capitalists in his essay

"On the Jewish Question" reflects, though in a distorted and anti-Semitic way, the class position that a certain portion of German Jewry had achieved in the context of relative political freedom. However, Marx's characterization of Jews resonated with older European stereotypes of Jews as usurers, getting rich in an un-Christian, immoral way. Such stereotypes prevailed across Europe, where, especially in the east, Jews were not allowed to own land, the historical source of much non-Jewish wealth.[3]

With social assimilation, the gendered public and private spheres that were part of bourgeois western European society became also part of Jewish culture. Jewish men came to be public, immersed in the secular world of business success. And Jewish women became domestic. As part of the assimilationist process, the good Jewish woman in France, Britain, and Germany, like her Christian counterpart, became the guardian of the home and of a woman-centered, domesticated religion. She thereby became also the guardian of the future of Judaism. In Western Europe then, Hyman suggests, Jewish identity came to be based on religion rather than on any ethnic distinctiveness of daily life. These Jews, especially those from Germany, made up the first wave of Jewish immigrants to the United States.

In sharp contrast, the arrival of capitalist modernity in Eastern Europe left no place for Jewish assimilation. Particularly in Russia, capitalism was accompanied by heightened anti-Semitism. Here, Russians were incited to violence, pogroms were organized, and segregation was justified by stereotypes of blood-sucking Jewish merchants. Eastern European Jews under Czarist rule had long been restricted to the so-called Pale of Settlement, a geographic area comprised of parts of Poland and western Russia, outside of which they were not allowed to take up residence. It was here, in the 1880s and 1890s, that they began to develop a secular Yiddish culture, *Yiddishkeit*, that provided a common link between Jews from different villages, regions, and nations and infused Jewish life with the intellectual, political, and artistic excitement of urban modernism. Yiddishkeit and capitalism's dislocations combined to break down the class divisions between the wealthy and learned on the one hand, and the ordinary manual workers on the other. These distinctions had governed *shtetl* (village) life before Jews became concentrated in cities.[4]

Because Russia's version of capitalism was anti-Semitic in the extreme, modern Yiddish culture, or Yiddishkeit, had a strong anticapitalist streak. Frozen out of class mobility and social assimilation, the Jew emphasized living a moral life developed in a communal, working-class, and decidedly leftist political direction. As a popular culture of the late nineteenth century, Yiddishkeit contained a synergistic mixture of religious and secular emphases on social justice that spoke to the Jews' new class- and racelike stigmatization in eastern Europe and the United States.

This popular culture also developed its own notions of Jewish womanhood. They were still patriarchal, but they also granted a measure of social mobility, political authority, and economic power to women, thus distinguishing the Yiddishkeit from western European ideals of Jewish womanhood. The Jewish *Haskalah* (Enlightenment movement), in Russia, encouraged secular education, including women's. However, its intellectuals opposed wage work for women, claiming that it supported the religious ideal of the Talmudic scholar and made husbands lazy. They also believed that it undermined women's domesticity and corrupted their morals. Of the political groups in the Jewish community, the Bund (the General Jewish Labor Union of Russia and Poland) attracted most women. Women were among its top leaders and even more numerous among the middle leadership and active rank and file. The Bund attracted many women seeking a new life and a break with the demands of their families, although they were still expected to do the cooking and caretaking. The Bund promised gender equality, even if women were expected to wait for its delivery by the revolution. Zionist ideologies of "muscular Judaism" and the exclusion of women from any public role attracted far fewer women, but they too talked about the ultimate equality of the sexes. All strains of Yiddishkeit "legitimated the presence of women in the world of commerce .

and artisanry as well as their cultivation of character traits that would ensure the survival of the family."[5]

From its birth then, modern eastern European Jewish culture encompassed the religious and secular and connected them through a common Yiddish language. That language sustained a rich secular literature, music, and theater that reflected the culture of their urban, working-class communities. Decidedly communal and ethnic in response to anti-Semitism, and secular in contrast to the family-centered religious assimilationism of the western European model, this is what eastern European Jews brought to America after 1880, where it developed and flowered in its own ways in the residential and occupational ghettos of the immigrant Jews who became part of America's working class.[6]

Working-class Jewishness in New York

The Lower East Side of New York City, which was "with the possible exception of Beijing, the most densely populated square mile on earth," was where most immigrant Jews first settled.[7] In the United States, in general, persistent racial segregation and labor force segmentation made working-class neighborhoods also racial and ethnic neighborhoods. The eastern European Jews who lived on the Lower East Side nevertheless had regular contact with the German Jews who had arrived earlier and whose neighborhoods were uptown; they were also separated by occupation, social status, and constructions of Judaism. Assimilated western European Jews, on the other hand, tended to look down on the new immigrants, harboring a mixture of embarrassment and charitable benevolence toward them.

Not surprisingly, the idioms by which Americans have expressed working-class consciousness have been racial and ethnic idioms. Historian Herbert Gutman was an eloquent pioneer in showing how working-class European immigrants fashioned their ethnic understandings and practices into an alternative culture that served as a world from which they developed their own critiques of capitalism.[8]

Jews were no exception. Even if they had been students, professionals, or intellectuals, Jewish immigrants all necessarily became part of a working-class Jewish community. As Gerald Sorin has shown, this reshaped their politics. Their kin, friendship, and work ties all bound them solidly to a community whose Jewishness was overwhelmingly proletarian.[9]

As Liebman argues so well, to live as a Jew in this community, especially before World War I, meant that one actively participated in a politicized working-class culture. It shaped one's options and one's ways of being a man or woman. It had local power, or hegemony, to shape daily relationships even across class lines. This was because, as Annelise Orleck put it, "[m]ost Jewish immigrant New Yorkers . . . were nourished on the same daily diet of socialist fundamentals."[10]

Jewish socialism shared a broad set of principles with the rest of the community: that everyday Jews were members of the working class and were exploited as workers; that Jews were stigmatized and discriminated against as a race; that Jewish workers had to organize and fight the bosses and the state for their due; that the goal of the international working-class struggle was to build a society based on reciprocal principles that fed the mind and spirit. And they shared a messianic faith that this would happen. The mass appeal of socialism gave it a hegemony in the Jewish community that it lacked in almost all of nonethnic America. Yiddish cultural practices and political views were working class. They provided a glimmer of alternative ways of constructing cross-class relationships and political practice by making them Jewish values. So perhaps the majority of Jews who had no allegiance to socialism, the Bund, or the Workmen's Circle were still likely to be quite antibourgeois and to have a working-class orientation simply by absorbing it through living in the Jewish community.[11]

But the Torah (biblical commandments) and Jewish religious traditions were also woven into the fabric of socialism. Just as a ghetto existence shaped the politics of identity in the Jewish community, so too did it shape its religion. Annelise Orleck describes Jewish women's activism as animated by "a heady mix of ideology gleaned from Isaiah, Marx and their mothers."[12] Jewish socialism and unionism together were at the center of the dense web of the community's institutional life, of mutual aid societies, like the Workmen's Circle, secular schools, choruses, literary and theater societies, and summer camps. The largest Yiddish daily newspaper in the world, the *Forward*, was socialist.

Political radicals were central actors in building community institutions right from the beginnings of Jewish immigration.

> Already by the 1890s, in the first years of Yiddish-language agitation, some of the most beloved speakers, editors and poets in the community were Socialists or anarchists who saw the struggles for unionization as the journey out of Egypt toward the Promised Land.[13]

The garment workers' unions were perhaps the institutions most important in making Jewish socialism a bedrock of political culture on the Lower East Side.[14] The International Ladies Garment Workers Union (ILGWU) and the Amalgamated Clothing Workers Union (ACWU) were built through huge waves of strikes that began with female shirtwaist makers in New York City in 1909 and continued in New York and Chicago especially, until 1914. The strikes unionized the clothing industry and institutionalized Jewish socialist politics among the unions' largely female membership. They organized their own social worlds around worker education, recreation, and Yiddish culture. They built residential cooperative apartments in the Bronx, the Rand School, the Workers' University, a Breadwinners' college, and the People's Institute at Cooper Union as well as a variety of self-help, literary, and music societies.

Unions were not the only Jewish groups to build social institutions to support a political community. Indeed, the idea of alternative communities was part of the life of Jewish political organizations. In New York City, whose population was over a quarter Jewish and the largest concentration of Jews in the United States, the concept took its most concrete form (no pun intended) in building. The 1920s saw a large wave of second-generation residential expansion as Jewish builders developed new Jewish neighborhoods. Although most of the building was for profit, some was not. Some of the most impressive undertakings were carried out by labor unions and political groups, especially in new areas of the Bronx. The ACWU built a large cooperative colony as well as financing other apartment houses designed for workers in the Bronx. The Sholem Aleichem Houses were built to preserve secular Jewish culture; the Labor Zionist Farband built co-ops; and left-wing socialists built the Workers Cooperative Colony. The Typographical Union and the Jewish Butchers Union also built cooperative housing projects. As Deborah Dash Moore has shown, "The cooperatives represented an ideological variation within the ethnic Jewish building industry, an example of Jewish builders uniting with Jewish workers to construct housing tailored to their socialist specifications. . . . In several cases the cooperatives created Jewish neighborhoods virtually overnight."[15]

Although Jewish culture was working-class conscious and heavily socialist, successful working-class politicians had also to identify themselves politically as Jewish.[16] The most widely known image of that fusion comes from the 1909 strike of shirtwaist makers in New York City. When Clara Lemlich, a leading organizer and striker, moved for a general strike at a mass meeting filled with young women garment workers, its chairman, Benjamin Feigenbaum, a socialist, asked the crowd in Yiddish to take the Hebrew oath to strike. But working classness and Jewishness did not fuse easily or naturally.[17]

It was not enough for a leader to be Jewish and socialist, as Arthur Gorenstein has argued in explaining why the Lower East Side in 1908 supported a Tammany candidate for Congress over the well-known unionist and Socialist Party leader Morris Hillquit. The Tammany candidate ran as pro-Jewish. Hillquit claimed:

> The interests of the workingmen of the Ninth Congressional District are therefore entirely identical with those of the workingmen

of the rest of the country, and if elected to Congress, I will not
consider myself the special representative of the alleged special
interests of this district, but the representative of the Socialist
Party.[18]

Gorenstein argues that Hillquit and the Socialist Party seriously underestimated the importance of Jewishness to the identity of working-class voters. This construction of Jewishness as
a response to racialization and anti-Semitism was particularly
clear in that election year. The Jewish community was then under attack at home and faced intense pogroms in Russia. American Jews mobilized against renewed efforts in 1907–1908 to
restrict immigration from Europe and Asia. And they felt the
weight of renewed racist stereotypes of Jews as a dirty and criminal people. Some of this, particularly an article by the NYC police commissioner, had a racist intent, but some also came from
"friends" like Eugene V. Debs and Lincoln Steffens, who wanted
to attack the dirty and dangerous conditions of the Lower East
Side rather than its people. The two were not easy for many Jews
to distinguish.

The Socialist Party's record on immigration was also less than
stellar. With one of its strongholds being white workers on the
West Coast, the party (including Hillquit) supported restricting
immigration from among "backward races" and those "who are
incapable of assimilation with the workingmen of the country
of their adoption." Hillquit claimed this was directed against
Asians, and that Jews should have no concern. However, Jews
had a great deal of concern and were strongly opposed to any
restrictions on immigration. Much of their opposition was based
on the assumption that any restriction would be extended to
Jews.

When, in 1910, the Socialist Party assumed a more explicitly Jewish and antiracist stance, it succeeded in reelecting its
candidate, Meyer London, a leader in the 1910 cloakmakers'
strike, to Congress. The Socialist Party's new position opposed
any restrictions on immigration. But London also ran as a rep-

resentative of the Jewish working class. Jewish workers did not accept the notion that a Jewish identity was peripheral to their working-class interests. In electing Meyer London, Gorenstein argues, they showed that they wanted a Jew who would represent specifically Jewish workers, and that Jewish workers did not believe that the interests of all workers were identical.[19]

The Dailiness of Jewish Working-class Culture

Jewish socialism on the Lower East Side was also a daily system of meaning and membership that gave a working-class character to the neighborhood. Historian Stephanie Coontz has argued that Euro-immigrant cultures employed categories of public and private but infused them with very different meanings than did their native-born middle-class counterparts. The cultural consciousness of a difference between "our" (private) world and "theirs" (public) in the working-class Jewish ghetto emerges most clearly in married women's daily responsibilities for family and household labor. Food in Jewish and Italian immigrant neighborhoods, wrote Elizabeth Ewen, "became an arena of contention between immigrant women and American society. . . . Social workers would write of their clients, 'Not yet Americanized, still eating Italian food.'"[20]

Stephanie Coontz argues that statements like this actually marked a real boundary between mainstream bourgeois culture and late-nineteenth-century working-class cultures that was recognized on both sides of the class and cultural divide. Working-class culture was a "clear-cut alternative to bourgeois individualism and work patterns."[21] Bourgeois culture insisted on a dichotomy between a public sphere of work, power, rationality, and maleness and a private sphere of domesticity, subordination, emotion, and femaleness. In contrast, within the working-class world, connections were paramount—among individuals, families and households, as well as between economy and affect. The language, Coontz notes, was confusing because both classes used the word "private" but meant different things by it. The working class used "private" to set off its ethnic cultural values from those of the bourgeoisie. The immigrant working class distinguished between its own community-based moral universe and that of the mainstream, between "our world" and "theirs."

Coontz suggests that "private life" applied to nonwork time, or "leisure time," and to values and practices governing that time. These practices contrasted with bourgeois practices based on hierarchy, alienated labor, competition, and individualism. Her point fits nicely with the observations of other feminist scholars that working-class women's perspectives bring family and community, work and politics together in a single sphere, which Coontz would characterize as the "private" world of working-class culture.[22] In contrast to bourgeois usage then, this working-class meaning of "private" did not mark a family or gendered sphere so much as it did community membership and separation from the social relations and values of mainstream American culture and the state.[23]

Following Gutman, I have argued elsewhere that if we focus on working-class women in trying to analyze class, it becomes clear that the American working class forms its culture and institutions in ethnic neighborhoods just as much as or more than it does in factories.[24] Irving Howe's *World of Our Fathers* is a classic portrait of the male part of this community. But working classness is also a complementary relationship between wage earners of both sexes and the mainly women who did the unwaged labor of transforming wages into necessary goods and services.

One's assigned contributions depended upon one's gender and stage of life. Daughters joined their fathers and brothers in shouldering responsibility for earning the family's wages. Often daughters were the main breadwinners, in part because they could more easily find work in the garment industry than could their more highly paid male kin.

Just how important were daughters' wages became clear when community and citywide relief committees visited the families of the young women who had been killed in the Triangle

Shirtwaist Company fire in 1911. They found that Jewish and Italian women "were supporting old fathers and mothers, both in this country and abroad; mothering and supporting younger brothers and sisters, sending brothers to high school, to art school, to dental college, to engineering courses."[25]

Single Jewish women were not seen as sexual beings in need of social and/or ritual regulation. Unmarried daughters, who were innocent of the pleasures of sex, "were seen as more socially neutral," and there were apparently few prohibitions on their mixing with men at work or in public, in Russia and in the United States.

Jewish anxieties about women's sexuality focused on married women. Because a woman became sexually wise once she married, she could not then go about so freely in public. If she were to attract the attentions of other men, she would threaten her husband's honor. The sexuality of men, married or single, carried few restrictions, nor was it ritually regulated. Their harassment of women workers seems to have been taken as part of male nature. In Jewish culture, married women were potential seducers whose behavior needed to be regulated socially and ritually. Since women's hair was believed to arouse erotic feelings, Orthodox women shaved their heads or covered their hair with a *shaitl* (wig). And they had to take a *mikveh* (ritual bath) each month after their period before they could resume sexual relations with their husbands.[26]

Consequently, married women frequently turned home-based activities into income-generating opportunities. Almost every Jewish household took in boarders at some time. This involved a great deal of work for the mother of the house, for she did all their cooking, washing, and ironing, perhaps helped by a daughter. Through boarding, single men and women were integrated into the community either as paying boarders or as "temporary" members of an integrated household economy under the direction of a mother. Household composition was a fluid mix of newly arrived immigrants, boarders, and kin, but households always needed a mix of waged and unwaged workers.

For widows with young children, like the mothers of future ILGWU leaders Pauline Newman and Rose Schneiderman, wage-earning, rent-paying boarders made the difference between poverty and homelessness. All four of Deborah Schneiderman's children served time in an orphanage when she could not feed them. Pauline and her sisters worked in factories from the time they were children, and their mother took in washing.

Such informal entrepreneurial activities were also important for the neighborhood economy. Domestic needs and resources varied over the course of a year and a life cycle, so some households were likely to be labor poor while others were labor rich at any given time. A household with small children was likely to need more domestic labor than a mother could supply, while one with older sons and daughters might have a labor "surplus" and be in a position to provide this kind of help. Direct reciprocity certainly existed, particularly between kin, but assistance could also be given in the form of a paid service. Although they appear to be "profit-seeking" ventures, informal economic activities like boarding or doing laundry operate on self-exploitation and are better understood as cash-mediated forms of reciprocity within working-class communities. That is how they were treated in women's neighborhood economies.

Within the neighborhood, married women and men engaged in a variety of more or less institutionalized but gender-specific reciprocal relationships that linked individuals and households to one another in complex networks of interdependence. Each Jewish neighborhood had its own little stores and pushcarts run by fellow immigrants, women and men, so that it was a somewhat self-contained world. Food shopping was a married woman's activity and a social activity, part of a vibrant street culture according to which one looked out for one's neighbors and the neighborhood, enforced norms of reciprocity, compared prices, bargained ferociously, watched the kids, and just socialized. The social relations of women's unwaged work were also central to the infrastructure of daily life.

Families were close. You just got up and visited. You knocked on the door. They opened it and you were one of the family. If someone got sick, the neighbor took care of them. My mother went for an operation and the neighbor took the younger children. They would shop and cook. Neighbors gathered in the halls, brought out their chairs and chatted. If someone was bad off, they made a collection.[27]

As Annelise Orleck shows so well, when we listen to women, it is obvious that Jewish working-class struggles were not confined to factories. Mothers had their own mighty struggles that centered on transforming wages into the wherewithal of life for their families. Women's mutual aid relationships and the mobilizations they sustained were key forms of the conscious working-class struggle.[28]

Nothing dramatized the cooperation of women on the Lower East Side in carrying out their household responsibilities as clearly as the meat boycotts, food protests, and rent strikes that rocked the city on and off from 1902 until the 1950s.[29] These were the strikes of the *balebostes*, the Jewish mothers who created their own version of Jewish socialist theory when they boycotted, marched, and threw the meat from the stores of offending butchers into the street. Their construction of themselves as strikers and their appeals to Marx, as Paula Hyman points out, dovetailed nicely with the Book of Isaiah's "warnings to the rich and haughty and its prophecies of judgment and cleansing"[30] and brought the secular and the religious together in the pursuit of social justice and the condemnation of greed.

When the price of kosher meat skyrocketed in 1902, women on the Lower East Side took to the streets. They called for a boycott and labeled themselves strikers. The police made arrests, the *New York Times* called it a riot, and 20,000 people turned out for a strike-support rally. The boycott spread to Jewish neighborhoods in Brooklyn and Harlem where women enforced it through patrols. But the strikers also appealed to male-run unions, benevolent and fraternal groups, to set up cooperative stores. Victory came in the form of price rollbacks almost to the original level.[31]

"Watching their mothers battle to improve their families' standard of living, it was clear to working daughters like Schneiderman [and] Newman . . . [that t]heir mothers saw their homes as directly linked to the larger economy and fought to keep them safe from deprivation."[32] So it is not surprising to learn that one of sixteen-year-old Pauline Newman's first big political actions was to organize a rent strike (with mixed results) on the Lower East Side.

> Taking her cue from a successful 1904 rent strike, Newman hatched an ambitious plan: to build a rent strike using both women's neighborhood and shop-floor networks. The result was the best organized of the early twentieth-century housewives' actions, and the largest rent strike New York had ever seen. Newman and her friends began by organizing their peers. By late fall they had assembled a band of four hundred self-described "self supporting women" like themselves, committed to rolling back rents. These young women soon found a sea of willing converts: the mothers of the Lower East Side.[33]

Between 1917 and 1920, women again took matters into their own hands against what many of them saw as food profiteering. An altercation on Orchard Street over the price of onions exploded when a peddler called upon his wife to beat up a woman customer. A crowd of women overturned his cart and scattered his vegetables in the street. Maria Ganz, a participant, left a vivid account of what happened: "It seemed only a moment before a mob of hundreds of women had gathered. Cart after cart was overturned, and the pavement was covered with trampled goods. . . . Policemen came rushing upon the scene, and they too were pelted with whatever was at hand." The women held a meeting of thousands, organized the Mothers' Anti-High Price League, and marched on City Hall, police attempts to disperse them notwithstanding. Here too, women had their own leaders, were able to enforce boycotts in their neighborhood, and spread them to other Jewish working-class neighborhoods in the city.[34] Food riots highlight the fact that women depended upon one another to execute successfully their responsibility for all those forms of unwaged labor by which they turned hard-earned dollars into onions, potatoes, and pot roast.

Food riots also made manifest the value of interdependence across class lines in the community. They showed everyone that merchants were accountable to community values of reciprocity. As Judith Smith said, "When ethnic retailers raised their prices, immigrants viewed such acts as an abandonment of the principles of community justice and particularly as a breach of reciprocity." It was "an injury to a customer loyally patronizing a *paesano* or *landsman*."[35]

Women held merchants and peddlers accountable to a Jewish working-class morality even though merchants and peddlers were not workers. The women insisted that the relationship between sellers and their customers was at least as much an ongoing personal relationship as it was a business one. Because of this personal relationships with peddlers, food rioters were doubly outraged at their prices and felt justified in expressing their moral indignation. They condemned those who behaved like bourgeois businessmen.

For men no less than women, their identities as Jewish and working class were formed in their neighborhoods as well as in factories. Men had their own forms of community-based networks that linked their work and domestic lives. These too were organized around the reciprocity of mutual aid. They centered on *landsmanshaftn*, unions, political parties, and the dense network of mutual aid institutions generated by these important community institutions. Secular and religious associations flourished in Eastern Europe in the latter nineteenth century. Jewish men combined artisan guilds, mutual aid, and Torah-reading in their associations. In the United States, Jews organized mutual benefit associations along lines of craft and town or region (landsmanshaftn) and, by the early 1900s, affiliated local chapters with more broadly based regional and national organizations. Landsmanshaftn most commonly provided medical and burial insurance and funds for wedding celebrations. A man's brothers in his landsmanshaft were expected to turn out for his wedding and other important events in his family life cycle. Although they were men's organizations and centers of male social life, a few had women's auxiliaries. Other forms of benefit organizations also existed. The secular and progressive Workmen's Circle grew rapidly after 1900 and ultimately developed chapters in many cities. Such organizations were crucial for integrating new immigrants into the worlds of waged labor, politics, cultural life, and the neighborhood. They helped them to find places to live, connecting them to jobs and to opportunities for social and cultural activities. Their role in providing medical and life insurance policies was important to maintaining families in the insecure context of working-class life. Moreover, the reciprocity upon which they were based provided a more general kind of social insurance. Although women and men may have had a certain amount of sex segregation in their community institutions, they both operated on the same principles of reciprocity, and both linked work and family life.[36]

Daily Hegemony of Working-class Culture

The hegemony of this working-class Jewish political identity in daily life emerges most clearly when we examine cross-class relationships within the Jewish community. Even though the large majority of Jews were workers, the immigrant community was not made up only of workers. Eastern European Jews soon became owners of garment factories, sooner still became contractors in the industry, and, most quickly of all, became "inside" contractors—that is, usually male workers who hired women "apprentices" and, under the guise of teaching them, paid them almost no wages for their work. Workers, contractors, and bosses were often tied by kinship, by membership in the same landsmanshaft, and by schul (temple). The community also had its merchants, local officials, and rabbis who stood both within and outside it. Under some conditions they functioned in accord with dominant working-class values; under others, they clashed with them.

Cross-class ties certainly complicated class struggle. Louis Painkin, a militant garment worker, noted:

> I had a relative who was in the raincoat business; he gave me a chance to learn the trade and subsequent to that I struck against him. . . . [W]e put him out of business. . . . He died of aggravation. And I was practically the leader of it. I was dedicated . . . [but] also too young to appreciate anything . . . done for [me]. You are involved in a cause, and the cause is paramount.[37]

Another point of view came from a letter writer to the *Jewish Daily Forward:* "I am a Socialist and my boss is a fine man. I know he's a capitalist but I like him. Am I doing something wrong?"[38]

By no means did ethnic loyalty and participation in the same community institutions stop Jewish bosses and Jewish workers from fighting each other. Garment manufacturers organized among themselves, and during strikes they frequently hired Jewish goons to attack the workers. Arnold Rothstein, a Jewish underworld boss, was the son of a manufacturer and behind some of the Jewish gangs that terrorized unionists. And Jewish leftists in the furriers' union led by Ben Gold helped get the gangsters jailed. Workers went on strike against their kin.

Moreover, most workers dreamed of becoming something other than a worker. One of the avenues closest to hand was that of garment contractor or manufacturer, so that yesterday's worker could be tomorrow's boss.[39] But contrary to received wisdom, neither aspirations such as these nor close ties to the "enemy" class proved a barrier to Jewish working-class radicalism. Indeed, Jews probably had a higher per capita count of petty and not-so-petty businessmen in their communities than did most other European immigrant groups. Yet they were also among the most radical.

Although mothers occasionally declared "war" on exploitative merchants, on a daily basis they were in the trenches insuring that peddlers and local merchants functioned as part of the moral world of the working-class community. Here is historian Elizabeth Ewen on the daily life of a peddler:

> Every week Mr. Lefkowitz called for his twenty-five cent installment [on a sewing machine]. Sometimes he got it, more often he didn't. . . . Years passed: he was still coming for his installments and had become an old friend. There were tears in his eyes when he received his last twenty-five cents (after eighteen years). . . . [He] was a neighborhood fixture, performing a variety of services as he put together his income. . . . [H]e supplied wine and whiskey by the gallon for family celebrations, he bought black cloth for those who must go into mourning; he sold lottery tickets; and yet with all these irons in the fire, he was almost as poor as any of us.[40]

Merchants, men and women, were first of all neighbors who provided goods and services to other neighbors at prices that were affordable within the neighborhood. For some men, peddling was an alternative to factory work. For many Orthodox Jewish men, the flexible schedule gave them time for Torah study. Although some hoped to become rich, few did. Their poverty in turn reinforced merchants' and customers' interdependence and strengthened a community infrastructure that had a leveling effect on income.[41]

The fact that local merchants were also members of the ethnic community was a powerful lever for demanding their accountability to a morality of reciprocity. Merchants who were not members of that ethnic community might be freer to behave like profit-seeking businessmen, and it might be much more difficult for communities to call them to account.

Ethnicity has been an important idiom by which working-class women have enforced their values, but it has not been the only one. Although storekeepers, rabbis, and teachers have not always sided with workers, it has happened often enough (and sometimes across ethnic lines) to demand an explanation. Mr.

Lefkowitz has plenty of company in the behavior of his occupational counterparts in other working-class communities. They have a good historical record of actively supporting many major industrial and social-justice struggles in the United States. From Appalachian textile towns and Rocky Mountain mining camps to East Coast neighborhoods of immigrant Europeans, shopkeepers, teachers, and clergy joined strikes, extending support and credit because their own survival lay with those who brought wages into the community. Their actions highlight the power of community morality on all who live in working-class communities.[42] Together with women's mutual aid networks this cultural value system is a class and ethnic political identity that has helped nineteenth- and twentieth-century working-class communities avoid the physical and moral isolation of households, incorporating them instead into community-based social universes in opposition to bourgeois organization and culture.

The working-class Jewish community as an economic and moral community has been larger than single neighborhoods. American patterns of racism and nativism have insured that ethnicity and culture transcend particular neighborhoods. Workers have depended upon far-flung social networks and voluntary associations made up of those of the same ethnicity for their jobs, housing, health, recreation, and marriage partners. Jews as well as other racially stigmatized people were constantly moving around within neighborhoods as well as into and out of them, so that ethnic communities have been simultaneously dispersed and local, with effective kinship networks in the nineteenth and twentieth centuries often spanning states and sometimes continents. Instead of a cash nexus dissolving reciprocity, working-class cultures used cash to expand its range. The widely understood moralities at the heart of political identification placed stringent constraints upon exploitative behavior. But they also helped ethnoracial working-class communities develop in new places and assisted people in their moves within and between them.

☐ *Jewish Womanhood*

Jewish working-class culture had its own ideas about woman-hood. They differed from those of the mainstream, not least by accepting women as strong economic and political actors. However, feminist scholars have pointed out that Jewish women were not the social equals of Jewish men, and that aspects of the community's notions of gender resonated with those of the mainstream. For example, patriarchal Jewish ideals of Talmudic scholarship for men and their right to economic support from women resonated with bourgeois values of patriarchal entitlement. Anzia Yezierska's novel *Bread Givers* is a moving portrait of a daughter's desperate struggle for independence from one such economically dependent father, an utter tyrant in his sense of entitlement to rule his family absolutely.[43]

Although the immigrant community buffered its members from daily contact with anti-Semitic stereotypes—of Jewish women as aggressive and coarse, and Jewish men as effeminate but lecherous knaves—charities, settlements, and other forms of uplift were an important point of contact with mainstream values. Charity was brought into the community largely by middle-class German Jews whose programs sought to make Jewish women more respectable and refined, and to make Jewish men more manly, more athletic, and brave.[44] When immigrants encountered their coreligionists' institutions of assimilation and uplift, this was the kind of Americanization they learned. There was also a strong assimilationist current in the Jewish socialism represented in the *Forward*, which was the most widely read paper in the community, and by a large part of the Socialist Party, which was quite influential in both garment unions. Nevertheless, real differences between Jewish and bourgeois ideals of domesticity persisted.

Even though Jewish women and bourgeois women were both expected to marry, and neither was expected to work for wages after marriage, *balebostes* (Jewish housewives) were not the same as their mainstream counterparts. A Jewish mother's sense of her work was similar to the preindustrial notion of mistress of a household, whom Alice Kessler-Harris has described as someone who has socially recognized skills and knowledge of the domestic arts, who organizes her own work and that of junior members of the household, and who also invents and carries out a mixture of unwaged and entrepreneurial activities.[45] For Jewish mothers like my grandmother, the home was a crowded workshop, hardly a haven in a heartless world.

Jewish mothers' conceptions of their work also challenged bourgeois notions of a woman's place. "In most working-class families it was common practice for the husband to turn over his wages to his wife."[46] Part of a Jewish mother's labor was to manage a complex household economy that depended upon several wage earners and her own nonwaged labor. By controlling all household income, married women asserted the importance of their work as well as its continuity with waged work. The centrality of a household economy in practice and as a working-class woman's cultural ideal departed from the prevailing individualist idea that a wage is paid simply for work done for employers and that only wage labor is real work. Women's household management also challenged bourgeois notions of men as decision-making heads of households.

That claim was undermined by wage-earning husbands especially, and by sons and daughters who struggled to withhold all or part of their wage packets for personal use.[47] Nevertheless, mothers' constructions of their labor as skilled work performed by adult women as part of their social place in a household and community economy was broadly upheld by the practices of women and men of the community.

As the history of rent strikes and food riots showed so dramatically, Jewish motherhood also contained the notion of political activism as part of women's responsibility to their families and community. This community also voted strongly for suffrage and supported Jewish feminist agitation.[48] Mothers' political activism stemmed from their domestic authority and responsibility to do whatever it took to provide that home for family and kin, as well as from the construction of "private" as encompassing the household as part of the working-class community.[49]

Silent films were a new medium at the turn of the century, and no one was more addicted to them than the immigrant working class. In New York City, notes Sharon Pucker Rivo, about a quarter of Manhattan's populace "frequented the city's 123 film houses, close to a third of which were located on the Lower East Side." The earliest non-Jewish moviemakers like D. W. Griffith and Mack Sennett, aiming at these audiences, tended to portray Jewish immigrants as innocent, "harmless and unthreatening," victims of a cruel and unjust society. The first Jewish, and mainly male, film portraits of Jewish women emerged from Hollywood studios and New York Yiddish film producers after World War I. Here, Jewish immigrant women become strong mothers and daughters, holding together their families, maintaining their cultures and communities in the face of adversity. Even though the Hollywood versions had more of an airbrushed quality, in both "the images flickering on the screen reflect the self-assurance and strong character of the women involved with making the films, both behind the scenes and on the silver screen—Fannie Hurst, Frances Marion, Vera Gordon, Anzia Yezierska, Rosa Rosanova, Molly Picon, and Lila Lee."[50]

Although Jewish women were believed to be intensely sexual, at least after marriage, the recent record has been fairly silent on that aspect of women's Jewishness. However, June Sochen has pointed us at places to look for exploring Jewish women's bawdy side. Early-twentieth-century "red hot mamas" like Sophie Tucker were a kind of Jewish and comic counterpart of African American mothers of the blues. Indeed, Tucker frequented Harlem and Chicago blues clubs and knew Bessie Smith. Tucker, who described herself as the last of the red hot mamas, was one of many remaining Jewish mamas who still performed in the 1950s.

"I Just Couldn't Make Ma Feelings Behave," one of her popular songs, declares an unspoken view in the 1910s and 1920s: that women have sexual feelings, that they have a right to them, and even further, could state them in public. Tucker was a large woman, probably weighing in at 180 pounds by 1916 when she opened at Riesenweber's, a new nightclub in New York; she did not fit society's image of a beautiful, desirable woman. Yet, like her black blues sisters, Tucker sang proudly of her needs and asserted her right to their fulfillment. All women, she implied, of whatever shape, had sexual natures. Besides Tucker, Millie DeLeon, Belle Barth, Belle Barker, Totie Fields, and many others operated within the bawdy comic genre. Contrary to the dominant representations of Jewish women, the bawdy Jewish woman entertainer has had a long history.

Sochen suggests that this tradition of "talking back" continues in Joan Rivers and Bette Midler.[51]

In Yiddish popular culture and daily expectations (if not in Hollywood), Jewish mothers were not expected to be ladylike. Mike Gold wrote of his mother, "How can I ever forget this dark little woman with bright eyes, who hobbled about all day in bare feet, cursing in Elizabethan Yiddish, using the forbidden words 'ladies' do not use, smacking us, beating us, fighting with her neighbors, helping her neighbors, busy from morn to midnight in the tenement struggle for life."[52] "Yiddishe Mamas" were often sentimentalized in story and song—from Scholem Asch to Sophie Tucker, and especially in Hollywood during the 1930s. Mother-blame was definitely not part of this culture.

Many years ago, Kamene Okonjo, in criticizing the sexism of Western treatments of Ibo political organization, pointed out the European incapacity to regard motherhood as a political status. Challenging Euro-American translations of Nigerian female leaders as queens, Okonjo noted, "In fact, she did not derive her status in any way from an attachment or relationship to a king. The word *omu* itself means 'mother,' being derived from . . . 'she who bears children.'" Unlike the bourgeois Western construct, Nigerian cultures recognize motherhood (in the sense of mother-of-one's-people) as a political status. So too did immigrant Jewish communities (and some recognized motherhood as a sexual status as well). In this they were similar to their immigrant Euro-American, African American, and Chicano/a counterparts.[53]

Expectations of Jewish daughters differed from those of their mothers, but also and even more sharply from those of bourgeois womanhood. If the womanhood of mothers centered around neighborhood, family relations, and unwaged labor, that of daughters centered around waged labor and the street, around a factory-based community and public leisure, both of which contravened confinement to a private sphere upon which bourgeois respectability depended.

Christine Stansell traced the roots of a widespread Euro-immigrant daughterhood to Irish immigrant youth culture of the streets. As Kathy Peiss has shown, Jewish women were among other young, immigrant women early in the twentieth century who used dress, style, and behavior to make a statement about who they were that rejected bourgeois notions of feminine refinement and domestic confinement. They created images of a working-class-conscious, heterosexual youth culture that grew up on the streets of New York. Jewish working girls participated fully in the commercial nightlife of dances, theaters, and eating places and especially in lectures and night school. Young working-class immigrant women claimed the streets and public spaces as theirs; they dressed to attract the attention of men. They frankly acknowledged their sexuality as expressive of power and subjectivity and as a means to get men to take them to the new public amusements they could not afford on women's low wages. The young Kate Simon gives us a rare look at young women's sense of themselves as sexual. Describing herself in the first fitted dress her mother made for her, after she had had her first menstrual period, she says:

> I might let Tony [a molesting barber] play his finger games under the sheet or punch his round belly. I might say "Son of a bitch" or even "You fucking bastard" to the humpbacked watchman if he tried to pinch my ass as I passed the factory, or dance around him, my skirt swirling flirtatiously, as he lumbered toward me. The next time I went to Helen Roth's house, her high-school brother would kneel and lay at my feet a sheaf of long-stemmed red roses.

Federico De Santis and his brother Berto would stick daggers into each other for rivalrous love of me.

I was ready for all of them and for Rudolph Valentino; to play, to tease, to amorously accept, to confidently reject.[54]

Sexuality and economics were interwoven in a direct challenge to parental notions of a household economy and authority over daughters. Jewish daughters struggled with themselves and their parents about how much, if any, of their wages to withhold for themselves.[55] Wages were the economic base of daughters' independence from both factory and family subordination. Jewish daughters did not have to assert their right to be working women or to be single for a period, but it was probably a struggle to be as independent of family demands as they might like to be.

Jewish daughterhood had its own characteristic forms of political activism, especially around unionization and fighting the garment bosses. In their struggles as wage earners, Jewish daughters were supported by their mothers and by more general community values. Wage earning was an honorable and expected contribution of sons and daughters equally. Their mothers' neighborhood networks provided the infrastructure for sustaining strikes and factory-based class militancy.

The immigrant Jewish daughters who animate recent historical work—and some of Barbra Streisand's most popular films, like *Yentl* and *The Way We Were*—are passionate beings. Their passions center around learning, independence, and personhood, but curiously, not around sexual expressiveness (which is not to be confused with romance).[56] Here even the feminist literature is relatively silent on specifically Jewish women's quests. We only know that daughters had an intense desire for learning and personhood. Community values rooted in eastern European secularism encouraged their passion for reading and for school, and mothers especially supported their daughters to the extent they could. Deborah Schneiderman was a single mother on the verge of starvation, but she worked nights in a factory and kept her daughter Rose in school until she could no longer find night work. Only then did Rose leave school for the garment factory. Although young women dreamed of independence and escape from the shops, maybe to becoming a teacher (and saw schooling as useful to upward mobility), the passion for learning was at least as much to nourish the soul. As Orleck observed, "Reveling in beautiful language and debating difficult ideas made them feel that they had defeated those who would reduce them to machines."[57]

If mothers supported their daughters' aspirations and unionization, daughters also learned from their mothers about political struggle and the importance of their struggle for food, clothing, and shelter. In the memoirs of their sons and daughters, immigrant Jewish mothers never appear housebound but rather as "mediators between the home and the larger society of school, work, and recreation" as well as supporting their daughters' "aspirations and desires for independence and education."[58] Maybe, like my grandmother and my mother, these immigrant mothers also supported their daughters' dreams even when they believed the odds were against them.

But how did mothers respond to their daughters running the streets in a heterosocial youth culture replete with music, strong drink, and unsupervised, late-night entertainments? Here the record is strangely silent for both Jewish mothers and daughters. Indeed, I found scarcely anything about sex and the Jewish girl! Did mothers worry about their daughters' respectability? Surely they were aware that the police and the social work establishment frowned on such behavior. Did they share in that standard? Or did mothers see that they shared their daughters' economic dependence on men and wish them well in their quest for pleasure and sweetness? We do not yet have answers to these questions.

Despite the relative freedom that Jewish women had in comparison to bourgeois women, Alice Kessler-Harris's pioneering study showed long ago that the Jewish men in positions of union and community leadership subscribed to keeping women's activism to a confined and appropriately gendered space. Labor leaders like Pauline Newman, Rose Schneiderman, Fannia Cohn, and Rose Pesotta spent their political lives in struggle with a sexist, recalcitrant, and fundamentally conservative, male, union leadership. Clara Lemlich is known in history books as the "wisp of a girl" who ignited the crowd and the 1909 uprising of 20,000 women's garment workers in New York City. She later married and "disappeared," in much the same way that the political activism of mothers disappeared in Jewish men's histories of working-class politics—until feminist scholars unearthed it.

Historians Annelise Orleck and Joyce Antler have recently shown us that the married Clara Lemlich Shavelson was anything but inactive. Indeed, she pushed the limits of the acceptable in the eyes of her family—although, significantly, apparently not in the eyes of the community.[59] Like a good Jewish mother, Shavelson raised her children, but she did not give up her activism. As a Communist Party member, "she turned her attentions to a group that had been utterly ignored by trade unionists, socialists, and communists alike: working-class wives and mothers. For the next thirty-eight years, they would be her constituency."[60] She built a political constituency on the platform of community-sanctioned Jewish motherhood. In the World War I period, as a soapbox speaker in Brownsville, Shavelson organized food riots, kosher meat boycotts, and rent strikes in response to wartime inflation. She built ongoing tenant and consumer organizations that spread throughout Jewish New York. She was one of the founders of the United Council of Working Class Housewives (UCWCH) and, with other Communist Party women, struggled unsuccessfully to get the party to recognize the importance of women's consumer struggles.

Indeed, Shavelson made much of her motherhood in organizing. She often pointed out her children when they passed her speaker's platform on the way home from school. Her daughter hated it.

> I would kind of slink by and my friends would say: "Oh look, there's your mother." And I would say, "Come on, hurry up!" . . . Here she

was pointing at you: "And we have before you my child! My little girl! My Ritala. Ritala, stand up! Raise your hand. This is my little girl Ritala. And over there. . . . " By that time I had disappeared.[61]

Shavelson's organizing came into its own during the Depression. As a member of the Unemployed Council, the UCWCH, and the Emma Lazarus Council, a tenant association in Brighton Beach, Shavelson was involved in huge mobilizations to demonstrate, to block evictions effectively, and to demand local unemployment compensation. Through the Communist Party women's networks, the UCWCH was able in 1935 to spark an extraordinarily powerful, nationwide meat boycott that began in New York City, in the black neighborhood of Harlem and in Jewish neighborhoods, to protest the high cost of living.[62]

Resistance to Shavelson came not from the community but from a Communist Party that in the late 1930s struggled mightily against its women and against politicization of the Jewish version of motherhood that its women had begun to take into the streets across the nation. Avram Landy inveighed against Mary Inman's argument that "motherhood was a socially constructed institution subject to change through political organizing. 'Motherhood,' he wrote, 'is a phenomenon of nature and not of society.'" Women could only become equal to men by wage work and union membership.[63]

But the mass of Jewish daughters who worked in the garment shops and who joined the ILGWU en masse were treated as anything but equals by the men who ran their union. Despite the fact that garment union memberships were up to three-quarters women, the leadership remained almost completely male. There were women organizers and activists like Clara Lemlich and Theresa Malkiel, and there was the occasional officer like Pauline Newman, Fannia Cohn, Rose Schneiderman, and Rose Pesotta. Although these women and the rank-and-file young women they tried to represent had their own ideas about what they wanted from a union, their ideas differed sharply from those of their male leadership.

Just as Jewish mothers' sense of themselves as household managers animated their struggles for bread, Jewish daughters yearned for independence from subordination to families and factories. This vision sustained their struggles to build a union and to shape it to serve their needs for an institution that supported the kind of social and intellectual life that would validate them as people.

Young women's dreams may be hard to reconstruct, but as Alice Kessler-Harris suggested over twenty years ago, the lives and struggles of the Jewish working-class women leaders who came out of the garment union provide a record of their sisters' aspirations and the ways they were circumscribed and thwarted by the male ILGWU leadership. Rose Schneiderman and Pauline Newman had stormy relations with an ILGWU that refused to recognize them as equals or to acknowledge their efforts on behalf of women. They had difficulties too from a white and middle-class Women's Trade Union League that supported them as women but often participated in the racism and elitism of the larger society.[64] "'Remember Rose,' wrote Pauline, 'that no matter how much you are with the Jewish people, you are still more with the people of the League.'" But she also acknowledged that "[t]hey don't understand the difference between the Jewish girl and the gentile girl."[65]

From their struggles we can learn something of Jewish daughters' aspirations for independence and their visions of what it meant to them, of an alternative to factory and marital subordination. Their vision, as Kessler-Harris points out, was of a community of working women that could provide institutional alternatives to family-based subordination. They wanted their union to do this, to build a community for single women, to support their peer groups and interdependence without domesticity, for most, for a short period, and for some like Newman, Cohn, and Schneiderman, for life.

Young women garment workers wanted more from their union than wages, and they struggled with their male leadership to make the union a center for the kind of social life they

envisioned: low-cost vacation places for working women, insurance, worker education, the kinds of things that would support
the independence and adulthood of single women.[66] A central
need was for a program of worker education. All the female leaders of the ILGWU built such programs—and did so over the ob-
jections of their male leadership. Fannia Cohn devoted her life
to worker education within and beyond the ILGWU. Moreover,
it was the women members of dressmakers' Local 25 of the
ILGWU whose efforts led to the creation of an educational department and to building Unity House, a union vacation house.
The men disparaged them, saying:

> "What do the girls know—instead of a union they want to dance."
> But the women persisted, insisting that the union would be better
> if the members danced with each other. The women proved to be
> right. By 1919 Unity House . . . had moved to quarters capable of
> sleeping 900 people and two years later Local 25 turned it over to
> a grateful International.[67]

It was Fannia Cohn who made the ILGWU's extraordinarily vibrant Workers' Education Department a center of daily working-
class life.[68] Women clearly built the ILGWU through their
militant actions and their strategic leadership, but except for an
occasional mention of their collective bravery or the young Clara
Lemlich's charisma, they are virtually invisible in prefeminist
Jewish labor history. Feminist scholars have started to show how
the impetus for making unions a center of working-class daily
life came from the ILGWU's women members, who craved for
themselves something of the intellectual, recreational, and as-
sociational life that the community's institutions already gave
to men, and they saw the union as their vehicle.[69]

That passion was also a quest for personhood and a resistance to domination that Orleck refers to as "industrial feminism." Suffrage was attractive to many immigrant daughters, who
recognized that the race-based benefits of feminine refinement
and male protection were white-only and never intended for
them. Jewish women strikers were beaten by police and thugs

on picket lines. They were treated by judges and employers as bad girls "whose aggressive behavior made them akin to prostitutes." When the "mink brigades" of wealthy feminists put an end to police brutality by just showing up on the picket line, their presence made clear that there was one sexual morality for white middle-class women and another for them, and that while the former might benefit from being dependent good girls, this was not even an option for working-class Jewish women.[70] Immigrant daughters' desire for suffrage stemmed in part from their recognition that they were the only ones who would or could end the abuses they faced, and in part from their desire for financial independence.

They also resisted domestic subordination to men. Although Jewish women struggled with their fathers and husbands, there seems to have been less resistance to rights for women among ordinary men than there was among the male union leadership. Men on the Lower East Side voted strongly in favor of suffrage, but the leadership of the ILGWU consistently opposed it as a legitimate issue for the working class. To understand this, we need to explore the limitations Jewish male culture placed on Jewish women's independence.

Orleck argues that the ILGWU's resistance to women was rooted in the fact that they subscribed to a unionism that was "a muscular fraternity of skilled male workers," in their case located unfortunately in an industry with a female workforce. For them, a largely female rank and file was a necessary evil whose vision was hardly worthy of consideration. These leaders were also leaders of the Socialist Party, and their practices necessarily represented those of Jewish socialism. When it came to women's places, they were also not that different from the Communist Party. The communists tried to limit the activism of mothers after 1930; the socialists did the same to daughters.

Together, they reflected the limits to women's assertiveness in working-class Jewish culture. Jewish women may have had more latitude than did bourgeois ladies, but they had less than Jewish men. Jewish daughters were expected to marry; their assertiveness and independence were temporary. Rose Schneiderman's mother warned "Rose that if she pursued a public life she would never find a husband. No man wants a woman with a big mouth."[71] To choose a lifelong career of activism and forgo marriage as Newman, Schneiderman, Cohn, and Pesotta all did was a hard path for a Jewish woman to take. Schneiderman and Newman kept quitting and returning. All four women were excluded from the informal male life of the union and continually struggled against loneliness.[72] There was no social place for grown women in the union because women were expected to find their place by marriage. In their struggles to make the union a social center for women, daughters were seeking at least a complement to marriage and family centeredness with its ultimate subordination of women.

☐ *Conclusion*

This chapter has explored the experience of Jewish working-class identity, the ways that it constructed Jewish men and women, and the ways that those constructions shaped their political activism. These immigrants distinguished the Jewish way of life from the dominant white middle-class culture by the nature of the relationships they created with each other. This does not mean that Jewishness was in full or even consistent opposition to bourgeois life, just that it more or less consistently marked itself as different and separate from it. This is especially true in the emphasis in Jewishness on reciprocity in structuring intracommunity institutions and relationships, and in working-class constructions of womanhood. These were key aspects of the social structure and values by which the Jewish community identified itself.

First and most generally, a culture of reciprocity underlay the creation of relationships and institutions. This was manifest in the centrality of mutual benefit and labor union organization to community structure, in the proliferation of housing cooperatives, in the structuring of same-sex social relations, in inter-household relationships, and in efforts to enforce reciprocal ideals upon local merchants. These ideals gave strength to class struggles against employers from their own ethnic community. When they did not behave as "landsmen," they were greedy bosses, beyond the pale of kinship. Leftist political organizing built upon this culture of reciprocity.

Second, women and most men rejected the ideals of bourgeois domesticity in favor of alternative measures of womanhood that supported women as wage earners, family managers, and political citizens within and beyond their communities. However, male-dominated socialist and union politics did not build upon this dimension of class consciousness. Indeed, the political cultures of the Jewish Left seem to have been blind to the alternative constructions of themselves that women developed. Political organizing certainly benefited from women's aspirations even without understanding them. However, the Jewish men's leadership undercut this emerging working-class feminist consciousness even as it built upon, or more accurately, appropriated it.

A Whiteness of Our ☐ CHAPTER 5
Own? Jewishness
and Whiteness in
the 1950s and 1960s

I f American Jews responded a century ago to being treated socially as nonwhites by developing a working-class socialist
form of Jewishness, then how have Jews responded to being extended the privileges offered to white members of the middle
class after World War II? How do we present ourselves to each
other as Jews and how do we present ourselves to a nation that,
in the main, sees us as white? That is the question this chapter
seeks to answer.

We have seen that not all Jews see the question this way.
Some resist the idea of white privilege; others do not see Jews
as white. The contentiousness about whether Jews are white is
only partly a collapse of racial assignment into racial identity.[1]
It is also about the ways Jews have responded to whiteness and
constructed themselves within this racial assignment.

This chapter explores the ways that American Jews understood their transformation. It is a very preliminary treatment of
the experience of Jewish whiteness from the late 1940s to the
mid-1960s.

I make two arguments about those understandings. The first and central argument is that a group of mainly Jewish public intellectuals spoke to the aspirations of many Jews in the immediate postwar decades, and in so doing developed a new, hegemonic version of Jewishness as a model minority culture that explained the structural privileges of white maleness as earned entitlements.[2] In the process, they constructed a male-centered version of Jewishness that was prefiguratively white, and a specifically Jewish form of whiteness, a whiteness of our own. They did not invent this Jewishness out of whole cloth. Indeed, elements of it had long been elements of American Jewishness. Animated by core Jewish concerns with social justice, these public intellectuals fashioned an interpretation of the postwar world and Jews' place in it. Because that interpretation resonated with and also reconciled the discomfort of many Jews' experiences of upward mobility, it came to be the most widely disseminated version of Jewishness. It was to Jewishness of the 1950s what Jewish socialism was to Jewishness at the turn of the last century. Although there were many forms of Jewishness in play in the postwar decades, they all recognized, responded, and reacted to this "whiteness" form of Jewishness, thus underscoring its hegemonic status. Further, the intellectuals' interpretations of Jewishness also influenced the way Americans came to think about race and ethnicity in general.

The second argument is that in their popular culture and their everyday life, Jews related to this version of Jewishness somewhat ambivalently. On the one hand, Jews had a justifiable wariness about the extent to which America's embrace was real.[3] They also had qualms about the costs of joining the mainstream to a Jewish sense of personal and social morality. On the other hand, they were ambivalent about Jewishness itself, about being too Jewish.[4] Was it an old-fashioned cultural morality that spoiled one's enjoyment of the mainstream party? Or was it a collective soul, an anchor in an atomized and materialist world? This ambivalence was expressed in literature, in self-parody, in social critique, and in "talking back."[5] It made Jews popular articulators of a larger American pattern in the 1950s of uneasiness about American affluence and capitalist modernity in general. As a consequence, from the late 1940s to the mid-1960s, Jewish artists and intellectuals found themselves in the unusual position of speaking in public forums as white Americans for white America, but also as white critics of the culture of 1950s whiteness.

☐ *The Setting*

Jews reshaped their identities after World War II in a social milieu full of crosscurrents. They emerged from the war scarred by the horror of a genocidal anti-Semitism that they could only gradually begin to discuss.[6] To speak of the Nazi Holocaust and to embrace the state of Israel became cornerstones of postwar Jewish identity. Yet, this was also a period when white America embraced Jews and even Jewishness as part of itself—you didn't have to be Jewish to love Levy's rye bread or to tell Jewish jokes. Jews could become Americans and Americans could be like Jews, but Israel and the Holocaust set limits to assimilation. Jews belonged to Israel and Israel belonged to Jews in a way that it did not belong to non-Jews. Especially in the 1950s and early 1960s, Israel represented a Jewish soul, albeit variously defined, in the face of seemingly limitless assimilationist possibilities.

For more than its first decade, Israel exerted a powerful appeal across the Jewish political spectrum partly because it represented different things to different Jews. The Jewish Left initially embraced Israel as a progressive nation born of the fight against Nazism. For socialists and Zionists, Israel gave birth to a new kind of idealistic Jewish man and woman who would renew the old fight against capitalism and provide an alternative to the smugness of American consumer society. Leon Uris's 1950s bestseller *Exodus* did it for me. Brave, idealistic—and secular—Zionist fighters for justice were such attractive and sexy ways of being a Jew that I applied and went to Brandeis with a newfound determination to embrace much more of my Jewish

heritage. In my case, it did not last past a few months of expo-
sure to a conservative Jewish university administration. For others Israel, especially its kibbutzim and new Jewish womanhood
and manhood, was progressive and appealing.[7] For conservatives,
its economic growth and, later, Israeli military power represented
Jewish success on a world scale, a nation among nations. And
at some level, for all Jews, Israel represented their determination never again to be victims and to unite as Jews of the
diaspora.

Thus, before the 1967 war, allegiance to Israel and fresh
knowledge of the Holocaust were defining experiences of Jewishness across the political spectrum. And yet, as Melanie Kaye/
Kantrowitz has noted, "Many Jews raised in the United States
in the wake of the Holocaust experienced it like a family secret—
hovering, controlling, but barely mentioned except in code or
casual reference."[8] Thus, both the Holocaust and Israel gave Jews
a degree of critical distance from mainstream American whiteness, a sense of otherness even in the midst of being ardently
embraced by the mainstream.

By the late 1940s, not only did economic and social barriers to Jewish aspirations fall away but the United States, perhaps in part from guilt about having barred Jews fleeing the
Nazis, perhaps in part from a more general horror of the Holocaust, became positively philo-Semitic in its embrace of Jewish
culture. Jews were prominent among public intellectuals; Jews
like Milton Berle, Sid Caesar, Sam Levinson, and Jack Benny
were even more widely visible because they were in the arts and
the new medium of television. Consider, for example, Calvin
Trillin's wonderful spoof "Lester Drentluss, A Jewish Boy from
Baltimore, Attempts to Make It Through the Summer of 1967":

> Soon Lester began to spot some signs of a trend himself—a boom
> in Jewish novels here, a Jewish Lord Mayor of Dublin there. He
> noticed an increasing use of Jewish mothers by comedians and of
> Jewish advisers by politicians. Scotch-Irish professors seemed
> undisturbed about being included in the category of "Jewish

intellectuals." The gentile movie stars who failed to convert to Judaism repented by donating their talents to Bonds for Israel benefits. . . . Lester's final decision came in February 1965 while he was reading an article in *Life* magazine about Robert Lowell, the New England poet. "Do I feel left-out in a Jewish age?" Lowell was quoted as saying. "Not at all. Fortunately, I'm one-eighth Jewish myself, which I do feel is a saving grace." Lester decided that the day a Boston Lowell bragged about being Jewish was the day a Baltimore Drentluss ought to let it be known that he was at least eight times as Jewish as Robert Lowell.[9]

Well into the 1960s, my circle of friends joked about our Jewish mothers, some of whom were African American and some of whom were white Protestant. Anyone could be a Jewish mother, and there were joke books full of ways to know one when you saw one. My high school newspaper was Jewish turf, even though less than half of the active staff was Jewish, and the non-Jewish majority joked that they were "assimilated Jews." In other words, non-Jewish whites joined Jews in adopting a commoditized cultural Jewishness as their own. Being Jewish was a way of being American.

It is not just that Jewishness was chic in mainstream circles, it also became mainstream. Observing that J. D. Salinger, Saul Bellow, Bernard Malamud, and Philip Roth were the great *American*—not great Jewish—writers of the period, Peter Rose notes that "[f]or perhaps the first time in American literary history, the Jew became everyman and, through a curious transposition, everyman became the Jew. . . . Most American Jews are part of the big wide—and white Establishment." Indeed, as Neil Gabler has argued for Hollywood up to World War II, Jews helped create white Americanness.[10]

And it wasn't only in the movies:

In the century of Calvin Klein, Ralph Lauren, and Dinah Shore, need we ask who but a Jew is best at packaging unwhiny blonde fantasy figures? I don't know about you, darlings, but ever since I found out that Kathie Lee Gifford was nee Epstein, I don't assume *anything*. Why be surprised, then, that Barbie, the ultimate *shiksa* goddess, was invented by a nice Jewish lady, Ruth Handler (with her husband Elliot, co-founder of Mattel)? Indeed, the famous snub-nosed plastic ideal with the slim hips of a drag queen is in fact named after a real Jewish princess from L. A., Handler's daughter, Barbara (who must have been hell to know in junior high school!). Her brother is named Ken.[11]

Being able to write and speak as white, and for non-Jews to accept Jews as white like them, was an important experience of Jewish maleness in the 1950s. As Alexander Bloom has shown so well, the New York public intellectuals who played a key role in shaping postwar American political and social thought were among those who exercised this ability. They were a very visible face of Jewishness between the 1940s and the first half of the 1960s. Almost all came from working-class Jewish families and were educated at City College and Columbia University. They saw themselves as outsiders and underdogs, as political and literary critics of the establishment, and as speakers for a working-class Jewish community that was already breaking up. The key players were almost all male (with the exceptions of Hannah Arendt, Midge Decter, and a young Susan Sontag) and Jewish (except for Daniel Patrick Moynihan): Lionel Trilling, Irving Howe, Philip Rahv, Norman Podhoretz, Daniel Bell, Irving Kristol, Norman Mailer, Sidney Hook, Nathan Glazer, and, somewhat later, Martin Peretz. Their journals were the *Partisan Review*, *Dissent*, and *Commentary*, the journal of the American Jewish Committee and their most important political forum in the immediate postwar decades.[12]

These intellectuals were interpreters of white America in the 1950s. They were embraced by its institutions, and some of them in turn embraced its institutions as their own. Some moved soon after the war into university jobs, where they played key roles in forging the postwar anticommunist liberal consensus—an agreement that ideological conflict had ended and that things were getting better for everyone. Some of them, like Nathan Glazer and Daniel Moynihan, shuttled off to Washington, but those who did not were still heard beyond the confines of the university.

Despite this seeming acceptance, many Jews remained uneasy. Was America's love affair with Jews temporary? Would the anti-Semitism of the 1920s and 1930s flare up again? This unease interacted in complicated ways with the growing political conservatism of the Cold War. Antiradicalism and anti-Semitism sometimes seemed to overlap in McCarthyite anticommunism, and did so most powerfully in the execution of Julius and Ethel Rosenberg. But Jews were also an important part of a wider cultural current of American unhappiness with conservatism and materialism that saw the loss of one's soul as among the fruits of success.

☐ *Model Minority, the New Racial Discourse, and Hegemonic Jewishness*

The word "ethnicity" did not come into use until after World War II, when it became the word of choice in academic and public-policy vocabularies to describe those who had been formerly discussed as members of a less-than-white race, nation, or people. The word "ethnicity" became a cornerstone of a new liberal consensus about the United States as a pluralist and democratic society. As has so often been pointed out, part of this consensus, especially in the eastern United States, was that the end of racial inequality was at hand, and soon African Americans and Puerto Ricans would be assimilated into a meritocratic and democratic society, just like the Jewish and other Euro-ethnic intellectuals who had developed these views. This was more than a self-serving perspective of the newly admitted (though it was that too).[13]

Ethnic pluralism gave rise to a new construction of specifically Jewish whiteness. It did so by contrasting Jews as a model minority with African Americans as culturally deficient. Ethnic pluralism also gave rise to a new, cultural way of discussing race. Sociologist Nathan Glazer was among those who developed these perspectives, and he was probably their most articulate spokesman in academic, policy, and general public venues. *Beyond the Melting Pot*, a work on New York City's major ethnic cultures coauthored with Daniel Moynihan, pulls together the strands of this viewpoint most clearly. Although Moynihan is usually thought of as the creator of the myth of the black matriarch, its seeds lay in Nathan Glazer's chapters on "Negroes" and Puerto Ricans. Glazer's contribution to the book—its conception and most of the chapters were his—was a sustained contrast between bad "Negro" and Puerto Rican cultures and not-so-good Italian culture on the one hand, and Jews as exemplary in their goodness on the other.

Model Minority and Jewishness as Prefigurative Whiteness

Glazer's treatment of Jews is a paean to their success at becoming solidly middle-class educationally and occupationally. This he attributes to a strong diaspora culture, strong families, little family breakup, and a "good" kind of voluntary self-segregation manifested especially in residential self-segregation and a low rate of intermarriage. Suburban, middle-class Jewish parents put their kids in Jewish schools and encourage them to participate in Jewish social centers in great numbers. "But the parents of these children do not want them to be any more religiously or consciously Jewish than is necessary, and that often means just enough to make them immune to marriage with non-Jews."[14] Jewish mothers may "hover" and make their sons neurotic, but neurosis seems to protect them from the psychoses non-Jews are heir to, like alcoholism. For example, Glazer would have us believe that at social events like bar mitzvahs everyone drinks before, during, and after the meal, "but the alcoholic and semialcoholic are nowhere in sight." Maintenance of ethnic belonging is important for Jewish upward mobility, but, Glazer argues, in other ethnic cultures it works against it.[15] In this effort,

Glazer was part of a larger discussion among Jewish intellectuals and academics about the reasons for Jews' obvious upward mobility, most of it male-centered and critical of Jewish mothers.

However, in her essay "In Defense of the Jewish Mother," Zena Smith Blau defended the stereotypic Jewish mother by trying to uphold both Jewish womanhood and Jewishness itself. In Blau's view, a Yiddish mama's control of her son through love and guilt might make him neurotic, but it also inculcated all those Jewish virtues that made Jews so successful. Not least, being tied to mama kept Jewish boys away from youth peer groups, and especially from "[g]entile friends, particularly those from poor, immigrant families with rural origins in which parents did not value education." And in the spirit of the benevolent paternalism with which Jewish intellectuals of the period treated African Americans, Blau notes that

> [m]ost lower-class parents who stress the value of education (one thinks of many Negro parents today) must contend with the fact that their children's friends and associates undervalue education, so that a parent who a) values education and b) encourages early independence (as most lower-class families do) is caught up in contradictory strategies. Children trained to be independent at an early age only become independent of parental influence and more dependent upon their peers.[16]

Glazer's chapter on Jews emphasizes their passion for education and their strong ethnic community bonds in business, intermarriage, and social life in general as the bases of their strength.

Glazer and other Jewish public intellectuals created this portrait of "good" Jewishness as much by contrast with "bad" African Americanness as by descriptions of Jewish culture itself. Not too unreasonably, he treated families as important institutions for cultural transmission. However, he paid little attention to Jewish families themselves. His treatment of African Americans includes a section entitled "The Family and Other Problems." In it, Glazer asks

[W]hy were schools that were indifferent to the problems of the children of other groups, forty and fifty years ago, adequate enough for them, but seem nevertheless inadequate for the present wave of children? Why is the strong and passionate concern of the Negro community and Negro parents for education so poorly rewarded by the children?

Glazer's answer lies "in the home and family and community," where the heritage of slavery and discrimination has stripped African Americans of any culture and destroyed the family. "[A] quarter [of New York's African American families] were headed by women. In contrast, less than one-tenth of the white households were headed by women. The rate of illegitimacy among Negroes is about fourteen or fifteen times that among white." Glazer believed that "it is probably the Negro boy who suffers in this situation. With an adult male so often lacking . . . his aspirations should be unrealistic, that his own self-image should be unsure and impaired."[17]

Although Puerto Rican families fared a little better, their mother-headed families were also problems to Glazer. And Italians seem to have been filtered through the awful stereotype of "amoral familism," developed by Edward Banfield.

> That form of individuality and ambition which is identified with Protestant and Anglo-Saxon culture, and for which the criteria for success are abstract and impersonal, is rare among American Italians. A good deal of this Italian-American orientation can be explained by looking at the family.[18]

Italian culture is not prefiguratively white, in the way Jewish culture—which Glazer has described as like Anglo-Saxon Protestant culture in valuing individuality and ambition—is.

A central thread of *Beyond the Melting Pot* is how African American, Puerto Rican, and Italian family cultures differ from Jewish culture so as to create barriers to this sort of ambition and success. For example, although Italians have strong families similar to Jews', Italian strength is said to produce only mafiosi and machine politicians.[19]

Other public intellectuals also elaborated the view that African Americans' problems lay with deficiencies in their culture just as Jewish success lay with the strengths of theirs.

Daniel Bell and Irving Kristol echoed Glazer's assertion that "the Negro middle class contributes very little, in money, organization, or involvement to the solution of Negro social problems," and that "institutions organized, supported, and staffed by Negroes might be much more effective than the government and private agencies that now deal with these problems."[20] They faulted middle-class African Americans for not serving the black poor and faulted the black community in general for not taking care of its own problems. Writing in the *New York Times* in 1964, Bell observed that a "cursory acquaintance with Jewish community life in New York City, for example, reveals the dense network of community organizations and services set up by the Jewish community itself . . . and the reason [the African American community lacks this structure] is that these tasks have been shirked or ignored by the Negro middle-class."[21] Glazer, Kristol, and Bell seem never to have noticed the contradiction between this problematic advocacy of African American middle-class organizational leadership and their outrage when African Americans took that leadership back from whites.

Norman Podhoretz's classic dissection of liberal racism "My Negro Problem—and Ours" adds masculinity explicitly to the mix. He analyzes the ways his childhood construction of African American men is implicated in his construction of his own white Jewish manhood. "For me as a child the life lived [by black boys] seemed the very embodiment of the values of the street— free, independent, reckless, brave, masculine, erotic." He contrasts all the good Jewish schoolboys living in a good home protected by their mothers' solicitousness, hot lunches, galoshes, and itchy woolen hats, with the free and defiant black boys, who "roamed around during lunch hour, munching on candy bars." Podhoretz lived in fear of these envied, bad black kids. But he also desired their masculinity: "most important of all, they were *tough*, beautifully, enviably tough."[22]

Podhoretz's construction of black men as tough and masculine resonates with the stereotypes that nineteenth-century white workers projected upon African American men. David Roediger argues that they were a distorted version of traits that had been valued in white, male artisan culture, but from which those workers sought to dissociate themselves in their efforts to be respectable. That is, they came to see themselves as sober workmen able to defer gratification and to support wives and children, in contrast to African Americans, whom they constructed as amoral, undisciplined, emotional, unable to defer gratification, and sexually uncontrolled. Where Roediger argues that white workers were ambivalent about their bourgeois respectability, Podhoretz admits to the same ambivalence. Even as he appreciated his galoshes, hot lunches, and good grades, he wished he had the masculinity of the bad black boys and feared being called a sissy. At least here, Podhoretz is more aware than Glazer that his version of black masculinity is his own projection.

> Did [any black boy] envy me my lunches of spinach-and-potatoes and my itchy woolen caps and my prudent behavior in the face of authority. . . . Did those lunches and caps spell for him the prospect of power and riches in the future? Did they mean that there were possibilities open to me that were denied to him? Very likely they did. But if so, one also supposes that he feared the impulses within himself toward submission to authority no less powerfully than I feared the impulses in myself toward defiance.[23]

By contrast with mythic African Americans, Glazer fashioned a Jewish culture as one with strong, two-parent families, with mothers at home taking responsibility for keeping their sons' (Jews seem to have had no daughters) noses in the books, away from bad peer influences, and inculcating very Protestant-like ambitions in them. Fathers went into business with relatives and were enmeshed in a dense web of community organizations dedicated to pulling each other up by their bootstraps and taking care of the unfortunate.

In contrast to prewar Jewishness, especially its progressive variants, which distanced itself from bourgeois society and culture, postwar Jewishness propounded by these male intellectuals celebrated its resonance with this mainstream. The virtues and rewards that they claimed for themselves as good Jewish sons depended upon showing how similar Jewish culture was to bourgeois cultural ideals and upon differentiating Jewish culture from a depraved and unworthy African American culture. What I see as white male privilege they saw as universal entitlements earned through the exercise of the virtues given them by their Jewish heritage.

Forgotten in the intellectuals' portrayals more than in those of the popular media was the Jewishness that idealized Yiddish mamas as strong, community-centered, and politically activist women (not unlike the African American matriarchs Moynihan later vilified). Forgotten too was the history of very unruly collective action, including rent strikes and meat riots, the Uprising of 20,000—in all of which women figured prominently—and Jewish socialism and Jewish unions, whose methods of uplift were hardly genteel or all male. The portrait of the Jewish immigrant woman as having been just a nagging version of the ideal mother and housewife for white motherhood demanded a real distortion and flattening of earlier key Jewish constructions of womanhood, even if parts of it did resonate with assimilationist constructions. As we shall see, the misogynist spin on strong mothers represented something of a rebellion by the sons of the assimilationist stream.

Model minorities and deficit cultures are like two hands clapping; they are complementary parts of a single discourse on race as a cultural phenomenon. The Jewish ethnicity that intellectuals claimed for themselves as model minorities was an immigrant version of bourgeois patriarchal domesticity characterized by values of hard work, deferred gratification, education, and strong two-parent families with the mothers full-time at home. It was the invention of a deficient African American culture that illustrated its exemplariness.

Model Minorities/Cultural Deficiency in Constructing Whiteness

The construction of Jewishness as a model minority is part of a larger American racial discourse in which whiteness, to understand itself, depends upon an invented and contrasting blackness as its evil (and sometimes enviable) twin. No one has been more eloquent on this point than Toni Morrison, whose pioneering work established the centrality of blackness for the existence of whiteness.

> In race talk the move into mainstream America always means buying into the notion of American blacks as the real aliens.

> There is no movement up—for blacks or whites, established classes or arrivistes—that is not accompanied by race talk. Refusing, negotiating or fulfilling this demand is the real stuff, the organizing principle of becoming an American. Star spangled. Race strangled.[24]

Sylvia Rodriguez's important new work on whiteness from the vantage point of New Mexico's triracial system illuminates the whiteness of tourists and "amenity migrants" to the "land of enchantment." As white Anglos come to dominate New Mexico's economy, Rodriguez argues, their "privilege entails the power to construct a fanciful racial order in which the downtrodden Indian is elevated to a quasi-supernatural position of spiritual superiority, while Mexicans are relegated to the unclean lower class." There are no Anglos in this picture because they are the viewers, appropriating the position of the unmarked norm. Their gaze, as Rodriguez demonstrates, is a romantic and antimodernist yearning for "transcendence and redemption through union with a spiritually suffused Indian Other"—another variety of race talk that also naturalizes white/Anglo appropriation and entitlement.[25]

Attention to the ways that whites have constructed whiteness by contrast with nonwhite Others, whether by distance and denigration or by elevation to noble savages, has become a major theme in American cultural studies in the last decade. Analyses of minstrelsy and working-class immigrant whitening expand the argument that inventing blackness and speaking for African or Indian America has been a conventional way that immigrants and working-class whites have made themselves white and American, "on the backs of blacks," as Morrison put it, and in so doing have added to or altered hegemonic constructions of American whiteness. For example, Michael Rogin and Eric Lott argue that Jews used the blackface of vaudeville tradition in the movies in much the same way that earlier Irish performers had used it on the stage. Noel Ignatiev has detailed the processes by which the Irish became white. Alexander Saxton has shown how white workers applied parallel stereotypes to Indians, Chinese, Japanese, and Mexicans in the West. He argues that the constellation of white farmers, frontiersmen, and workers in the nineteenth century who demanded an egalitarian republic wherein all white men were equal, and from which Native Americans and blacks were to be excluded, made an original, self-serving contribution to American politicoracial discourse.[26]

Although Glazer, Bell, and Kristol conducted their whitening in the world of high culture and public policy, they too invented their own Jewish form of whiteness by reinventing blackness as monstrous and proclaiming their distance from it: I'm good, you're bad; I'm white, you're black.[27] Popular culture and personal memoirs like Podhoretz's could simultaneously cop to and critique the whiteness they embraced by expressing envy and admiration for the blackness they publicly disavowed and despised. But social science analyses like Glazer's, which were the stuff of political advocacy, were flatter, less nuanced. Still, these Jewish intellectuals and nineteenth-century white workers managed to create versions of patriarchal whiteness that were not that different from one another.

Jewish intellectuals in the postwar decades and racist white workers of the nineteenth century were also socially similar in another way. Both were somewhere between wannabes and nouveau arrivistes, accepted as white, but not securely. Both saw themselves as underdogs, the one in class terms, the other in ethnoracial terms. Neither felt part of, or unambivalently friendly to, the upper-class establishment that seemed to look down its collective nose at them. Despite the complexity of cultural communication these forms embed, Jewish intellectuals, like white male workers, have fought more often to sit at the table with capitalists, even if only as sergeants-at-arms, than to accept kinship with workers who are not white. White artisans struggled mightily against a capitalism that sought to degrade them, they thought, by using nonwhite labor against them. Postwar intellectuals had no desire to return to the ghetto or to join any struggle against capital; they liked their newfound respectability, but they also knew that they were not to the manor born and needed to create a place for themselves there.

Cultural Race, Ethnicity, and Whiteness

The dominant postwar discourse on ethnicity also had a progressive aspect. Its emphasis on culture, which stressed the possibilities of change and assimilation, challenged older ideas that race was biological and that social inequalities were biologically based (and hence both socially proper and inevitable).

However, the postwar concept of ethnicity had one chemistry when attached to blackness and quite a different one when attached to whiteness. Like many liberal whites in the early 1960s, Glazer did not believe that African Americans had an ethnic culture of their own; they were just a race of black Americans.

[I]t is not possible for Negroes to view themselves as other ethnic groups viewed themselves because—and this is the key to much in the Negro world—the Negro is only an American, and nothing else. He has no values and culture to guard and protect. He insists that the white world deal with his problems because, since he is so much the product of America, they are not *his* problems, but everyone's. Once they become everyone's, perhaps he will see that they are his own too.[28]

The racism of this passage notwithstanding, when it came to African Americans, ethnic pluralists had strong doubts about whether they had any cultural stuff with which to assimilate. When directed at blackness, the discourse of ethnicity produced its own, new, cultural variety of racism, which prevails today. Instead of asserting the inherent biological inferiority of some races, it asserted the inherent cultural inferiority of some ethnicities.

When it came to combining whiteness and ethnicity, postwar intellectuals developed a worldview that helped a broad swath of Catholic as well as Jewish Euro-ethnics reconcile their ethnic identities with the privileges of white racial assignment. At one level, the words "white" and "ethnicity" are complementary: one can both claim the privileges of whiteness and embrace the institutions and values of a particular heritage. On another level, the two words are an oxymoron. The entitlements of whiteness depend upon their denial to nonwhites. Those who became Euro-ethnics in the late 1960s and 1970s—Irish, Jews, Poles, and Italians, for example—have as part of their ethnic heritage a racial assignment as not really white. For white ethnics to claim their whiteness would seem to depend upon denying equal entitlements to nonwhites.

At least some of the politics of white ethnicity have continued that pattern of denial in word and deed. For example, Nathan Glazer defended the right of white ethnics to exclude people of color from their neighborhoods and social institutions on the grounds that this was simply continuing an old "American" pattern of voluntary ethnic clustering. Yet he simultaneously attacked affirmative action as undermining the universalist meritocracy that was equally American. For Glazer, exclusion and particularism are unacknowledged privileges of ethnic whites. Thus, when African Americans wanted to exclude whites from leadership and then membership in African American civil rights organizations, Glazer answered that such exclusion was racist. Apparently Jews had the right to self-segregate, but African Americans did not. In a parallel fashion, when African Americans demanded affirmative action in higher education, Glazer answered that they had to earn it as individuals by their grades, as Jews had done.

> We are moving into a diploma society where individual merit rather than family and connections and group must be the basis for advancement, recognition, achievement. . . . Thus Jewish interests coincide with the new rational approaches to the distribution of rewards.[29]

He forgot, however, that when Jews got into college on their grades, anti-Semites argued that the real qualifications for college entry were good breeding and well-roundedness, which Jews lacked. For them, Jews manipulated an insignificant technicality (grades) to rob their white sons and daughters of their (presumed) rightful places in college. The Bakke decision more recently made a similar argument against affirmative action— namely, that admission of students of color based on criteria that include more than grades and test scores is unfair because it deprived a white man of his rightful place in the medical school of the University of California at Davis. Bakke "deserved" entry only on the basis of selected criteria.

Prewar Roots of Jewish Whiteness

Part of the force of postwar hegemonic Jewishness came from its ability to refashion themes that had been parts of American Jewish culture long before the war. Jews advanced a variety of cultural claims to Americanness long before these were granted. For the most part, these claims were efforts to assimilate the values of mainstream America. The ways in which these efforts were woven into Jewish culture gave a kind of authenticity to their postwar configurations.

Postwar intellectuals drew upon the earlier assimilationist strand of prewar Jewishness. For example, Neil Gabler has written of the self-made, immigrant, Jewish movie moguls and how their Hollywood creations of the 1920s and 1930s gave several varieties of ideal America to the world. Locked out of the white corporate elite by anti-Semitism, movie producers invented a parallel Jewish universe of bourgeois American whiteness different from the East Coast Jewish ghettos many of them had fled but also different from the old-money whiteness to which they aspired.[30] If the Jewish studio magnates lived a whiteness of their own, they also presented a Hollywood version of Jewishness that was just as white and equally "American." Sharon Rivo argues that Hollywood films of the 1930s show Jewish immigrant culture through the rose-colored glasses of "nostalgia for the good old days of family unity and the warmth of traditional family and communal life. The images of the Jewish women frequently mirror those of the male characters: the more virtuous characters are hardworking, sacrificing toilers who shun easy economic and personal gain for family and communal good."[31]

In the 1930s, radio, the other mass medium, portrayed a similarly nostalgic view in the serial initially called *The Rise of the Goldbergs*, then simply *The Goldbergs* (and finally *Molly* when it became a 1950s TV show). This show transfixed a mass national audience and garnered Pepsodent toothpaste as its sponsor. Donald Weber argues that both Gertrude Berg and her show were

> a gigantic effort to bridge the space between these dual ethnic and American identities, to soften the jagged edges of alienation through the figure of Molly Goldberg and her special accommodating vision—a vision of a loving family, of interdenominational brotherhood, of middle-class ideals, of *American* life. . . . Berg's Molly is no . . . "red-hot mama" like the young Sophie Tucker, who, along with her cohort of early vaudeville entertainers, drew on her ethnic identity to construct a distinctive, often unbuttoned comedy of satire and sexual innuendo. . . . [Instead, she] offered a soul-inspiring

testament to the wonder-working powers of the American way, a daily chapter in the saga of hope and perseverance that struck a profound answering chord in the hearts of her millions of listeners in the 1930s and beyond.[32]

By 1949, Molly moved not only to TV but out of the Bronx and into the suburb, appropriately named Haverville, where her accent became much less Yiddish and where little in the show marked it as Jewish. Indeed, Weber argues that much of the show's popularity lay in its valorization of mainstream middle-class values.

This is also what Lester Friedman has argued with respect to Hollywood's postwar construction of Jewishness. In the 1947 production of *The Gentleman's Agreement*, a film that is critical of anti-Semitism, Jews are portrayed as no different from any other white Americans—"underneath surface differences, Jews, Catholics and Protestants (and by extension other minority-group members) all think alike."[33]

Although Jewish women were presented in a favorable light in movies and the radio, it was only a small segment of Jewish women who appeared. Rivo notes that there were no

> political or union activists; no Zionists, no Emma Goldmans, no Henrietta Szolds. There is also a lack of upper-middle-class society women: affluent reformers, settlement house or welfare patrons, professional women. There are no disapproving images of Jewish women: no vamps or villains.[34]

David Levering Lewis has analyzed a second strand of assimilationism among the turn-of-the-century German Jewish elite. For this group, the desire to assimilate brought with it a reluctance to fight the growing anti-Semitism directly for fear of jeopardizing their place in society. Lewis and Hasia Diner both argue that the resultant tension was in part resolved by supporting African American struggles, in which German Jews sought to fight anti-Semitism "by proxy" in Diner's words; by "remote control" in Lewis's.[35]

A third strand of assimilationism comes from eastern European immigrant communities. Many Jewish socialists held a commitment to Americanness. They sought to eliminate separate Yiddish-speaking branches of the Socialist Party, seeing the struggles of Jewish workers as no different from those of native-born American workers. Socialists and communists held Jewish womanhood to middle-class ideals. The very bourgeois notions about gender and womanhood that were expressed by Jewish socialist leaders in the garment unions and by Communist Party leadership in the 1930s have been discussed in the previous chapter. Such notions undergirded postwar male intellectuals' understandings of Jewish womanhood.

Jewish community leaders were heavily involved in the civil rights of African Americans between the world wars. Hasia Diner has suggested that their participation was, among other things, part of their effort to present Jews as more American than were native-born whites, precisely because Jewish concerns with social justice heightened their dedication to American ideals of social justice and democracy.

Then too, as Deborah Dash Moore and Paula Hyman tell us, many ordinary Jews in the 1920s and 1930s expressed their desire for assimilation and upward mobility by joining temples. These temples, which served as community centers, promoted a woman-centered version of Jewishness through a range of secular, middle-class family activities rather than serving as a site for neighborhood, male Talmudic bonding. Later claims by intellectuals that Jewish culture was prefiguratively white also resonated with this middle-class and domestic construction of Jewishness.[36]

Although assimilationist aspirations and these ways of being Jewish were shared by growing numbers of ordinary Jews in the decade before World War II, they did not have the hegemonic status they came to possess after the war. In part, this was no doubt because Jews before the war knew that they did not *have* the privileges of white, gentile Americans. This knowledge supported the earlier range of hegemonic constructions of Jews as workers and as not white. For the committed Jewish Left, this may have meant that Jews were in antiracist and class conflict with capitalist America. But, as Arthur Liebman has argued, for most ordinary Jews, socialism embodied a particularly Jewish relationship of critical distance from capitalist America.[37]

☐ Gender, Jewishness, and the Unbearable Ambivalence of Whiteness

How did such ordinary Jews respond to the arrival of the white welcome wagon after the war? It was one thing to enjoy arguments that celebrated Jewish culture as prefiguratively white and of Jewish men as model minorities who had earned the entitlements of white manhood as individuals through their Jewish cultural inheritance. But it was quite another to translate this into a way to love, live, and raise families. My parents had no doubt about their Jewishness, and my brother, Henry, and I had no doubt about our whiteness, but the two didn't combine as seamlessly as our public intellectuals said they should. My parents' social world was virtually all Jewish; Henry's and mine were mixed. Also, where Jewish male intellectuals ignored women in constructing an almost single-sexed model minority, it was a little harder to keep women out of popular Jewish cultural productions of the 1950s and 1960s, and virtually impossible to ignore ourselves in real life.

What follows are some preliminary thoughts. They come from reading Jewish reflections from and about the 1950s against each other in the context of my own background. In Jewish literature and popular culture, there seems to be an ambivalence about assimilation that was expressed in misogyny, in self-satire, and in social critique.

Jewishness itself also changed rapidly in the postwar decades. In 1957, when Glazer was developing his ideas, only 3.5 percent of all Jews married non-Jews. This was as low a level as when Jews were segregated by anti-Semitism. However, that figure masked changes that were already in motion. By the 1980s, Jews were marrying non-Jews as often as Jews, and by the 1990s, more Jews married non-Jews than married Jews. Outside of New

York, Jewishness seems to have lost much of its salience. By the 1970s, the danger that Jews as a people might disappear because of their very success in becoming part of the white mainstream became a real possibility.[38] It rapidly became clear that a white Jewish identity and lifestyle weren't as easy to live as the idea of Jewishness as prefigurative whiteness made it seem.

My parents worried that Henry and I would have no Jewish heritage. Once in a while my mother asked me, *pace* Glazer, if I wouldn't like to join the local synagogue's youth group—maybe so I could marry a nice Jewish boy, maybe so I could remember I was Jewish. But both my parents remained adamantly secular, uninterested in Jewish organizations. They had mixed feelings about white mainstream suburban values too. They loved having their own house and car, but they frowned on the excesses of consumer culture and the driving ambitions of material success. These were "goyishe," non-Jewish, in contrast to the more humane and moral Jewish way of life. Like many ordinary middle-class Jews, they had reservations about aspects of Jewish culture (including its materialism) as well as mainstream white society. And they remained ambivalent about their intellectual spokesmen's rosy view of both.

Thus, when ordinary adult Jews in the 1950s and 1960s looked inward, they faced the issue of whether Jewishness and whiteness were compatible with each other in daily life and in a form they could transmit to their children. I suspect that they also confronted each part of the package, Jewishness and whiteness, separately and often in contrast, as they asked what they found attractive in each. Anxieties about how to be white *and* Jewish, and ambivalence about whether either alone was a desirable way to live, surfaced explosively in stereotypes about Jewish womanhood. I suggest that these became ways Jewish men expressed their fears about Jewishness, whiteness, and masculinity.

Jewish Mothers and JAPs

Recent analyses suggest that stereotypes of Jewish mothers and Jewish American princesses (JAPs) are the two faces of an ambivalence about whiteness and Jewishness. Why would men who some twenty years earlier had idealized Jewish mothers for their strength in the community and their dedication to their families turn around and give the world some of its most misogynistic images of smothering and emasculating mothers (of sons; no daughters here either) and self-centered, withholding, materialistic, and asexual wives?

In an important series of articles, Riv-Ellen Prell has examined gender conflict in postwar American Jewish literature as portraying the struggle to remain Jewish while becoming part of the American mainstream.[39] She and Paula Hyman both suggest that such images reflect Jewish men's own struggles with their desires for the privileges that white masculinity held out to them—remember, GI benefits and postwar opportunities were for white *men*, not women—and their anxiety about the loss of their own Jewishness that their embrace of those privileges might carry.

Jewish men's ambivalence revolved around the promise and the reality of patriarchal domesticity, upon which so much of 1950s white masculinity depended. Jewish mothers in the 1950s and 1960s were the first victims, as their sons sought to free themselves from the Jewishness embodied by their mothers in order to possess the fruits of the mainstream. Jewish wives replaced them and became Jewish American princesses in the 1970s, as Jewish men confronted the hollowness of the materialism they had achieved and projected it onto their wives. Paula Hyman uses Philip Roth's novels to show how we went from praise songs about loving and effusive, lovable, and tough Jewish mothers to jokes and stereotypes about Portnoy's mother, the loud, domineering wife of a henpecked husband and the smotherer of her son's masculinity.

> Philip Roth's self-pitying Alexander Portnoy fantasizes himself as a child saying to his father, "Deck her, Jake. Surely that's what a *goy* would do, would he not? . . . Poppa, why do we have to have such guilty deference to women—you and me—when we don't! We mustn't! Who should run the show, Poppa, is *us*!"[40]

Women bought into this stereotype too. Some tried not to be Jewish mothers; others like Blau defended the stereotype by inverting it, arguing that smothering and nagging was good for their sons and good for Jews in the long run.

Jewish women became the lightning rod for the electricity of Jewish men's ambivalence, Hyman argues, in part because of the way that Judaism had been adapting to Jewish upward mobility long before World War II. In the middle-class Jewish New York neighborhoods where upwardly mobile Jews began to move, temples catered to whole families as a way of retaining some kind of Jewishness in the face of weakening bonds of working-class community interdependence. The ritual and cultural heart of this new Judaism came to rest in the home.

The task of not only making a Jewish home but of transmitting a Jewish sense of meaning and morality to the children was increasingly turned over to women. This was an enhancement of women's religious worth and of their importance in the family and to the community. It represented a shift from men to women in day-to-day responsibility for the continuity of Jewish identity.[41] Yet, as Hyman reminds us, it was also a reconstruction of Judaism that was consonant with white, middle-class notions of domesticity. Jewishness became still more woman-centered and domesticated during the two decades after the war, as men left the neighborhood, along with the temple, to move further afield in pursuit of worldly success.

The tension around assimilation, about losing a valuable heritage that gave meaning to life in exchange for a culture of limited or dubious value, was itself not new, but its particular gendering was a postwar product. As part of their responsibility for preserving Jewish culture, Jewish mothers were supposed to make sure their sons became nice Jewish boys along the lines that Norman Podhoretz described himself, bringing home nice Jewish wives. But Podhoretz was not the only Jewish man to aspire to masculinity. Some perhaps aspired to non-Jewish trophy wives as visible and seductive symbols of their masculinity and of their success in entering the white mainstream.

The misogyny reflects hostility to Jewish women. Its message about Jewish mothers projects on them their sons' anxieties about combining worldly success and loyalty to Jewishness even as the sons are experiencing their own ambivalence about both their Jewishness and their whiteness.[42]

Jewish American princesses (JAPs) are different creatures from Jewish mothers. Where the Jewish mother stereotype developed in the 1950s, that of JAPs peaked in the 1970s. As Riv-Ellen Prell so insightfully argues, JAPs are Jewish men's projections of their own nightmares about whiteness onto Jewish women. Such projections of course neatly avoid confronting the thought that men might have the same values themselves. Where Jewish mothers hovered and smothered and guilt-tripped their sons into forsaking the hard-earned pleasures of white middle-class masculine materialism, JAPs were the metastasizing cancer of that materialism. Perhaps they emerged a decade or two after the Jewish mother stereotype because they reflected anxieties that came from several decades of life in mainstream consumer culture. A JAP's only passion is to materialism and her own adornment.

> What does a JAP make for dinner?
> Reservations.
>
> How do you give a JAP an orgasm?
> Scream "Charge it to daddy."[43]

No red hot mamas here.

Prell finds the birth of the Jewish American princess in Herman Wouk's *Marjorie Morningstar* and Philip Roth's *Goodbye, Columbus*. In the latter, upwardly aspiring Neil Klugman becomes sexually involved with princess-to-be Brenda Patimkin, daughter of a wealthy Jewish businessman. Brenda is not yet a Jewish princess. She is athletic—she sweats and isn't ashamed of it—erotic, sexual, and playful. Contemplating his relationship, Neil says:

What is it I love lord? Why have I chosen? If we meet You at all, God, it's that we're carnal and acquisitive, and thereby partake of You. I am carnal and I know You approve, I just know it. But how carnal can I get? I am acquisitive. Where do I turn now in my acquisitiveness? Which prize is you? . . . Which prize do you think, shmuck? Gold dinnerware, sporting goods trees, nectarines, garbage disposals, bumpless noses, Patimkin sinks, Bonwit Teller. . . .

But, alas, Brenda and her sinks are not to be Neil's. When her mother discovers their relationship, she lets Brenda know that if she chooses Neil she loses her family's wealth. "Brenda will reject Neil, her right to sexuality, and her independence in order to stay in the orbit of material affluence and leisure."[44] In rejecting sexuality for "stuff," Prell argues, Brenda became the prototype for the Jewish princess. Neil can't have her, but he does assert his manhood by rebelling against the bargain she makes. Neil's moral of the story is that Jewish women are all that stands in the way of Jewish men having it all—whiteness and Jewishness too.

The projection of Brenda trading her soul for gold dinnerware also reveals a great deal of ambivalence about the white American dream, about the emptiness of consumerism and the loss of an authentic, sensual, active Jewish self. As with other projective stereotypes, these stereotypes of Jewish women are nightmare reminders to Jewish men of a Jewishness they would forsake and a whiteness they would embrace. The Jewish mother stereotype is a perversion of Jewish strength and love, and Jewish princesses embody the horrors of the too-white and joylessly passive consumer culture. Projecting this double bind onto women absolves Jewish men from coming to grips with their own ambivalence—not all that different from the psychodynamics of white working-class racism.

But Prell argues that we must also recognize that these works of literature are about the rebellions of Jewish sons against the second-generation Jewishness of their fathers. In them, however, the Jewishness appears as remarkably "white," in that fathers are hardworking producers and paterfamilias. The fathers in Herman Wouk's *Marjorie Morningstar* and Philip Roth's *Goodbye, Columbus* "were manufacturers, occupations involving unrelenting work with no apparent intrinsic value beyond the affluence it brought the family." The sons, Noel Airman (an apt translation of the Yiddish *luftmensch*, one who disdains such mundane toil) and Neil Klugman, struggle against these ideals.

> As these men tasted the sweet fruit of desire and sexuality, they began to lose their autonomy and independence! o the taskmaster of hard work. As they lost these women, they won their freedom from fathers and productivity. . . . [E]ach refused the middle class by refusing its daughter. They fled the triptych of Jewish life: hard work, personified by the father-producer; the creation of a family, personified by the beautiful, sexual daughter; and the maintenance of Judaism, personified by the mother.[45]

But the Jewishness that is rejected here is the assimilationist Jewishness of prefigurative whiteness. As we shall see below, this stance links Wouk and Roth to the wider 1950s white male rebellion against domesticity. Jewish women were the butt of Jewish men's ambivalence—Henny Youngman's "Take my wife. Please."—in many of the same ways that white wives and mothers became the butt of white male rebellion.

Jewish Women Respond

What about Jewish women? Did they go as lightly into that great good night of bourgeois domesticity as Jewish misogyny alleged? If my family is any guide, even those who tried had a hard time. How did Jewish women respond to the gender wars waged by these stereotypes? Many ways. Jewish women expressed their own anxieties about their Jewishness and their womanhood in the 1950s epidemic of nose jobs and in their obsession with bodily deficiencies. But Jewish female popular writers of the 1970s and 1980s "talked back," Riv-Ellen Prell argues, to Roth's and Wouk's women as "beautiful prizes to be bestowed by fathers on stand-in sons." The comic protagonists in Susan Lukas's *Fat Emily*, Louise Rose Blecher's *The Launching of Barbara Fabrikant,* or Myrna Blythe's *Cousin Suzanne* give voices to those prizes. They are "funny, outrageous, ironic women" struggling to find love and marriage to a Jewish man who will give them the identity they need to be a Jewish woman. But they see their bodies as "grotesque," as working against them—because they are too fat or because their nose is too big. The struggle to control a body out of control, or one that always threatens to become so, is a struggle to contain one's Jewishness so that it conforms to whiteness. Mostly it doesn't work. These heroines are "imperfect, uncontrollable, and unlovable by her own cultural double, the Jewish male."

The beauty and self-assurance of Roth's and Wouk's Jewish princesses become in these novels portraits of "women who express seething frustration at their inability to become what is expected and their disappointment in love that is never realized." At the same time they refuse to be the wifely prizes of the 1950s script.

> As classic "losers" these women are funny; their voices control the novels, providing commentaries on contemporary Jewish life, the family, and the impossible dilemmas that beset women. Drawing on familiar styles of Jewish performance—self-effacing, comic, hyperbolic, and iconoclastic—they transform the language of hopelessness into power. These writers not only talk back to Philip Roth and others, they appropriate their writing.

> In the 1970s, assimilation, and the family fell apart, these women writers appropriated and reformulated the loser/outsider as a woman bursting out of cultural restraints. Jewish women writers declared themselves capable of narrating lives at the same time that their narratives asserted that the future will not be as they imagined it as children.[46]

We get a more subversive woman's retrospective on 1950s Jewish manhood in Nora Ephron's 1980s classic portrait of a Jewish American prince, *Heartburn*.

You know what a Jewish prince is, don't you? If you don't, there's an easy way to recognize one. A simple sentence, "Where's the butter?" Okay. We all know where the butter is, don't we? The butter is in the refrigerator. . . . But the Jewish prince doesn't mean "Where's the butter?". He means "Get me the butter." He's too clever to say "Get me" so he says "Where's". And if you say to him (shouting) "in the refrigerator" and he goes to look, an interesting thing happens, a medical phenomenon that has not been sufficiently remarked upon. The effect of the refrigerator light on the male cornea. Blindness. "I don't see it anywhere." . . . I've always believed that the concept of the Jewish princess was invented by a Jewish prince who couldn't get his wife to fetch him the butter.[47]

But in the 1950s and 1960s, when Jewish women first began to rebel against this misogyny, they did so more as white middle-class women than as Jewish women. Betty Friedan's *The Feminine Mystique* and Wini Breines's *Young, White and Miserable*, an analysis of the birth of a slightly younger cohort of middle-class feminists, are two cases in point. Friedan and Breines told their stories as whites and were silent about their Jewishness. But as Melanie Kaye/Kantrowitz has argued, Jewish women were a significant part of the early, white, feminist movement and of the New Left. In this, some (myself included) followed one strand of an older pattern of Jews on the left, where, despite the fact that a disproportionate part of the white communists in the 1930s and New Left members of the 1960s were Jews, they identified politically as white, while downplaying their Jewishness.[48]

Friedan was also silent about her radicalism and her Jewishness. She describes herself as a white, middle-class, college graduate, married—a mother trapped in suburbia. Not radical; not Jewish. Daniel Horowitz has recently argued that "if Rosa Parks refused to take a seat at the back of a segregated bus not simply because her feet hurt, then Friedan did not write *The Feminine Mystique* simply because she was an unhappy housewife." Horowitz restores Friedan's radical political history as a labor journalist and progressive activist in New York City. She learned her feminism in the progressive wing of the union movement.[49]

But he only hints at restoring her Jewishness, which was part of her early identity. Born in Peoria in 1921, Friedan felt out of place "as a Jew, a reader, and a brainy girl" until she went off to Smith College in 1938.[50] Much later, she struggled to arrive in the promised land of the white suburban world, only to be confronted with its emptiness for Jewish women. In this context, can we reread Friedan's plaintive "Is this all there is?" as particularly Jewish, even though her Jewishness and Jewish radicalism are not part of her own story?

In the late 1950s and early 1960s, Friedan could not escape the Jewish mother stereotype any more than Zena Smith Blau could. Where Blau accepted it as an accurate description of Jewish womanhood and gave it a positive spin, Friedan took the smothering and hovering as an accurate description of white middle-class motherhood and gave it a negative spin. Where Blau saw Jewish mothers as creating nice Jewish boys, Friedan saw middle-class housewives creating homosexual sons. She claimed that male homosexuality was a pernicious rebellion—a cautionary tale—against overprotective mothers and domineering wives. Friedan's argument for feminism rested squarely on homophobia: that the privileges that white domesticity gave to Jewish men created monstrous Jewish mothers who cost men their heterosexual masculinity.[51] So, even as Friedan criticized domesticity, her homophobia still prescribed nuclear, heterosexual coupling as the only way to live, and in the process underlined whiteness, masculinity, and Jewishness as explicitly heterosexual.

Jewish Whiteness as American Whiteness

Jewish whiteness became American whiteness in three ways: when Jewish images like Jewish mothers and JAPs were adopted by mainstream white America to form misogynist versions of white womanhood; when Jews spoke as white and spoke for whites, whether as Ken and Barbie or as artists and intellectuals; and when Jewish public intellectuals constructed Jewishness as white by contrasting themselves with a mythic blackness.

Although Jews hardly invented the homophobia and mother bashing so prevalent in white America in the 1950s—one needs only to reread Dr. Spock—the Jewish mother stereotypes were particularly ethnic offerings of newly white Jewish men to this wider, patriarchal, white culture. Jewish mother jokes came to be enjoyed by all—especially ethnic whites—as their way of participating in the more general white climate of mother bashing. You didn't have to be Jewish to love Jewish offerings to white America. And you didn't have to be Jewish to be called a Jewish mother. Jewish mother and JAP stereotypes resonated with all of American whiteness. A larger non-Jewish audience embraced themes presented as specifically Jewish. Gilda Radner's version of a Jewish princess, Rhonda LaVondadonda, was a national favorite on *Saturday Night Live* in the 1970s. And Jewish women were very numerous among those who responded warmly to a feminism presented as generically white.

Daniel Horowitz suggests that we read Friedan's *The Feminine Mystique*—and her silence on her radical past—as a white middle-class woman's counterpoint to white male social critics who saw suburban and corporate life as emasculating. Both spoke for a broad swath of non-Jewish, middle-class, white America that was also anxious and alienated from the psychic emptiness of economic prosperity. In this reading, *The Feminine Mystique* stands as a white woman's counterpoint to *The Hidden Persuaders*, *The Lonely Crowd*, and *The Man in the Grey Flannel Suit*.

Barbara Ehrenreich's *Hearts of Men* reminds us that domesticity in the 1950s was a man's ideal as well as a woman's. Her work locates the roots of 1960s white radicalism in men's prepolitical rebellions against the suburban domesticity of the 1950s. Some of these men held on to their middle-class privileges when fleeing suburbia, as Ehrenreich argues, by flocking to a newly constructed pleasure-seeking white bachelorhood of the sort that was being popularized by *Playboy* magazine.

Where Alexander Portnoy was ambivalent about the masculinity of middle-class suburbia, the poets and critics of the Beat
generation, like *Playboy*, actively rejected it, Wini Breines argues. Their ideals were black men and working-class white gangs,
whom they saw as truly liberated from bourgeois life, as real men
rather than the emasculated lawn-mowing, henpecked, corporate-
clone husbands they were expected to become. Breines's *Young,
White and Miserable* expands on white middle-class teens' attraction to and appropriation of African American rhythm and
blues music in the 1950s and 1960s, first by the Beats, then by
masses of teens. Listening to the music and imitating real and
imagined African American culture became ways of rebelling
against the emptiness and constraints of suburban domesticity.
Breines argues that these fantasy images of glorified blackness
and working-class white masculinity became personas of white
middle-class 1960s activists and gave those movements a particularly masculine, band-of-brothers character.[52]

Breines also argues that girls created their own alternatives
through the men they chose to be with rather than through the
women whom they chose to be like. Girls manifested their dis-
satisfaction by romanticizing black and working-class white bad
boys, by helping to create ideals of masculinity like Marlon
Brando and James Dean, but "definitely not the man in the grey
flannel suit" or, I might add, the nice Jewish boy.[53]

However, there was another current of women's dissatisfac-
tion that was manifested in a shift in whom girls wanted to be
like. Jewish women were prominent among those who sought
another kind of womanhood in radical political communities.
Our first glimmerings of that womanhood were in the civil rights
movement in the 1950s. Televised battles over school and bus
integration made it clear that African Americans were not just
the latest group of "immigrants," the newest ethnicity on the
urban block and the last in line for the fruits of upward mobility. It was obvious that white America was enormously more re-
sistant to including black Americans than it was to including

people like me and my family. As Sarah Evans and Melanie Kaye/ Kantrowitz have shown, many white feminists' first glimmerings of an alternative womanhood came from their participation alongside black women in the civil rights movement. We had our own version of romanticized blackness in constructions of strong, independent black womanhood. In rebellion as in racism, white womanhood and manhood depended once again upon inventions of African American womanhood and manhood, this time as romanticized positive models. White feminism was part of a wider, white, New Left romantic appropriation of blackness that critiqued the white middle-class mainstream.[54] And white Jewishness was part of that feminism.

Because much of Jewish white middle-class America shared the same anxieties and ambivalences as their non-Jewish white counterparts, they could tell many stories about themselves equally well as stories about generalized whiteness or as stories about Jewishness. Like Ken and Barbie, those nonbiodegradable plastic icons of Anglo-Saxon whiteness invented by Jewish entrepreneurs, the Jewish origins of the ideas aren't obvious, but those who produced them were nevertheless inventing ways of being simultaneously Jewish (though not too Jewish) and white. Just as Jewish novelists spoke for a white America that was not ethnic, so too did Jewish artists, social critics, feminists, and leftists. To ask, But is this a Jewish point of view? is to miss the point that Jews were helping to define whiteness as they became part of it.

Conclusion: White Jewishness as Experience

I have reinterpreted my father's question: Is a Jewish identity a white identity now that Jews' ethnoracial assignment is white? I have tried to show that postwar public intellectuals sometimes came dangerously close to a "yes" answer when they stressed the cultural similarities between Jewish culture and white bourgeois ideals. I've also suggested that ordinary Jews said "yes and no" in a variety of ways, or, like my parents, found the question strange. Although everyday Jews embraced many of these formulations, they were more ambivalent than their intellectual spokesmen about Jewishness and whiteness in general, and men were ambivalent about their masculinities in particular. Where intellectuals ignored Jewish women, Jewish popular culture stereotyped them as Jewish mothers and JAPs. Jewish women seem to have spoken their own ambivalence about Jewish womanhood directly through images of their bodies, and sometimes about Jewish whiteness in general. Ambivalence about whiteness also surfaced in the mix of demonizing and romanticizing stereotypes of African Americans.

All these responses to ethnoracial reassignment were in play at the same time. Model minority entitlement called forth responses: Portnoy's ambivalence, nose jobs, Betty Friedan's "Is this all there is?" expression of the emptiness of whiteness, the Beats' rejection of middle-class whiteness as suffocating meaninglessness. If white entitlement depended upon distinguishing whites' predominantly masculine subjects from blackness and femaleness, romantic appropriations of blackness filled the void that was part of these same subjects' experience of whiteness.

What all these varieties of ambivalence had in common, however, was a sense of Jewishness as an earthly system of morals and meaning somehow embodied in good works and social justice. This underlay the ambivalence on the part of ordinary Jews like my parents to mainstream affluence, as well as the heavy concentration of Jews in the progressive movements of the 1960s and 1970s. However, this same sense of social justice also animated the self-righteousness of the opposition to affirmative action by many Jewish intellectuals and mainline Jewish organizations.

The clash over the meaning of social justice was inevitable. It exploded in the latter 1960s, in the wake of the 1967 Arab-Israeli Six-Day War, which opened up a new era of struggles over the meanings of Jewishness. A proper discussion of the Jewish New Left is beyond my scope here, but it is important to note that it came into being at least in part as a response to the conservatism of 1950s hegemonic Jewishness.

Part of where one stood in the Jewish culture wars depended upon the way in which one understood the relationship between ethnoracial assignment and ethnoracial identity. For the most part, Jews on the left acknowledged in some way that they had been socially assigned to whiteness and accorded its privileges. Their view of social justice demanded making those privileges universal entitlements. More conservative Jews conflated assignment and identity, insisting, as Glazer did, that Jewish privileges were earned and that social justice demanded others do likewise.

Jews on the left since the 1960s have been no more homogeneous than leftist Jews have ever been. Some, like me, rejected Jewishness in reaction to the conservatism of organized Jewry and retained a Jewishness of memory. Some left their Jewishness at home and acted politically as generic white folks. In this respect, both followed, ironically, an early-twentieth-century assimilationist path—of Jews joining the English-speaking Socialist Party and Communist Party instead of the Yiddish-speaking branches or their equivalents. Morris Schappes and Paul Buhle have both argued that this strategy led to impoverished forms of resistance and a loss of social and cultural alternatives, which were better preserved in the richer and more vital Yiddish-speaking Left.[55]

Other Jews confronted politically conservative but hegemonic forms of Jewishness as part of their struggle for social justice. Since 1967, many Jews who felt caught between anti-Zionism on the left and anger at the conservatism and sexism of establishment Jewry, formed a variety of underground Jewish student newspapers and groups. Some, like Peace Now, New Jewish Agenda, and Jews for Racial and Economic Justice, had longer lives; others lasted only a short time. All of them sought to challenge the hegemony of politically conservative Jewish organizations, insisting on the legitimacy of radical *Jewish* voices. Jewish women's struggles against male bias and misogyny in

Jewish religious practices, and struggles by gay and lesbian Jews, were key parts of a strong and lasting current working to make Jewishness and Judaism more reflective of democratic world-views.[56] These currents continue to have real and enduring impacts on many Jewish institutional practices.

Conclusion ☐

I n the last hundred years, Jews in the United States have been shuttled from one side of the American racial binary to the other. Their sense of Jewishness responded to and reflected their various social places. This book has sought to explore how being assigned a particular place in the American racial structure has affected Jewish collective attempts to create a Jewish ethnoracial identity.

We have seen that the Jews' unwhitening and whitening were not of their own making. Rather, the movements were effected by changes in national economic, institutional, and political practices, as well as by changes in scientific and public discourses about race in general and Jews in particular. In this larger historical matrix, race, class, and gender have been mutually constituting aspects of social being, an organizing principle that has produced and reproduced a bifurcate populace, a "metaorganization of American capitalism" and the American way of constructing nationhood.

☐ Race and the Metaorganization of American Capitalism

This idea of nation has been built around the myth that its populace consists of two mutually exclusive kinds of people who are defined by mutually exclusive ways of being women and men.

The first are white ladies and gentlemen, mothers of the nation and thinking citizens. The second are nonwhite and savage "hands," male and female workers "of an industrial grade suited only to the lowest kind of manual labor," in the words of General Francis Walker, Chief of the U.S. Bureau of Statistics, director of the U.S. Census, and professor of political economy and history at Yale in the 1890s.[1]

As the popular 1920s Kansas journalist William Allen White (quoted in chapter 3) attested, the racial nature of womanhood is precisely what distinguishes those who are fit for democracy from those who are not: "And as the Aryans of Greece tried democracy with their bondwomen and failed, and the Aryans of Rome tried a Republic with slaves and failed, so they who came to America from Latin countries failed in this new world because their new world homes were half-caste and not free, and the liberty they sought was license and not sacrifice."[2]

The alleged virtues of white womanhood and those of white manhood have justified not only the natural rightness of patriarchal and heterosexual domesticity, but also the superior class positions that are entitlements of whiteness. The alleged character deficiencies and lack of sharp gender distinctions among peoples designated as nonwhite have been portrayed as confirmation of the myth that nonwhites are not fit to be actors on the national stage or to parent the nation's children, that their only place is to produce—but not to consume—its wealth. Looked at from this angle, capitalist democracy does have parallels with ancient Athenian democracy, but they are not pretty: both are democracies for the few, built upon the labor of those excluded from the circle of national democracy.

This is an extraordinarily powerful myth. It is part of what anthropologists used to call "national character," that somewhat inchoate constellation of beliefs and values that marked Americans as American or Japanese as Japanese.[3] There has been a return of interest in how nations construct their identities and their histories, and renewed struggles over which histories will be told and by whom. Although scholars emphasize that national identities are continually contested, they also recognize that there are beliefs and values that have a kind of hegemony or cultural dominance in nations and in-groups within them. Hegemonic beliefs, as Antonio Gramsci called them, are usually those of the powerful, but they are also part of everyone's cultural repertoire. Their power comes from the fact that everyone learns them and learns to think with them. The United States is far from unique in this regard. There is a growing multidisciplinary body of scholarship on the racial and gendered construction of national belonging in Europe, and in nations that were its former colonies, that show marked parallels. One might almost think of the American metaorganization as a variant on a larger, "Atlantic-centered" set of racial ways of constructing national belonging (especially in settler colonies based on expropriation) and of organizing societies along capitalist lines of unequal economic and political entitlements.[4]

As a constitutive myth, this bipolar view of the American populace works in complex ways. It is a widely shared set of cultural categories that organizes the ordinary distinctions we make every day; it organizes the way we explain our actions to ourselves and others, and it becomes the way to frame public explanations, decisions, and arguments. It enables our analysis and it limits it. It explains the way things are and the way they must be. It is also practiced institutionally, in the way school districts and election districts are drawn, in the ways employers recruit their labor force, and in the ways that immigration, labor, and welfare laws are constructed. And the discourse that shapes these institutions is in turn strengthened as the institutions and policies create a social landscape that makes the categories seem natural, and makes racism and sexism seem like common sense.

I argued that this metaorganization, the logic underlying the construction of nationhood, has its historical roots in an economy and culture built upon slavery and expropriation. A kind of unholy trinity of corporations, the state, and monopolistic media produces and reproduces patterns and practices of whiteness with dreadful predictability. Its continued persuasiveness rests upon the pervasive social, spatial, occupational, and residential segregation that makes our bifurcated social structure seem like a natural phenomenon. This is why racist stories and categories are an easy sell and why countering them is so difficult. Thus, when people set out to embrace or to resist this organization, the political identities by which they construct themselves as social actors are cast in terms of the bifurcated cultural grooves of ethnicity, race, class, and gender.

When immigrants learn that the way to be American is to claim white patriarchal constructions of womanhood and manhood and a middle-class or bourgeois outlook for themselves, they are adapting patterns and practices that were here long before they were. These are the patterns and practices by which the United States has continually redefined itself as a nation of whites (however variably white has been defined).

American racial stereotypes of native good and alien evil tell an old story that grows in power every time it is told and with every variation in the telling. The images and the story go back to colonial times, when settlers reinvented themselves as American natives by murdering and expropriating Native Americans. It is a tale of Manichaean contrasts between the virtuous and the unworthy, good and evil, real Americans and intruding aliens. Its moral is how the American nation was built. One version, the hard-core racist one, has told how an American "we" kept unassimilable barbarians out. The other, liberal, melting pot or salad bowl version has been about how assimilable "we"/"they" were and how race is a transitory state. But fluidity and assimilation have meant assimilation into the practices and meanings of whiteness, of the dominant culture and values, of creating oneself as worthy by contrast with blackness.

☐ I have sketched this portrait of the racial metaorganization of American capitalism by synthesizing the insights of several decades of critical scholarship across the disciplines. Its utility is to help us to understand why that metaorganization seems to continually reconstitute itself so "naturally." But it also helps to challenge and change it by showing the central role that segregation plays in the construction of what has been called racist common sense.[5]

By segregation I mean occupational and residential segregation by race and sex. In chapters 2 and 3, I examined some of the practices by which corporations and the state have reproduced occupational segregation. We also saw how challenges to segregation, especially in the case of the Bell System, were transformed into new patterns of racial and gender job resegregation. It would seem then that "separate and unequal" continues to govern the practices of major American institutions. This analysis challenges some forms of conventional wisdom about strategies to bring about change. For example, the conventional wisdom of the American labor movement has been to organize around the issues that affect the broadest swath of its constituency (such as wages or job security).[6] Such programs have historically privileged the needs of white workers, usually men but sometimes women, at the expense of all others. They also allow employers to establish new patterns of resegregation and job degradation. If the labor movement put more effort into challenging job segregation and race- and gender-based job degradation directly, it might be more effective in the long run. Such a strategy would prevent corporations from eroding workers' gains by reghettoizing work and degrading the jobs they have defined as nonwhite. Opposition to occupational segregation would also help to undercut and denaturalize racist and sexist "common sense."

☐ *Ethnoracial Identity, Whiteness, and Its Alternatives*
Of course, things have never really been the way the myth of American nationhood implies they are. The myth is not even an accurate mirror of the social structure, much less a mirror of real people. Most obviously, people bear very little resemblance to the stereotypes attached to them. In addition, there are all sorts of people "out of place," some struggling to get out

of the awful places to which they have been assigned, others struggling equally hard but unsuccessfully to stay in more socially desirable statuses. Some groups, as we have seen in the case of American Jews, develop their own cultures that provide ethnoracial ideals of womanhood and manhood that differ from mainstream white ideals as well as from mainstream negative stereotypes (I will return to this below). And, of course, some even try to change the social order.

For Zygmunt Bauman, lack of fit, in this case, of real people into the American scheme of ethnoracial, class, and gender classification is about power rather than about the adequacy of the classification scheme. He has argued that classification as an instrument of control, as the imposition of a conceptual and a political order, is central to the condition of modern social life, but that such imposed order never works completely.[7] This suggests the possibility of thinking about some ways of being "out of place"—women soldiers and African American lawyers, for example—as forms of resisting or stretching imposed and expected social places. In the same vein, constructions of ethnoracial cultures by people assigned to the nonwhite side of the American racial binary might be thought of as another form of resistance to those same classifications. However, just as all forms of agency are not resistance, neither are all forms of ethnoracial culture. Indeed, in chapter 5, I argued that one very influential form of Jewish whiteness has been more about belonging and support for the American system of control than resistance to it.

But part of Bauman's point is also to suggest that the modernist enterprise of classification is itself flawed, that even those who would eagerly embrace their social places and identities cannot fully do so. Such classification, he suggests, works better for containment, for boundary marking, than as a social space within which to live. The inherent unsatisfactoriness of this modern system of classification is at the root of what he sees as the ambivalence of modernity.

This ambivalence derives from the particular binary way of seeing the world that developed in the European Enlightenment.

I touched upon it in discussing nineteenth-century evolutionary theories like Herbert Spencer's, which contrasted primitive savages and civilized Europeans. These theories sorted the then current world's populace into one or the other category. They were ideologically key to justifying colonialism and other forms of exploitation. But Rousseau's and Engels's critiques of this social order were equally modernist in their construction. For them, noble savages were the heroes, and their destruction confirmed the decadence of civilization.

Not only are both versions, Spencer's and Rousseau's, modernist, they are both necessary parts, the two hands clapping, of the modernist edifice of classification as control. What this means is that each symbol, in this case savage and civilized, has a positive and a negative aspect built into it. Other important contrastive pairs are similarly constructed. Thus, the country and the city, as Raymond Williams told us, have each been described in this dual manner. The countryside has alternatively been a site of meaning and connectedness and also a site of backwardness and stifling conformity. Similarly, the city has been a place of freedom and excitement and a source of sin and alienation. As so many have pointed out, the concepts of country, city, savagery, and civilization are each a metaphor for the West's culturally structured ambivalence about its own society and culture, about the embrace of individualist success and freedom from communal constraints, on the one hand, and the simultaneous yearning for a missing connectedness to a moral community, on the other. Contrastive pairs define each other and in the process constitute a discourse for expressing that ambivalence.[8]

This love/hate relationship with the modern condition is part of the experiential fabric of capitalism. "All that is solid melts into air"—Marshall Berman borrowed the phrase from Karl Marx to describe the experience of capitalist modernity, the excitement of the promise, the new, of constant change, but also the emptiness of continual loss, of discovering that reality does not match the promise. This sense of loss often manifests itself as nostalgia, as a longing for a golden age of an allegedly stable moral community—whether Engels's Iroquois society, William Allen White's tribal Teutons, or Walt Disney's Main Street America. It is an always present underside of the excitement, freedom, and independence associated with modern life.[9]

Whiteness as Ambivalence

Jews experienced the ambivalence of modernism acutely in the immediate post-World War II period. My parents, like many other ordinary Jews, sought the comforts of a middle-class life and the freedom and independence it promised. They also understood their newfound success as the result of their own efforts. My teenage quest was for the normalness, the perfect pageboy hairdo and camel-hair coat that seemed to be the birthright of the "blond people." Yet we lived with a certain skeptical stance about that which we embraced. We were not entirely sure that we wanted to be "blond" people. We shared in the feeling, widespread in the 1950s, that mainstream culture was somehow materialistic and shallow, lacking in real meaning, leaving one with Friedan's lament: "Is this all there is?" For Jews, the fruits of success seemed to come at the cost of a meaningful Jewish community, cultural identity, and the loss of an authentic Jewish soul.

Although Jewish ambivalence resonated with that of already white Americans over what they understood to be the modern condition, Jews experienced that ambivalence as specifically ethnoracial in two ways. They expressed its different sides as a conflict between Jewishness and whiteness, and between white Jewishness and blackness. In so doing, I suggest, they revealed ambivalence to be part of the experiential structure of whiteness itself. Ambivalence was expressed in the counterpoint between Jewish intellectuals' embrace of whiteness and the more ambivalent responses to whiteness in Jewish popular culture.

The eagerness to be white is not hard to understand, since whiteness is a state of privilege and belonging. The Jewishness created by postwar Jewish intellectuals laid Jewish claim to these privileges and to belonging to the mainstream. It did so in part by reinventing *Yiddishkeit*, the culture of Jewish immigrants, as very Anglo-Saxon-like, as the positive cultural stuff that was the secret of Jewish success at melting so easily into the national pot. Their version of Jewishness as prefigurative whiteness put an attractive spin on whiteness. As with the positive spin on civilization as progress, this one depended upon an invented, opposite blackness. For Jewish whiteness to be unambivalently embraceable, as Toni Morrison argues about whiteness in general, it needed a blackness that was its repellent opposite. Glazer's construction of African American culture as inherently deficient helped meet this need.

A negative spin on whiteness is also part of the dialectic of racialized ambivalence, like civilization in the descriptions of Rousseau and Engels. This spin too depends for its existence upon contrast with an invented blackness. If the positive take on whiteness justifies and naturalizes a system of racial privilege, the negative one critiques it by romantic inversion. Thus the Beats and 1960s leftists framed their critique of systemic racial and class privilege as a romantic portrait of noble and defiant black masculinity, while their feminist counterparts constructed invulnerable, autonomous black women as part of their critique of feminine dependency and institutional sexism.

In the previous chapter I suggested that ordinary Jews found this way of understanding one's place in the world—by defining oneself in contrast to an invented Other—difficult to live. Like the Midas touch and Patimkin sinks, embracing the privileges of whiteness seemed to cost them the loss of a meaningful Jewish cultural identity.[10] Efforts to have it all, to avoid those costs and contradictions, were not pretty. First of all, in the popular and scholarly imagination of the 1950s and 1960s, the Jewish quest for whiteness and its privileges was a quest by a Jewish male subject. In the attempt to construct a suitably masculine white and Jewish subject, Jewish women became the prime scapegoats for men's *and* women's ambivalence about whiteness. Jewish mother and Jewish American princess stereotypes, as well as homophobia, served as public (and publicly embraced) projections of that ambivalence and anxiety about whiteness itself. These projections also revealed whiteness as exclusively patriarchal and heterosexual.

Second, it is also worth pointing out that none of these moves was particularly successful. The same limited repertoire of strategies for escaping the double bind of whiteness have been reinvented over and over: affirmation by invidious contrast; experience of one's "choice" as empty of meaning; symbolic or rhetorical rejection (but seldom economic or political rejection) of that choice by romantic contrast. Jewish versions are but a small part of the larger American history of reinventing whiteness in familiar grooves by those who are eager for its privileges and who obsessively but unsuccessfully seek to escape its contradictions. In one sense, the experience of whiteness is an experience of ambivalence, of having to choose among unsatisfactory or partially satisfactory choices. On an individual level, ambivalence lies in believing that life demands choosing among alternatives that are necessarily less than fully satisfactory.

Ambivalence is also collective. That is, part of whiteness is participation in a shared social understanding that this limited repertoire of unfulfilling alternatives is indeed the full universe of human social possibilities. The moral universe of whiteness is the moral of the modernist story that it is the human condition to want more than it can have—for example, that it is the human condition to wish for individuality and communitas despite the "fact" that it is not possible to have a world where they coexist in mutually supporting ways.

The whiteness of modernist culture lies in the socially structured grooves for justifying one "choice" as worthy by constructing the other as unworthy because it is attached to genetically or culturally unworthy people. Invidious comparisons are the way to define oneself, one's ethnoracial group, gender, or sexual orientation, and to reconcile one to a status quo acknowledged to be unsatisfactory. We call this last move a realistic view of the world.

Resisting Whiteness

It is worth thinking about the realism of resignation in relation to the messianism of turn-of-the-century Yiddishkeit. Can the latter provide an alternative to the former and, if so, in what ways? There are many calls today to abolish whiteness as a system of privilege.[11] Such calls are moves in the right direction, even if they sometimes play down the ways racial privilege is institutionalized through economic, political, occupational, and residential apartheid. If white ambivalence comes from believing that there is something inevitable about the injustices of the social order, this ambivalence also rationalizes white privilege: if inequality is natural, then giving up one's power and privilege only means that someone else will take them. To "abolish," or at least to put a dent in, this aspect of whiteness takes the presence of alternative systems of organization and meaning.

The Yiddishkeit that was hegemonic within turn-of-the-century urban American Jewish neighborhoods contained worldviews and values that differed from modernist ones. When Jews in the 1950s experienced the ambivalence of whiteness as a specifically ethnoracial ambivalence—how to be Jewish and white; or how Jewish to be—they were experiencing whiteness not in relation to a fictionalized blackness but in relation to that real culture of Yiddishkeit. Reexamining those values reveals that the existential ambivalence deriving from modernism's repertoire of "choices" is anything but necessary or natural.

It is true that Jewishness was employed as a contrastive form, to mark reservation, ambivalence, and a limit on the embrace of whiteness. It is also true that Yiddishkeit was imbued with the modernism of the dominant culture.

But that is not all there was. There were also things within Jewishness that made it meaningful and hard to give up in the quest for whiteness and belonging.

I do not think that Yiddishkeit is unique in this respect. Rather—as Paul Gilroy has argued for the polyphonic cultures of the Black Atlantic, as Robin Kelley has claimed for African American cultures, and as Paul Buhle and Jonathan Boyarin have supported in different ways Jewish perspectives—the ethnoracial cultures of many subordinated peoples also embed funds of experience and alternatives to modernity.[12]

The Yiddishkeit of the not-quite-white, urban, working-class Jewish community provided one such alternative. Perhaps Jews of my generation who have grown up white hold on to fragments and memories of that Jewishness as our ethnoracial identity precisely because it represents an alternative to the contradictions of whiteness. Yiddishkeit did not rest upon invidious comparison for its existential meaning, and it held out a different and more optimistic vision than that of modernity (even as it also participated in modernity). Instead of having to choose between individual fulfillment and communal belonging, it expected Jews to find individual fulfillment *through* responsibility to the Jewish community. That was the path for becoming an adult woman and man. This understanding was shared across the community's religious and political spectrum, from the nonobservant, socialist Left to the Orthodox and Zionist Right and by all combinations in between. To do good works (however understood) for a community larger than one's family and self is still at the center of Jewishness as a this-worldly system of meaning.

Although Yiddishkeit did not regard women as the equals of men, neither did it construct them as ladies. They were not delicate of constitution or psyche. They were sexual (even if the histories do not tell us much about their sexual agency). And they were social actors valued as individuals, as were men, through their contributions to the political, economic, and social life of the community.

Part of the psychic damage done by whiteness is that it is a worldview that has difficulty envisioning an organization of social life that does not rest upon systematic and institutionalized racial subordination. In this effort, the heritage of Yiddishkeit has much to recommend it. Not least is its messianic faith in the inevitability of a just world to be brought about by human agency, and the view that honor and success come from serving the community. Other working-class ethnic cultural heritages can be interrogated in the same way—not as prospective models for the future, where we scrutinize and evaluate one or another aspect of the culture according to how well it fits a particular preconceived notion of the good life.

We should look at our histories not as models to emulate but for insights, new ideas and conversations—for resources and tools for thinking with—for beginning to envision alternatives to whiteness, capitalism, modernism, and the stultifying organizations of social life they support.

For American Jews, this requires confronting our present white racial assignment. The Yiddishkeits of memory were forged under conditions in which Jews were considered less than fully white. Those ghettoized conditions forced Jews to depend on one another. Part of what gave meaning to that interdependence was a value system shared by Talmudic scholars and socialists that human worth was measured by service to the community rather than by wealth or recognition in the wider world. This was part of what made you a Jew. Reciprocally, the forced interdependence compelled Jews to behave that way—or at least to justify their behavior in terms of that value system.

The privileges of whiteness, especially occupational and residential mobility, which were extended to American Jews after World War II, dissolved that forced interdependence. If external racism contained the class, religious, and political differences that have always marked Jewish communities, what will preserve those aspects of the culture today? Many Jews of my generation who grew up white did not experience the forced reciprocity and community obligations that constituted a coercive side of Jewish identity. One of the things I know as an anthropologist is that our parents and grandparents did not enact these cultural precepts because they were inherently better people than we are. They had to do it in ways that we do not—because we are white and therefore do not have to do it. The challenge for American Jews today is to confront that whiteness as part of developing an American Jewishness that helps build an explicitly multiracial democracy in the United States.

NOTES ☐

Introduction

1. Throughout the book, I use "race" and "ethnicity" more or less interchangeably and combine them in the adjective "ethnoracial." Both terms have had a variety of definitions attached to them in the scholarly and popular literatures in play at any given time. "Ethnicity" is a relatively new word, coming into use mainly after World War II. It replaced "people" and "nation" and served as an alternative to "race," which was associated with biology, eugenics, and other theories of scientific racism. In this discourse, "ethnicity" emphasized cultural attributes in contrast to biological ones. More recently, "ethnicity" has been used to describe the cultural heritages of Europeans, while "race" has been used for everyone else's heritage. Because the meanings of each term have varied, and because both have been used to describe socially salient identities and identifications, I also put them together as "ethnoracial" or "racial-ethnic."

2. For the classic portrait on African American double vision, see Du Bois 1903. Jewish double vision is not the same.

3. Dinnerstein 1987; Dinnerstein 1994, 105–127.

4. On the Clarion, Utah, colony, see R. Goldberg 1986. I thank Bert Silverman for telling me about the history of *kucheleins*.

5. Markowitz 1993 gives a full picture of the culture, backgrounds, and politics of New York City's Jewish teachers.

6. Rich 1976.

7. Dill 1979; Fikes 1999; E. N. Glenn 1987; Palmer 1989; Rollins 1985; Romero 1992.

8. On Gloria Richardson, see Cook 1988; on Ella Baker, see Cantarow and O'Malley 1980. On black and white motherhood in the 1960s, see Polatnick 1996; E. B. Brown 1989. On African American women in the civil rights movement as inspirations for white feminists, see Evans 1980 and Kaye/Kantrowitz 1996.

9. Morrison 1993; see also 1988 and 1990.

10. Anzia Yezierska's character Hannah Breineh, in her short story "The Fat of the Land" (Kessler-Harris 1979), comes close.

CHAPTER 1   *How Did Jews Become White Folks?*

1. Gerber 1986; Dinnerstein 1987, 1994.
2. On the belief in Jewish and Asian versions of Horatio Alger, see Steinberg 1989, chap. 3; Gilman 1996. On Jewish culture, see Gordon 1964; see Sowell 1981 for an updated version.
3. Not all Jews are white or unambiguously white. It has been suggested, for example, that Hasidim lack the privileges of whiteness. Rodriguez (1997, 12, 15) has begun to unpack the claims of white Jewish "amenity migrants" and the different racial meanings of Chicano claims to a crypto-Jewish identity in New Mexico. See also Thomas 1996 on African American Jews.
4. Higham 1955, 226.
5. M. Grant 1916; Ripley 1923; see also Patterson 1997; M. Grant, quoted in Higham 1955, 156.
6. *New York Times*, 30 July 1893, "East Side Street Vendors," reprinted in Schoener 1967, 57–58.
7. Gould 1981; Higham 1955; Patterson 1997, 108–115.
8. It was intended, as Davenport wrote to the president of the American Museum of Natural History, Henry Fairfield Osborne, as "an anthropological society . . . with a central governing body, self-elected and self-perpetuating, and very limited in members, and also confined to native Americans [*sic*] who are anthropologically, socially and politically sound, no Bolsheviki need apply" (Barkan 1992, 67–68).
9. Quoted in Carlson and Colburn 1972, 333–334.
10. Synott 1986, 249–250, 233–274. For why Jews entered college earlier than other immigrants, and for a challenge to views that attribute it to Jewish culture, see Steinberg 1989.
11. Ibid., 229.
12. Synott 1986, 250. On anti-Semitism in higher education, see also Steinberg 1989, chaps. 5 and 9; Karabel 1984; Silberman 1985.
13. Synott 1986, 239–240.
14. Although quotas on Jews persisted into the 1950s at some of the elite schools, they were much attenuated, as the postwar college-building boom gave the coup de grace to the gentleman's finishing school.
15. Steinberg 1989, 137, 227; Markowitz 1993.
16. Silberman 1985, 88–117. On Jewish mobility, see Sklare 1971, 63–67; see M. Davis 1990, 146 n. 25, for exclusion of Jewish lawyers from corporate law in Los Angeles. Silberman 1985, 127–130.
17. Gerber 1986, 26.
18. Steinberg 1989, chap. 5.
19. Ibid., 225. Between 1900 and 1930, New York City's population grew from 3.4 million to 6.9 million, and at both times immigrants and children of immigrants were 80 percent of all white heads of household (Moore 1992, 270 n. 28).
20. This census also explicitly changed the Mexican race to white (U.S. Bureau of the Census 1940, 2:4).
21. Sifry 1993, 92–99.
22. Nash et al. 1986, 885–886.
23. On planning for veterans, see F. J. Brown 1946; Hurd 1946; Mosch 1975; "Postwar Jobs for Veterans" 1945; Willenz 1983.

24. Wynn 1976, 15.
25. G. B. Nash et al. 1986, 885; Eichler 1982, 4; Wynn 1976, 15; Mosch 1975, 20.
26. Willenz 1983, 165.
27. J. Nash et al. 1986, 885; Willenz 1983, 165. On mobility among veterans and non veterans, see Havighurst et al. 1951.
28. Keller 1983, 363, 346–373.
29. Silberman 1985, 124, 121–122; Steinberg 1989, 137.
30. Silberman 1985, 121–122. None of the Jewish surveys asked what women were doing. Silberman claims that Jewish women stayed out of the labor force prior to the 1970s, but the preponderance of women among public school teachers calls this into question.
31. Steinberg 1974; 1989, chap. 5.
32. Steinberg 1989, 89–90.
33. Willenz 1983, 20–28, 94–97. I thank Nancy G. Cattell for calling my attention to the fact that women GIs were ultimately eligible for benefits.
34. Willenz 1983, 168; Dalfiume 1969, 133–134; Wynn 1976, 114–116; K. Anderson 1981; Milkman 1987.
35. Nalty and MacGregor 1981, 218, 60–61.
36. Wynn 1976, 114, 116.
37. On African Americans in the U.S. military, see Foner 1974; Dalfiume 1969; Johnson 1967; Binkin and Eitelberg 1982; Nalty and MacGregor 1981. On schooling, see Walker 1970, 4–9.
38. Hartman (1975, 141–142) cites massive abuses in the 1940s and 1950s by builders under the Section 608 program in which "the FHA granted extraordinarily liberal concessions to lackadaisically supervised private developers to induce them to produce rental housing rapidly in the postwar period." Eichler (1982) indicates that things were not that different in the subsequent FHA-funded home-building industry.
39. Dobriner 1963, 91, 100.
40. For home-owning percentages and the role of merchant builders, see Eichler 1982, 5, 9, 13. Jackson (1985, 205, 215) gives an increase in families living in owner-occupied buildings, rising from 44 percent in 1934 to 63 percent in 1972. See Monkkonen (1988, 184–185) on the scarcity of mortgages. See Gelfand (1975, chap. 6) on federal programs. On the location of highway interchanges, as in the appraisal and inspection process, Eichler (1982, 13) claims that large-scale builders also often bribed and otherwise influenced the outcomes in their favor.
41. Weiss 1987, 146; Jackson 1985, 203–205.
42. Jackson 1985, 213; Abrams 1955, 229. See also Gelfand 1975; Tobin 1987; Lief and Goering 1987, 227–267; Sansbury 1997, 30–31.
43. Eichler 1982. See also *Race and Housing* 1964.
44. Quoted in Foner 1974, 195.
45. Berman 1982, 292.
46. On urban renewal and housing policies, see Greer 1965; Hartman 1975; Squires 1989. On Los Angeles, see Pardo 1990; Cockroft 1990.
47. Jackson 1985, 206; D. Brody 1980, 192. Not only did suburbs proliferate, they also differentiated themselves into working and middle class based on the income disparities of occupations; see Berger 1960 for a case study.
48. Jackson 1985, 197. These ideas from the real estate industry were "codified

and legitimated in 1930s work by University of Chicago sociologist Robert Park and real estate professor Homer Hoyt" (Ibid., 198–199).
49. See Gans 1962.

CHAPTER 2 *Race Making*

1. This is not to say that there was no anti-Semitism. Before race became fully institutionalized, the American colonies marked Jews as non-Christians. Early anti-Semitism in the United States was part of the European anti-Jewish heritage that settlers brought to the colonies.
2. Brundage 1994, 21–23.
3. On racialization of the Irish, see the pioneering work of Leonard Liggio (1976) and Theodore Allen (1994), both of whom argue that British racialization of the Irish as nonwhite was a precursor for the creation of African Americans as a black race. On the early history of European patterns of racializing conquered peoples and putting them to work, see C. Robinson 1983.
4. Fields 1990; T. Allen 1994.
5. Ignatiev 1995, chap. 4; see also Roediger 1991, chap. 7.
6. Brecher 1972; Steinberg 1989, 36. As was seen already, latent fear of revolution, distrust of foreigners, including immigrants, and anti-working class sentiments by the general U.S. population coalesced in the Red Scare of 1919. Economic depression, massive strikes, and unsettling news of the Bolshevik revolution in Russia raised the specter of communism even in government circles. Several hundred working-class strike leaders were deported. Among those deported to the Soviet Russia was Emma Goldman, an anarchist firebrand, who had come to the United States in 1886 as a young girl, and had been involved in the anarchist movement since the 1890s. She had been jailed during the war for pacifist and anti-government activities.
7. Brundage 1994, 21–23; see diLeonardo (1984, 153–156) on Italians in Northern California.
8. Steinberg 1989, 36, citing the U.S. Immigration Commission 1911.
9. Carpenter 1927, 271, table 121.
10. Dubofsky 1988, 24.
11. Eckler and Zlotnick 1949, 97.
12. D. Brody 1980, 129.
13. Ibid.
14. D. Brody 1960, 120. Sometimes brotherly inclusion was extended to male immigrant workers, as in the eastern coal-mining and Chicago meatpacking unions that welcomed immigrants. However, as Patricia Cooper's (1987) analysis of the transformation of the cigar-making industry from the province of skilled men to one dominated by "unskilled" immigrant women shows, craftsmen had a particularly difficult time making common cause with immigrants who were women.
15. It is worth indicating that Montgomery's (1979) description of the turn-of-the-last-century European immigrant proletariat applies equally well to the eve of the twenty-first century, when Latin American and Southeast Asian immigrant workers labor in newly reorganized service industries and deunionized, reorganized manufacturing industries. The resurrection of piece rates, casualization of the workforce, rollbacks of unions, denial of benefits and social services since the 1980s evokes an eerie parallel between immigrants of the 1890s and 1990s, and the new loss of manufacturing jobs formerly available to African Ameri-

cans evokes the nineteenth-century pattern of excluding African Americans from industrial jobs.

16. On domestic work, see Palmer 1989. On immigrant women's work generally, see Carpenter 1927, 292. For detailed patterns of women's occupational segregation by sex in cotton mills and apparel factories and for ethnic variations in women's work patterns, see Lamphere (1987). See especially E. N. Glenn's (1985) important article for the argument that women of color have been defined as workers.

17. Carpenter 1927, 292. See also Amot and Matthei 1991; K. Anderson 1996. See Lamphere 1987 for Polish and French Canadian women about 1915; Ruiz 1987 for Mexican American women in the 1930s; S. Glenn 1990 for Jewish women.

18. Miller 1988, 10, also 16 for ethnic segregation in specifically men's jobs.

19. Newman 1988, 192–194.

20. Bodnar 1980, 48–49.

21. "[T]he distinction between white and colored" has been "the only racial classification which has been carried through all the 15 censuses." "Colored" consisted of "Negroes" and "other races": Mexican, Indian, Chinese, Japanese, Filipino, Hindu, Korean, Hawaiian, Malay, Siamese, and Samoan. (U.S. Bureau of the Census 1930, 2:25, 26). See also Haney Lopez 1996 for changes in who was considered white.

22. Sabel 1982.

23. Steinberg 1989, 94; Sorin 1985, 19.

24. Orleck 1995, 25.

25. Howe 1980, 155; Rischin 1962, 233, 241.

26. Howe 1980, 155.

27. Ibid.; Steinberg 1989, 99.

28. Howe 1980, 156–157.

29. Steinberg 1989, 98–99. Unfortunately, this data is not broken down by sex. Skilled workers among the largely rural Southern Italian, Irish, and Polish immigrants represented only 15, 13, and 6 percent respectively.

30. Rischin 1962, 231; Brandes 1976, 1.

31. Rischin 1962, 231.

32. David Roediger (1991) makes a parallel contrast for antebellum, white, working-class racism that equated servility, slavery, and blackness as a threat to free white manhood. Young women in the early-nineteenth-century textile mills also drew parallels between their wage slavery and the bondage of African Americans, although in their case, it was to support abolition of slavery (Sacks 1976).

33. Bonacich 1972; 1976.

34. Ignatiev 1995, 109.

35. Ibid., 111.

36. Ibid., chaps. 4–6.

37. V. Green 1995. I thank Vivian Price for showing me this.

38. Ibid., S113.

39. Ibid., S120, S121.

40. Ibid.

41. Hacker 1979, 539; quoted in V. Green 1995, S124.

42. For an excellent case study of a union that may have been well intentioned but was utterly insensitive to the circumstances of its women members, see Remy and Sawers 1984.

43. E. Williams 1966; see also Blackburn 1996 for recent support for Williams's argument.
44. Bennett 1970; Jordan 1974; E. Williams 1966; Davidson 1961. See also Toni Morrison 1988 for her inspired rereading of *Moby Dick*—its "unspeakable unspoken" central theme of race and racism—and her analysis of her own work. I thank Barrie Thorne for showing me this.
45. Fields 1982; 1990, 101–109.
46. Smedley 1993, 303.
47. This is the argument of Du Bois (1935, chaps. 1–7); see esp. pp. 24 and 89 for the impact of Frederick Douglass's abolitionist work in generating antislavery sentiment and an effective anti-intervention movement among English workers, and to find Karl Marx and John Stuart Mill as key activists in this movement. That African slavery in the New World was a form of capitalism is also Eric Williams's (1966) thesis, in contrast to a strand of white Marxism that regards New World slavery as a kind of precapitalism.
48. Jones 1985, 18. See also E. N. Glenn 1985.
49. Steinberg 1989, 25, n. 37; Montgomery 1993, 13; E. Williams 1966, 19; Dubois (1935, 9) gives nineteen dollars a year as the total cost for "maintenance of a slave in the South."
50. Higginbotham 1992, 257.
51. James 1963; G. B. Nash 1986, esp. chaps. 2 and 4.
52. Lieberson 1980, 5, quoting the *Report of the National Advisory Commission on Civil Disorders* (1968, 143–145), formed by President Johnson to investigate the urban uprisings of the 1960s. For a visually striking demonstration of the impact of this policy on the racial shape of the labor force, see Carpenter 1927, 276–277, who describes the complementary geographic distribution of African Americans and European immigrants, the former confined to the South, the latter virtually absent in the South but present everywhere else.
53. Steinberg (1995, 205–210) has argued that the reconstruction and industrialization periods were two key historical moments of opportunity not taken to end racism.
54. Almaguer (1994, 56) notes that the California constitution enfranchised "[w]hite male citizens of the United States and every White male citizen of Mexico, who shall have elected to become a citizen of the United States."
55. Ibid., 57.
56. By 1940, however, Mexicans were again presumed to be white. See Foley (1996) for efforts of the League of United Latin American Citizens to litigate for Mexican Americans' civil rights in Texas between 1920 and 1960, on the basis that Mexicans are white.
57. Sanchez 1993, 258.
58. E. N. Glenn 1985; Takaki 1989, 89–92, 132–176. Joel (1984) uses the work of Andrew Lind to show that Hawaiian planters deliberately recruited "as many nationalities as possible on the plantation"—from Japan, Korea, the Philippines, Spain, Portugal, Germany, Norway, Puerto Rico, Russia, and Poland. Although done to divide and conquer, those labor practices created races.
59. Rosenblum 1973, 74; Reich 1981, 24–25. Although African American agricultural workers were largely tenants and sharecroppers, their conditions of labor were intensely driven and, especially in cotton and sugar production, which together dominated Southern agriculture, were organized as gang labor, with women and children often forced to participate (Jones 1985, 79–109).

60. On law and earlier changes in the American ethnoracial map, see Haney Lopez 1996. On immigration law, see Ong 1994. On labor and immigration, see Ong, Bonacich, and Cheng 1994; Takagi 1983.
61. Wright 1994, 50–51.
62. See Morsy 1994 for an excellent perspective on "honorary whiteness."
63. See Harrison 1995 for an excellent review of the literature; see Steinberg 1995 on the rollback of civil rights gains. A sample of studies I have found useful include: on economic inequality, Wilson 1980, 1987; Oliver and Shapiro 1995; on residential segregation, Massey and Denton 1987; 1993; Bullard, Grigsby, and Lee 1994; Sugrue 1995. For a Los Angeles profile see Grant, Oliver, and James 1996; Allen and Turner 1997 (I thank Mike Davis for making this last available to me). On the drug wars and its consequences, see Baum 1996.
64. Sanjek 1994, 107, 113.
65. Ibid., 115–116.
66. Cooper 1989, 28.
67. Carter and Carter (1981) argue that one of the bitter fruits of women's entry into formerly all-male professions like law and medicine is the fact that their success has facilitated the emergence of a more factory-like organization of professional work where professionals lose much of their autonomy to corporate managers. Murphree 1984 and Machung 1984 show parallel transformations of clerical work from white male entry-level managerial jobs to dead-end front office work by white women and de-skilled, intensely supervised, paper assembly lines staffed by women of color.
68. Omi and Winant 1994.

CHAPTER 3   *Race, Gender, and Virtue in Civic Discourse*

1. Montgomery 1979, 13.
2. E. N. Glenn 1994; Brackette Williams 1989; 1996. The literature is huge, is growing rapidly, and spans the disciplines. Over the years, I have found the following particularly instructive: Anzaldúa 1990; Bolles 1995; E. B. Brown 1989; Christian 1988; Collins 1990; Dill 1979; Giddings 1984; Gilkes 1988; E. N. Glenn 1985; Glenn, Chang, and Forcey 1994; Harris 1995; King 1988; Moraga and Anzaldúa 1983; Mullings 1997; Ruiz 1987; Zavella 1987; Asian Women United of California 1989. Valuable pioneering theories include Cade 1970; Beal 1970; Ladner 1970.
3. Patterson 1997.
4. Kessler-Harris 1982, 4–6.
5. Bederman 1995, 20.
6. J. D. Brody 1996, 154. See also K. M. Brown 1996; Higginbotham 1992; Crenshaw 1988.
7. Higginbotham 1992.
8. Mullings 1997, 111.
9. Jewell 1993, 36.
10. Bederman 1995, 28.
11. Ibid., 50.
12. White 1985, 41–61.
13. There are large anthropological and postcolonial studies literatures on the subject. See Sacks 1978 for an early treatment of the anthropological. I have found Patterson 1997; Said 1979; Mohanty, Russo, and Torres 1991; and Stoler 1989

particularly helpful in bringing critical anthropological and postcolonial perspectives together.

14. Spencer 1899, 725.
15. Ibid., 374–375. See Sacks 1978, chap. 1, for a discussion of evolutionary thinking.
16. For twentieth-century parallels, see Banfield 1958. See Harney 1985 on Canadian and U.S. "Italophobia."
17. Quoted in Carlson and Colburn 1972, 328–329.
18. Bederman 1995, 30. See also Takaki 1989, 101; Carlson and Colburn 1972, 177–178; Rotundo 1990.
19. Hall 1979.
20. These stereotypes can work in extraordinarily complex ways. See Mullings 1997, 109–127; Jewell 1993; Carby 1987; Bederman 1995 for the United States; Stoler 1989; Mohanty et al. 1991 for postcolonial critiques.
21. Ehrenreich and English 1973.
22. Quoted in Andreu Iglesias 1984, 175. I thank Bonnie Urciuoli for this source.
23. Palmer 1989, 138.
24. Jones 1985, 14.
25. White 1985, 102.
26. Jones 1985, 22–89; A. Davis 1981; White 1985.
27. Jones 1985, 23, 27.
28. Spruill 1938; Jones 1985, 22–29.
29. G. Lerner 1969.
30. Carpenter 1927, 271, table 121.
31. D. Goldberg 1989, 2–3.
32. Carpenter 1927, 271, table 121.
33. Benson 1986; V. Green 1995; Norwood 1990.
34. Quoted in Carlson and Colburn 1972, 344.
35. Omi and Winant 1994 coined the term "racial state" to describe the way in which the government has made a person's fundamental rights and entitlements depend on the race to which he or she is assigned. See also Green and Carter 1988. See Boris 1995; Crenshaw 1988; Harris 1995 on critical race theory. See MacKinnon 1987 on feminist jurisprudence. On the many ways in which the state is simultaneously racial and gendered, see Boris and Bardaglio 1991; Crenshaw and Morrison 1992. Katznelson 1981 suggests that, when Americans are constructed as public actors, they are constructed racially. Haney Lopez 1996 argues that law—especially marriage, immigration, and naturalization law—have given phenotypic reality to race.
36. Kessler-Harris 1990, 19–20.
37. D. Brody 1960, 98, 101–103; Byington 1974.
38. D. Brody 1960, 98.
39. Montgomery 1979.
40. N. E. Rose 1993, 103; 1994.
41. N. E. Rose 1993, 83–85, 101–103. See also Abramovitz 1988; Mink 1995; Boris 1993.
42. N. E. Rose 1993, 35.
43. Kessler-Harris 1995.
44. Mink 1995, 171.
45. Jones 1992, 3; Boris and Bardaglio 1991; N. Rose 1994.
46. Abel 1997, 1809, 1813.

47. Kerber 1995; Sarvasy 1992.
48. Coontz 1992, 132 (emphasis in original).
49. Cameron 1993, 172.
50. Coontz 1992, 135.
51. Petchesky 1985.
52. Ladd-Taylor 1994, 138.
53. Coontz 1992, 136. See also Naples 1991 and 1994; Boris 1993.
54. Amot and Matthei 1991, 77; K. Anderson 1996, 110–111; Chan 1991, 115.
55. Solinger 1992, 18.
56. Ibid. See also Kunzel 1994.
57. Solinger 1992, 10.
58. Moynihan 1965.
59. Naples 1997, 40–41, 43.
60. L. Gordon 1994.

CHAPTER 4 *Not Quite White: Gender and Jewish Identity*
1. For similar distinctions, see Blauner 1991; Mullings 1984, 23–24.
2. Although examining Jewish ethnicity might tell us something about European ethnicity more generally, Jews are not its measure. Together with Finns, they seem to have been the most radical of the European immigrants. Other Euro-ethnicities, and sometimes ethnic ghettos in particular cities, were known as more or less conservative or more or less radical. See Buhle 1980, 9; D. Goldberg 1989, 34–35, 70–71, 109–110, 206–207, and passim.
3. Marx 1978.
4. See also Epstein 1969, 4–5; S. Glenn 1990; Howe 1980; Rischin 1962.
5. Hyman 1995, 67–71, 75–84, 144–146.
6. Epstein 1969, xli–xlii, 1–8; Howe 1980, 14–26; Sorin 1985, 10–46.
7. Orleck 1995, 26.
8. Gutman 1976; Strikwerda and Guerin-Gonzales 1993, 27–29.
9. Almost 70 percent of the political activists whom Gerald Sorin (1985) studied had worked in the garment industry, and for almost 60 percent that industry was their life's work. When they came to the United States, most stayed with family or friends who helped them set up house, find work, and get integrated into New World ways. See also Epstein 1969; Mendelsohn 1976, 150–177; Trunk 1976, 342–393.
10. Orleck 1995, 27. Liebman 1979 is the major source. See also Buhle 1980; Epstein 1969; Howe 1980; Rischin 1962; Sorin 1985; Schappes 1978.
11. Liebman 1979; Buhle 1980; Diner 1977; Howe 1980; Kann 1993; Schappes 1978; Sorin 1985. Even on the Left, the immigrant community was far from politically harmonious. There were at least three often mutually hostile currents of socialism in early-twentieth-century Jewish communities: the more assimilationist and "class first" social democracy of the "right wing" of the Socialist Party and of the *Forward*; the Yiddishist "left wing," many of whose members joined the Communist Party when it was founded and who read the *Freiheit*; and the Labor Zionists, who sought to build a Jewish socialist state. There was also a convervative Zionist paper, the *Taggeblatt*, which was also very widely read and supported the Tammany Hall political machine.
12. Orleck 1995, 30.
13. Buhle 1980, 14.
14. Rischin 1962, 236; Sorin 1985; Buhle 1980, 15. Socialists were not the only

radicals among the immigrants. There were also many kinds of anarchists and internationalist socialists, utopian farmers, Zionist socialists, and syndicalists.

15. Moore 1981, 53–55.
16. Although Howe (1980) has argued that Jewishness compromised working-class values and politics, Schappes 1978 and Buhle 1980 have argued more persuasively that the Jewishness of its socialism was "an enrichment and concretization of class reality" (Buhle 1980, 15–16). See also Sorin 1985, 35; Vanneman and Cannon 1990; Kelley 1990 for similar arguments on the complementarity of class and ethnicity.
17. Sorin 1985, 81, 92.
18. Ibid., 211.
19. Ibid., 221.
20. Ewen 1985, 175.
21. Coontz 1988, 287.
22. See Ackelsberg 1984, 1988; Bookman and Morgen 1988; Kaplan 1982; Collins 1989, 1990.
23. Coontz 1988, 287, chap. 8.
24. Sacks 1989.
25. S. Glenn 1990, 83.
26. Ibid., 81–82, 145–148.
27. Ewen 1985, 162.
28. Orleck 1995, 27. See J. A. G. Robinson 1987; D. Frank 1985 for two important case studies of women's community-based activism.
29. Orleck 1995, 27–30.
30. Ibid., 27; Hyman 1980.
31. Orleck 1995, 27–28; Hyman 1980. On food and rent strikes, see also D. Frank 1985; S. Glenn 1990, 176, 211.
32. Orleck 1995, 25–26.
33. Ibid., 29.
34. Ewen 1985, 178, 180–183. In Providence in 1910, Judith Smith (1985, 156–158) described a similarly successful kosher meat boycott by women who demanded "respectable treatment," fresh meat, and clean wrapping paper, as well as a pasta protest by men in 1914. In each of these instances, women "acted together—for themselves, for their families, for their neighborhoods, and in defense of their world."
35. Smith 1985, 156.
36. See Parr 1990 for an excellent analysis of Canadian family and community bases of men's working-class consciousness. On landsmanshaftn, see Weisser 1985. Howe 1980s vivid picture of New York's Jewish community centers on men's lives; see Sorin 1985.
37. Sorin 1985, 100.
38. Ibid.
39. Schappes 1978, part 1, 37, part 2, 31; Sorin 1985, passim, for many personal stories.
40. Ewen 1985, 170.
41. This perspective raises the question of whether small business entrepreneurs who are members of working-class ethnic communities are capitalists or something else. The answer would depend on the importance of the business to the household's overall livelihood. But there is a deeper issue about the na-

ture of these small businesses and the aspirations of their developers. Although the point is beyond the scope of this work, small-scale entrepreneurs in working-class communities are not always the same as small capitalists. Largely due to circumstance and social ties, their practical goal tends to be net income rather than profit. By this I mean that the income from small businesses is plowed into household subsistence rather than being reinvested. It is money, not capital, and while small merchants may gouge and exploit, they are constrained by the needs of their kin and by the limiting circumstances of a working-class clientele.

Working-class merchants have existed in different forms in different times and places. Their businesses have included pushcarts in nineteenth-century northeast United States; regional systems of marketing and specialized food preparation by women in Latin America, Africa, Southeast Asia, and the Caribbean; and swap meets and flea markets in late-twentieth-century North American cities. For the most part, they function as supermarkets for working-class consumers and are largely staffed by working-class sellers, very few of whom can support themselves or their households by that labor alone.

42. For example, see Dubofsky 1988, 30, on "Anglo-Saxon" miner strikes in Coeur d'Alene, Idaho; Hall et al. 1987 on Appalachian textile workers' struggles; Cameron 1985, 1993, on European immigrants in Lawrence; Chafe 1981; Carson 1981 on black student sit-ins; and J. A. G. Robinson 1987 on the Montgomery bus boycott.
43. Yezierska 1975.
44. Hyman 1995, 107–108.
45. Kessler-Harris 1982, 7–8.
46. Ewen 1985, 98, 100–104; Mintz and Kellogg 1988, 84–95.
47. Sacks 1984, 15–38.
48. Hyman 1995, 112.
49. These constructions of womanhood are quite widely shared. See Fisher and Tronto 1990 for a discussion of work as part of caring. For a discussion of this theme in contemporary African American motherhood, see Braxton 1990; Collins 1990, chap. 6.
50. Rivo 1998, 34, 42, 30–42.
51. Sochen 1998, 74, 68–76.
52. Gold, quoted in Hyman 1995, 128.
53. Okonjo 1976, 48, 45–58. Feminists of color developed the idea of motherhood as political citizenship in a way that overlaps with, but is distinct from, the maternalist politics of white women. Central to the approaches of women of color is the notion that motherhood is a political as well as a domestic status. See E. N. Glenn 1994; Collins 1990; Pardo 1990; Braxton 1990.
54. Simon 1982, 178.
55. Stansell 1986; Peiss 1985.
56. For differing readings on Streisand, see Sochen 1998 and Herman 1998 in *Talking Back*, Joyce Antler's welcome new volume on Jewish women in popular culture.
57. Orleck 1995, 41.
58. Ibid., 131.
59. See Kessler-Harris 1976; Orleck 1995; Antler 1995.
60. Orleck 1995, 216.

61. Ibid., 227–228.
62. Ibid., 217–239; Antler 1995, 271.
63. Orleck 1995, 241.
64. Kessler-Harris 1976, 6, 5–23.
65. Ibid., 13.
66. MacLean 1982. See Norwood 1990 for a discussion of the importance of single women's peer groups and women's communities in the formation of the Boston telephone operators' union.
67. Kessler-Harris 1976, 17.
68. Rischin 1962, 242.
69. MacLean 1982.
70. Orleck 1995, 62.
71. Ibid., 37.
72. Orleck 1995; Sorin 1985, 124–135.

CHAPTER 5   *A Whiteness of Our Own? Jewishness and Whiteness in the 1950s and 1960s*

1. See M. Lerner 1993 for an argument that Jews are not white.
2. On New York intellectuals, see Bloom 1986; Teres 1996; Kessner 1994.
3. Ginsberg 1993.
4. On being "too Jewish," see Kleeblatt 1996.
5. On Jewish talking back, see Antler 1998, a valuable collection of popular representations of Jewish women.
6. For personal testimonies, see Kaye/Kantrowitz 1996; Lauter 1996.
7. Liebman 1979, 351–353, 417–419.
8. Kaye/Kantrowitz 1996, 108.
9. Trillin 1969, 496.
10. P. Rose 1969, 12–14; Gabler 1988. See also Rogin 1996.
11. Lieberman 1996, 108.
12. Later, *The New York Review of Books* and *Ramparts* were founded by Jewish public intellectuals who broke with the neoconservative politics of this circle and identified with those of the New Left. On this group, see Bloom 1986; Teres 1996.
13. See Handlin 1952, 203, on the adoption of ethnicity and the dropping of race. For critical discussions of sociological approaches to American ethnicity, see Bonacich 1980; Rose and Rose 1948, 5; A. M. Rose 1951, 434; M. G. Smith 1982.
14. Glazer and Moynihan 1963, 163–164.
15. Ibid., esp. 160–165.
16. Blau 1969, 66.
17. Glazer and Moynihan 1963, 50, 51.
18. Ibid., 194–195. Edward Banfield's *The Moral Basis of a Backward Society*, about southern Italian culture, was one of the first of these postwar works of cultural denigration. Banfield argued that Italy was undeveloped because of its culture of "amoral familism" and that this explained the discrimination and poverty among turn-of-the-century Italian immigrants to the United States. Presumably, Italians jettisoned those cultural deficiencies after World War II. Banfield later went on, as Nixon's urban advisor, to argue for policies of "benign neglect" as the best way to correct a similar set of alleged cultural deficiencies in African American families.

19. Ibid., 198–199.
20. Ibid., 53.
21. Bell 1964, 31; Glazer 1967; Kristol 1965, 98; 1966, 138.
22. Podhoretz 1992, 113.
23. Ibid.
24. Morrison 1993, 57; see also 1988 and 1990.
25. Rodríguez 1997, 3.
26. See Rawick 1972 for an early analysis of this counterpoint. Delgado and Stefancic 1997 offer a wide-ranging collection of recent studies on whiteness. See Fishkin 1995; Stowe 1996 for reviews of the whiteness literature. See Harris 1995 for critical legal/race theory. See Ware 1992; diLeonardo 1992 on whiteness and womanhood. See also Dominguez 1986 and 1993; Fine, Weis, Powell, and Wong 1997. On Jews' racial in-betweeness, S. Horowitz 1994 is particularly insightful. On Jewish whiteness in anthropology, see G. Frank 1998. In general, see Brettschneider 1996a and 1996b; Edelman 1996; Rubin-Dorsky and Fishkin 1996; Frankenberg 1993; Gabler 1988; Rogin 1996. On language and whiteness, see Urciuoli 1991. On the Irish, see Ignatiev 1995; Roediger 1991; Lott 1993. On the U.S. West, see Saxton 1971 and 1990; Rodríguez 1997.
27. See reviews by Saxton 1977 and Schappes 1973.
28. Glazer and Moynihan 1963, 53.
29. Glazer 1967, 31. But see Glazer 1997 for a reversal of this position. On white ethnic politics of Jews and Italians in Brooklyn, see Rieder 1985.
30. Gabler 1988.
31. Rivo 1998, 43.
32. Weber 1998, 91.
33. Friedman 1991, 24; see also Friedman 1987 for a full treatment of Jews in American films.
34. Rivo 1998, 47.
35. Diner 1977; Lewis 1992. See also G. Frank 1997.
36. On upward mobility and temples as community centers, see Moore 1981; 1992; Hyman 1995, chap. 4. See also Gabler 1988, 108–109, 195–198. Liebman 1979, 357–443, argues that the cooperation between the elite and the Left around World War I relief efforts for Jews in Europe, together with upward mobility among children of immigrants, heightened the importance of assimilation into the dominant society within the still predominantly working-class Jewish community.
37. Ginsberg 1993 also speaks to this point. It is of course central to the vast literature dealing with Jews and modernity. See Hyman 1995 for an interpretive synthesis of some of the major themes. Guttmann 1971 treats the ways that marginality and assimilation play out in Jewish literature.
38. Glazer and Moynihan 1963, 160, on intermarriage rate; Prell 1993 on the salience of Jewishness in and outside New York. In the last twenty-five years, these fears have surfaced in the research agendas of Jewish social sciences and of research sponsored by Jewish organizations: What is the rate of intermarriage with non-Jews? Are out-marrying Jews lost Jews? Are their children lost to Jewishness or is intermarriage an enhancement of the Jewish population? Jewish organizations sponsor surveys of membership in temples and worry about how to make Judaism more relevant. See Cohen 1988 and Kosmin and Scheckner 1992 for discussions of these issues.
39. Prell 1990; 1993; 1996; 1998.

40. Quoted in Hyman 1995, 159.
41. Hyman 1995; Moore 1981; 1992. Cohen 1988 is a good guide to the social science literature.
42. See Gilman 1991 and Biale 1992 as well as Hyman 1995 for a guide to the history and interpretation of anti-Semitic stereotypes of Jewish men as feminized.
43. Prell 1996, 77–80.
44. Ibid., 89
45. Prell 1998, 127.
46. Ibid., 134, 138.
47. Quoted in Prell 1990, 263.
48. Breines 1992; Friedan 1963. On the New Left, see Kaye/Kantrowitz 1996. On the Jewish Left, see Buhle 1980; Liebman 1979, 67–69, and chap. 2. On the Communist Party, see Horne 1996; Naison 1983.
49. D. Horowitz 1996, 30. From the time of her graduation from Smith College in 1942 and the beginning of her work on the book in 1957, Friedan wrote frequently about feminist issues in addition to critiques of racism, chronicling workers' struggles and the radical history of worker unionization in the course of her work for the United Electrical Workers' newspaper.
50. Ibid., 3.
51. Friedan 1963, 274, 276.
52. Ehrenreich 1983; Breines 1992.
53. Breines 1992, 145, 13–22.
54. Evans 1980; Kaye/Kantrowitz 1996. On African American women's leadership, see Cantarow and O'Malley 1980; Cook 1988; J. A. G. Robinson 1987.
55. Buhle 1980. But see Liebman 1979 for a counterargument.
56. Brettschneider 1996a; S. Horowitz 1994. See Porter and Dreier 1973 for a worldwide list of groups and newspapers as well as early essays on Jewish radicalism.

Conclusion

1. Quoted in Carlson and Colburn 1972, 308.
2. Ibid., 311.
3. Ruth Benedict's *The Chrysanthemum and the Sword* is perhaps the best-known and most sustained anthropological work in this genre.
4. See Brackette Williams 1989 for a superb review of the literature. On the "Black Atlantic," see Gilroy 1993. On history and national identity, see Hobsbawm and Ranger 1983; Anderson 1983; Brackette Williams 1996. Excellent new case studies include Bays 1999; Fikes 1999; Medina 1999; Stoler 1989.
5. Hall cited in Twine 1997, 3; Castles 1996, 30–32.
6. As in the title of AFL-CIO chief John Sweeney's book, *America Needs a Raise*.
7. Baumann 1991. I thank Sandra Harding for showing me this.
8. Raymond Williams 1973. Most of the great nineteenth- and early-twentieth-century thinkers wrestled with these dichotomies: Karl Marx's treatment of bourgeois freedom as the alienation of workers from control over the means of production; Herbert Spencer's treatment of savagery versus civilization; Emile Durkheim's mechanical and organic solidarity; Tonnies's *gemeinschaft* and *gesellschaft*; and Freud's eros and civilization come to mind.
9. Berman 1982. See Jordanova 1981 for an early discussion of the Enlightenment as a gendered cultural system. Harding 1991; 1993; and Patterson 1997

offer excellent discussions of how the Enlightenment has shaped the class, racial and gender system of science.

10. I am not suggesting that whites are oppressed, simply that there is a price, however willingly it is paid, for their unacknowledged privileges. See Segrest 1996 for a provocative analysis of the emotional costs of white privilege.

11. Fine et al. 1997; Roediger 1994; Ignatiev and Garvey 1996. This was also a major theme at the conference on "The Making and Unmaking of Whiteness" sponsored by the Department of Ethnic Studies at the University of California, Berkeley, 11–13 April 1997.

12. Gilroy 1993, 1–40; Kelley 1990, 1997; Buhle 1980; Boyarin 1996, 211–214.

BIBLIOGRAPHY ▢

Abel, Emily K. 1997. "Taking the Cure to the Poor: Patients' Responses to New York City's Tuberculosis Program, 1914–1918." *American Journal of Public Health* 87 (11):1808–1815.

Abramovitz, Mimi. 1988. *Regulating the Lives of Women: Social Welfare Policy from Colonial Times to the Present.* Boston: South End Press.

Abrams, Charles. 1955. *Forbidden Neighbors: A Study of Prejudice in Housing.* New York: Harper & Brothers.

Acklesberg, Martha. 1984. "Women's Collaborative Activities and City Life: Politics and Policy." In *Political Women: Current Roles in State and Local Government,* ed. J. Flammang. Beverly Hills: Sage Publications, 242–259.

———. 1988. "Communities, Resistance, and Women's Activism: Some Implications for a Democratic Polity." In Bookman and Morgen 1988, 297–313.

Alba, Richard D., and Gwenn Moore. 1982. "Ethnicity in the American Elite." *American Sociological Review* 47, 3:373–382.

Allen, James P., and Eugene Turner. 1997. *The Ethnic Quilt: Population Diversity in Southern California.* Northridge: The Center for Geographical Studies, California State University, Northridge.

Allen, Theodore W. 1994. *The Invention of the White Race.* London: Verso.

Almaguer, Tomás. 1994. *Racial Fault Lines: The Historical Origins of White Supremacy in California.* Berkeley: University of California Press.

American Quarterly 47, 3. Special issue on whiteness.

Amot, Teresa, and Julie Matthei. 1991. *Race, Gender and Work: A Multicultural Economic History of Women in the United States.* Boston: South End Press.

Anderson, Benedict. 1983. *Imagined Communities: Reflections on the Origin and Spread of Nationalism.* London: Verso.

Anderson, Karen. 1981. *Wartime Women.* Westport, Conn.: Greenwood.

———. 1996. *Changing Woman.* New York: Oxford University Press.

Andreu Iglesias, Cesar. 1984. *Memoirs of Bernard Vega: A Contribution to the History of the Puerto Rican Community in New York.* Translated by Juan Flores. New York: Monthly Review Press.

Antler, Joyce. 1995. "Between Culture and Politics: The Emma Lazarus Federation of Jewish Women's Clubs and the Promulgation of Women's History, 1944–

1989." In *U.S. History as Women's History: New Feminist Essays*, ed. L. Kerber, A. Kessler-Harris, and K. Sklar. Chapel Hill: University of North Carolina Press, 267–295.

———, ed. 1998. *Talking Back: Images of Jewish Women in American Popular Culture*. Hanover, N.H.: University Press of New England for Brandeis University Press.

Anzaldúa, Gloria, ed. 1990. *Making Face, Making Soul/Haciendo Caras*. San Francisco: Aunt Lute Books.

Asian Women United of California, eds. 1989. *Making Waves: An Anthology of Writings by and About Asian American Women*. Boston: Beacon Press.

Baker, Lee. 1996. "D. G. Brinton: Rising to Power along the Color-Line." Paper presented at the annual meeting of the American Anthropological Association, San Francisco.

———, and Thomas Patterson. 1994. "Race, Racism and the History of U.S. Anthropology." *Transforming Anthropology* 5, 1 and 2:1–7.

Banfield, Edward. 1958. *The Moral Basis of a Backward Society*. With the assistance of Laura Fasano Banfield. Glencoe, Ill.: Free Press.

Barkan, Elazar. 1992. *The Retreat of Scientific Racism: Changing Concepts of Race in Britain and the United States Between the World Wars*. New York: Cambridge University Press.

Baum, Dan. 1996. *Smoke and Mirrors: The War on Drugs and the Politics of Failure*. Boston: Little, Brown.

Bauman, Zygmunt. 1991. *Modernity and Ambivalence*. Cambridge, U.K.: Polity Press.

Bays, Sharon. 1999. "What's Culture Got to Do with It?: 'Cultural Preservation' and Hmong Women's Activism in Central California." *Transforming Anthropology* 8, 1.

Beal, Frances. 1970. "Double Jeopardy: To Be Black and Female." In *Sisterhood Is Powerful*, ed. Robin Morgan. New York: Vintage, 340–352.

Bederman, Gail. 1995. *Manliness and Civilization: A Cultural History of Gender and Race in the United States, 1880–1917*. Chicago: University of Chicago Press.

Bell, Daniel. 1964. "Plea for a 'New Phase' in Negro Leadership." *New York Times Magazine* (31 May).

Benedict, Ruth. 1946. *The Chrysanthemum and the Sword: Patterns of Japanese Culture*. Boston: Houghton and Mifflin Co.

Bennett, Lerone. 1964. *Before the Mayflower. A History of the Negro in America*. Chicago: Johnson.

———. 1970. "The Making of Black America." *Ebony* 25 (August): 71–77.

Benson, Susan Porter. 1978. "The Clerking Sisterhood: Rationalization and the Work Culture of Saleswomen." *Radical America* 12, 41–55.

———. 1986. *Counter Cultures: Saleswomen, Managers, and Customers in American Department Stores 1890–1940*. Urbana: University of Illinois Press.

Berger, Bennett. 1960. *Working Class Suburb: A Study of Auto Workers in Suburbia*. Berkeley: University of California Press.

Berlowitz, Marvin, and Ronald Edari. 1984. *Racism and the Denial of Human Rights: Beyond Ethnicity*. Minneapolis, Minn.: MEP Publishers.

Berman, Marshall. 1982. *All That Is Solid Melts into Air: The Experience of Modernity*. New York: Simon and Schuster.

Biale, David. 1992. *Eros and the Jews: From Biblical Israel to Contemporary America*. New York: Basic Books.

Binkin, Martin, and Mark J. Eitelberg. 1982. *Blacks and the Military.* Washington, D.C.: Brookings Institution.

Blackburn, Robin. 1996. *The Making of New World Slavery: From the Baroque to the Modern.* London: Verso.

Blau, Zena Smith. 1969. "In Defense of the Jewish Mother." In Peter Rose 1969, 57–68.

Blauner, Bob. 1991. "Racism, Race, and Ethnicity." Draft paper for thematic session "Reexamining the Commonly Used Concepts in Race/Ethnic Relations," American Sociological Association.

Blewitt, Mary H. 1988. *Men, Women and Work.* Urbana: University of Illinois Press.

Bloom, Alexander. 1986. *Prodigal Sons: New York Jewish Intellectuals and Their World.* New York: Oxford University Press.

Bodnar, John. 1980. "Immigration, Kinship, and the Rise of Working-class Realism in Industrial America." *Journal of Social History* 14, 1:45–65.

————. 1985. *The Transplanted: A History of Immigrants in Urban America.* Bloomington: Indiana University Press.

Bolles, A. Lynn. 1995. "Decolonizing Feminist Anthropology." Paper presented at the annual meeting of the American Anthropological Association, the Association of Feminist Anthropologists invited session "From an Anthropology of Women to the Gendering of Anthropology," Washington, D.C., November 15–19.

Bonacich, Edna. 1972. "A Theory of Ethnic Antagonism: The Split Labor Market." *American Sociological Review* 37, 5:547–559.

————. 1976. "Advanced Capitalism and Black/White Relations in the United States: A Split Labor Market Interpretation." *American Sociological Review* 41, 1:34–51.

————. 1980. "Class Approaches to Race and Ethnicity." *Insurgent Sociologist* 10, 2 (fall):9–23.

Bookman, Ann, and Sandra Morgen, eds. 1988. *Women and the Politics of Empowerment.* Philadelphia: Temple University Press.

Boris, Eileen. 1993. "The Power of Motherhood: Black and White Activist Women Redefine the 'Political'." In *Mothers of a New World: Maternalist Politics and the Origins of Welfare States*, ed. Seth Koven and Sonya Michel. New York: Routledge, 213–245.

————. 1994. "Gender, Race, and Rights: Listening to Critical Race Theory." *Journal of Women's History* 6, 2:111–124.

————. 1995. "The Racialized Gendered State: Constructions of Citizenship in the United States." *Social Politics* 2, 2:160–180.

————, and Peter Bardaglio. 1991. "Gender, Race, and Class: The Impact of the State on the Family and the Economy, 1790–1945." In *Families and Work*, ed. Naomi Gerstel and Harriet Gross. Philadelphia: Temple University Press, 132–151.

Boyarin, Jonathan. 1996. "The Tree of Knowledge and the Tree of Life." In Brettschneider 1996b, 207–218.

Boynton, Robert S. 1995. "The New Intellectuals." *The Atlantic Monthly* 275, 3 (March): 53–70.

Brandes, Joseph. 1976. "From Sweatshop to Stability: Jewish Labor between Two Wars." *YIVO Annual of Jewish Social Science* 16, 1–149.

Braxton, Joanne. M. 1990. "Ancestral Presence: The Outraged Mother Figure in Contemporary Afra-American Writing." In *Wild Women in the Whirlwind:*

Afra-American Culture and the Contemporary Literary Renaissance, ed. Joanne M. Braxton and Andree Nicola McLaughlin. New Brunswick, N.J.: Rutgers University Press.

Brecher, Jeremy. 1972. *Strike: The True History of Mass Insurgency From 1877 to the Present*. San Francisco: Straight Arrow.

Breines, Wini. 1992. *Young, White, and Miserable: Growing Up Female in the Fifties*. Boston: Beacon.

Brettschneider, Marla. 1996a. *Cornerstones of Peace: Jewish Identity Politics and Democratic Theory*. New Brunswick, N.J.: Rutgers University Press.

————. 1996b. *The Narrow Bridge: Jewish Views on Multiculturalism*. New Brunswick, N.J.: Rutgers University Press.

Brodkin, Karen. 1998. "Motherhood Is Not an Entry-Level Job." In *The Family Track*, edited by Constance Coiner and Diana Hume George. Urbana: University of Illinois Press.

Brody, David. 1960. *Steelworkers in America: The Nonunion Era*. New York: Harper Torchbooks.

————. 1980. *Workers in Industrial America: Essays on the Twentieth Century Struggle*. New York: Oxford University Press.

Brody, Jennifer Devere. 1996. "Rereading Race and Gender: When White Women Matter." *American Quarterly* 48, 1:153–160.

Brown, Elsa Barkley. 1989. "Mothers of Mind." *Sage* 6, 1: 4–11.

Brown, Francis J. 1946. *Educational Opportunities for Veterans*. Washington, D.C.: Public Affairs Press, American Council on Public Affairs.

Brown, Kathleen M. 1996. *Good Wives, Nasty Wenches and Anxious Patriarchs: Gender, Race and Power in Colonial Virginia*. Chapel Hill: University of North Carolina Press.

Brundage, David T. 1994. *The Making of Western Labor Radicalism: Denver's Organized Workers, 1878–1905*. Urbana: University of Illinois Press.

Buhle, Paul. 1980. "Jews and American Communism: The Cultural Question." *Radical History Review* 23 (spring):9–33.

Bullard, Robert D., J. Eugene Grigsby III, and Charles Lee, eds. 1994. *Residential Apartheid: The American Legacy*. Los Angeles: Center for Afro-American Studies, University of California.

Byington, Margaret. 1974 [1910]. *Homestead: The Households of a Mill Town*. Pittsburgh: University Center for International Studies.

Cade, Toni, ed. 1970. *The Black Woman: An Anthology*. New York: New American Library.

Cameron, Ardis. 1985. "Bread and Roses Revisited: Women's Culture and Working-Class Activism in the Lawrence Strike of 1912." In *Women, Work and Protest*, ed. Ruth Milkman. Boston: Routledge and Kegan Paul, 42–61.

————. 1993. *Radicals of the Worst Sort: Laboring Women in Lawrence, Massachusetts, 1860–1912*. Urbana: University of Illinois Press.

Cantarow, Ellen, and Sharon O'Malley. 1980. "Ella Baker: Organizing for Civil Rights." In *Moving the Mountain: Women Working for Social Change*, ed. Ellen Cantarow. Old Westbury, N.Y.: The Feminist Press.

Cantor, Milton. 1978. *The Divided Left: American Radicalism 1900–1975*. New York: Hill and Wang.

Carby, Hazel. 1982. "White Woman Listen." In *The Empire Strikes Back: Race and Racism in 70s Britain*. Centre for Contemporary Cultural Studies. London: Hutchinson.

————. 1987. *Reconstructing Womanhood: The Emergence of the Afro-American Woman Novelist.* New York: Oxford University Press.

Carlson, Lewis H., and George A. Colburn. 1972. *In Their Place: White America Defines Her Minorities, 1850–1950.* New York: Wiley.

Carpenter, Niles. 1927. *Immigrants and Their Children 1920: A Study Based on Census Statistics Relative to the Foreign Born and the Native White of Foreign or Mixed Parentage.* Census Monographs 7. Washington, D.C.: U.S. Government Printing Office.

Carson, Clayborne. 1981. *In Struggle: SNCC and the Black Awakening of the Nineteen Sixties.* Cambridge, Mass.: Harvard University Press.

Carter, Susan B., and Michael Carter. 1981. "Women's Recent Progress in the Professions, or Women Get a Ticket to Ride after the Gravy Train Has Left the Station." *Feminist Studies* 7, 477–504.

Castles, Stephen. 1996. "The Racisms of Globalization." In E. Vasta and S. Castles 1996, 17–45.

Chafe, William. 1981. *Civilities and Civil Rights: Greensboro, North Carolina and the Black Struggle for Freedom.* New York: Oxford University Press.

Chan, Sucheng. 1991. *Asian Americans: An Interpretive History.* Boston: Twayne Publishers.

Chateauvert, Melinda. 1994. "A Response to 'Gender, Race, and Rights'." *Journal of Women's History* 6, 2:125–132.

Cheng, Lucie, and Edna Bonacich. 1984. "Introduction" to *Labor Immigration under Capitalism.* Berkeley: University of California Press, 1–56.

Christian, Barbara. 1988. "The Race for Theory." *Feminist Studies* 14, 1 (spring):7–80.

Cockcroft, Eva. 1990. *Signs from the Heart: California Chicano Murals.* Venice, Calif.: Social and Public Art Resource Center.

Cohen, Steven M. 1988. *American Assimilation or Jewish Revival?* Bloomington: Indiana University Press.

Collins, Patricia Hill. 1987. "The Meaning of Motherhood in Black Culture and Black Mother-Daughter Relationships." *Sage* 4, 2:3–10.

————. 1989. "The Social Construction of Black Feminist Thought." *Signs* 14, 4:745–773.

————. 1990. *Black Feminist Thought.* New York: Unwin Hyman.

Cook, Melanie B. 1988. "Gloria Richardson: Her Life and Work in SNCC." *Sage,* student supplement, 51–53.

Coontz, Stephanie. 1988. *The Social Origins of Private Life: A History of American Families 1600–1900.* New York: Verso.

————. 1992. *The Way We Never Were.* New York: Basic Books.

Cooper, Patricia A. 1987. *Once a Cigar Maker: Men, Women, and Work Culture in American Cigar Factories, 1900–1919.* Urbana: University of Illinois Press.

————. 1989. "Recasting Labor History: A Response to Philip Scranton." *International Labor and Working-Class History* 35 (spring):23–30.

Cornford, Daniel, ed. 1995. *Working People of California.* Berkeley: University of California Press.

Crenshaw, Kimberle Williams. 1988. "Race, Reform, and Retrenchment: Transformation and Legitimation in Antidiscrimination Law." *Harvard Law Review* 101: 1331–1387.

————, and Toni Morrison, eds. 1992. *Race-ing Justice, En-gendering Power: Essays on Anita Hill, Clarence Thomas and the Construction of Social Reality.* New York: Pantheon Books.

Dalfiume, Richard M. 1969. *Desegregation of the U.S. Armed Forces: Fighting on Two Fronts, 1939–1953*. Columbia: University of Missouri Press.

Darden, Joe T. 1993. "African American Residential Segregation: An Examination of Race and Class in Metropolitan Detroit." In Massey and Denton 1993, 82–94.

Davidson, Basil. 1961. *Black Mother: The Years of the African Slave Trade*. Boston: Little, Brown.

Davis, Angela Y. 1981. *Women, Race and Class*. New York: Random House.

Davis, Mike. 1990. *City of Quartz*. London: Verso.

Delgado, Richard, and Jeanne Stefancic, eds. 1997. *Critical White Studies: Looking Behind the Mirror*. Philadelphia: Temple University Press.

diLeonardo, Micaela. 1984. *The Varieties of Ethnic Experience: Kinship, Class and Gender Among California Italian Americans*. Ithaca: Cornell University Press.

———. 1992. "White Lies, Black Myths: Rape, Race, and the Black 'Underclass'." *Village Voice* (22 September).

Dill, Bonnie Thornton. 1979. "The Dialectics of Black Womanhood." *Signs* 4, 543–555.

Diner, Hasia. 1977. *In the Almost Promised Land: American Jews and Blacks, 1915–1935*. Westport, Conn.: Greenwood Press.

Dinnerstein, Leonard. 1987. *Uneasy at Home: Anti-Semitism and the American Jewish Experience*. New York: Columbia University Press.

———. 1994. *Anti-Semitism in America*. New York: Oxford University Press.

Dobriner, William. M. 1963. *Class in Suburbia*. Englewood Cliffs, N.J.: Prentice-Hall.

Dominguez, Virginia R. 1986. *White by Definition: Social Classification in Creole Louisiana*. New Brunswick, N.J.: Rutgers University Press.

———. 1993. "Questioning Jews." *American Ethnologist* 20, 3:618–624.

———. 1994. "A Taste for 'the Other': Intellectual Complicity in Racializing Practices." *Current Anthropology* 35, 4:333–348.

Dublin, Thomas. 1979. *Women at Work*. New York: Columbia University Press.

Dubofsky, Melvyn. 1988. *We Shall Be All: A History of the Industrial Workers of the World*. 2d ed. Urbana: University of Illinois Press.

Du Bois, W.E.B. 1903. *The Souls of Black Folk*. Chicago: A. C. McClurg and Company.

———. 1935. *Black Reconstruction in America, 1860–1880*. New York: Harcourt, Brace, and Company.

Eckler, A. Ross, and Jack Zlotnick. 1949. "Immigration and the Labor Force." In *Reappraising our Immigration Policy*, edited by Hugh Carter, 92–101. Philadelphia: The Annals of the American Academy of Political and Social Science.

Edelman, Marc. 1996. "Devil, Not-Quite-White, Rootless Cosmopolitan: Tsuris in Latin America, the Bronx, and the USSR." In *Composing Ethnography: Alternative Forms of Qualitative Writing*, eds. Carolyn Ellis and Arthur Bochner. Walnut Creek, Calif.: Altamira Press.

Edwards, Richard. 1979. *Contested Terrain: The Transformation of the Workplace in the Twentieth Century*. New York: Basic Books.

———, Michael Reich, and T. Weisskkopf, eds. 1972. *The Capitalist System*. Englewood Cliffs, N.J.: Prentice-Hall.

Ehrenreich, Barbara. 1983. *The Hearts of Men: American Dreams and the Flight from Commitment*. Garden City, N.Y.: Anchor Press.

———, and Deirdre English. 1973. *Complaints and Disorders*. Old Westbury, N.Y.: The Feminist Press.

————, and Dierdre English. 1978. *For Her Own Good*. New York: Pantheon.

Ehrlich, Judith Ramsey, and Barry J. Rehfeld. 1989. *The New Crowd: The Changing of the Jewish Guard on Wall Street*. Boston: Little, Brown.

Eichler, Ned. 1982. *The Merchant Builders*. Cambridge, Mass.: MIT Press.

Eisenstein, Sarah. 1983. *Give Us Bread, But Give Us Roses Too*. Boston: Routledge and Kegan Paul.

Eisenstein, Zillah, ed. 1979. *Capitalist Patriarchy and the Case for Socialist Feminism*. New York: Monthly Review Press.

Epstein, Melech. 1969 [1950]. *Jewish Labor in the USA: An Industrial, Political and Cultural History of the Jewish Labor Movement, 1882–1914*. 2 vols. in one. New York: KTAV Publishing House, Inc.

Ernst, Robert. 1949. *Immigrant Life in New York City*. New York: King's Crown Press.

Evans, Sara. 1980. *Personal Politics: The Roots of Women's Liberation in the Civil Rights Movement and the New Left*. New York: Vintage.

Ewen, Elizabeth. 1985. *Immigrant Women in the Land of Dollars: Life and Culture on the Lower East Side, 1890–1925*. New York: Monthly Review Press.

Feagin, Joe R. 1994. "A House is Not a Home: White Racism and U.S. Housing Practices." In Massey and Denton 1993, 17–48.

Feldberg, Roslyn, and Evelyn Nakano Glenn. 1983. "Technology and Work Degradation: Effects of Office Automation on Women Clerical Workers." In *Machina ex Dea: Feminist Perspectives on Technology*, ed. J. Rothschild. New York: Pergamon, 59–78.

Fields, Barbara Jean. 1982. "Ideology and Race in American History." In *Region, Race, and Reconstruction: Essays in Honor of C. Vann Woodward*, ed. J. Morgan Kousser and James M. McPherson. New York: Oxford University Press, 143–177.

————. 1990. "Slavery, Race and Ideology in the United States of America." *New Left Review* 181: 95–118.

Fikes, Kesha. 1999. "Domesticity in Black and White: Assessing Badia Defiances to Portugese Ideals of Black Womanhood." *Transforming Anthropology* 8, 1.

Fine, Michelle, Lois Weis, Linda C. Powell, and L. Mun Wong, eds. 1997. *Off White: Readings on Race, Power, and Society*. New York: Routledge.

Fink, Leon. 1994. *In Search of the Working Class*. Urbana: University of Illinois Press.

Fisher, Berenice, and Joan Tronto. 1990. "Toward a Feminist Theory of Caring." In *Circles of Care*, ed. Emily K. Abel and Margaret K. Nelson. Albany: SUNY Press, 35–62.

Fishkin, Shelley Fisher. 1995. "Interrogating 'Whiteness,' Complicating 'Blackness': Remapping American Culture." *American Quarterly* 47, 3:428–467.

Fishman, Sylvia Barack. 1998. "Our Mothers and Our Sisters and Our Cousins and Our Aunts: Dialogues and Dynamics in Literature and Film." In Antler 1998, 153–170.

Foley, Neil. 1996. "Mexican Americans and the Faustian Pact with Whiteness in the Southwest, 1920–1960." Paper presented at the annual meeting of the American Studies Association (November).

Foner, Jack. 1974. *Blacks and the Military in American History: A New Perspective*. New York: Praeger Publishers.

Frank, Dana. 1985. "Housewives, Socialists, and the Politics of Food: The 1917 Cost of Living Protests." *Feminist Studies* 11, 2:255–285.

Frank, Gelya. 1997. "Jews, Multiculturalism and Boasian Anthropology: Ambiguous Whites and the Founding of an Anti-Racist Science." *American Anthropologist* 99, 4:731–745.

Frankel, Linda. 1984. "Southern Textile Women: Generations of Struggle and Survival." In Sacks and Remy 1984, 39–60.

Frankenberg, Ruth. 1993. *White Women, Race Matters: The Social Construction of Whiteness*. Minneapolis: University of Minnesota Press.

Friedan, Betty. 1963. *The Feminine Mystique*. New York: W. W. Norton.

Friedman, Lester D. 1987. *The Jewish Image in American Film*. Secaucus, N.J.: Citadel Press.

———. 1991. "Celluloid Palimpsests: An Overview of Ethnicity and the American Film." In *Unspeakable Images: Ethnicity and the American Cinema*, ed. Friedman, 11–38. Urbana: University of Illinois Press.

Gabler, Neal. 1988. *An Empire of Their Own: How the Jews Invented Hollywood*. New York: Anchor.

Gans, Herbert. 1962. *The Urban Villagers*. New York: Free Press of Glencoe.

———. 1967. *The Levittowners*. New York: Pantheon.

Gelfand, Mark. 1975. *A Nation of Cities: The Federal Government and Urban America, 1933–1965*. New York: Oxford University Press.

Gerber, David, ed. 1986. *Anti-Semitism in American History*. Urbana: University of Illinois Press.

Giddings, Paula. 1984. *When and Where I Enter*. New York: Bantam.

Gilkes, Cheryl. 1988. "Building in Many Places: Multiple Commitments and Ideologies in Black Women's Community Work." In Bookman and Morgen 1988, 53–76.

Gilman, Sander. 1991. *The Jew's Body*. New York and London: Routledge.

———. 1996. *Smart Jews: The Construction of the Image of Jewish Superior Intelligence*. Lincoln: University of Nebraska Press.

Gilroy, Paul. 1993. *The Black Atlantic: Modernity and Double Consciousness*. New York and London: Verso.

Ginsberg, Benjamin. 1993. *The Fatal Embrace: Jews and the State*. Chicago: University of Chicago Press.

Gittler, Joseph B. 1981. *Jewish Life in the United States: Perspectives from the Social Sciences*. New York: New York University Press.

Glazer, Nathan. 1967 [1964]. "Negroes and Jews: The New Challenge to Pluralism." In *The Commentary Reader*, 388–398. New York: Atheneum.

———. 1987. *Affirmative Discrimination: Ethnic Inequality and Public Policy*. Cambridge, Mass.: Harvard University Press.

———. 1997. *We Are All Multiculturalists Now*. Cambridge, Mass.: Harvard University Press.

———, and Daniel Patrick Moynihan. 1963. *Beyond the Melting Pot*. Cambridge, Mass.: M.I.T. Press.

Glenn, Evelyn Nakano. 1985. "Racial Ethnic Women's Labor." *Review of Radical Political Economics* 17, 3:86–108.

———. 1987. *Issei, Nissei, War Bride: Three Generations of Japanese American Women in Domestic Service*. Philadelphia: Temple University Press.

———. 1994. "Social Constructions of Mothering: A Thematic Introduction." In Glenn, Chang, and Forcey 1994, 1–29.

———, and Roslyn Feldberg. 1977. "Degraded and Deskilled: The Proletarianization of Clerical Work." *Social Problems* 25, 1:520–564.

————, Grace Chang, and Linda Rennie Forcey. 1994. *Mothering: Ideology, Experience and Agency*. New York: Routledge.

Glenn, Susan. 1990. *Daughters of the Shtetl: Life and Labor in the Immigrant Generation*. Ithaca: Cornell University Press.

Goldberg, David J. 1989. *A Tale of Three Cities: Labor Organization and Protest in Paterson, Passaic, and Lawrence, 1916–1921*. New Brunswick, N.J.: Rutgers University Press.

Goldberg, Robert Alan. 1986. *Back to the Soil: The Jewish Farmers of Clarion, Utah, and Their World*. Salt Lake City: University of Utah Press.

Goldscheider, Calvin. 1986. *Jewish Continuity and Change: Emerging Patterns in America*. Bloomington: Indiana University Press.

————, and Goldstein, S. 1985. *Jewish Americans: Three Generations in a Jewish Community*. Bloomington: Indiana University Press.

Gordon, Albert I. 1959. *Jews in Suburbia*. Boston: Beacon Press.

Gordon, Linda. 1994. *Pitied but Not Entitled: Single Mothers and the History of Welfare, 1890–1935*. New York: The Free Press.

Gordon, Milton. 1964. *Assimilation in American Life: The Role of Race, Religion and National Origins*. New York: Oxford University Press.

Gorenstein, Arthur. 1960. "A Portrait of Ethnic Politics: The Socialists and the 1908 and 1910 Congressional Elections on the East Side." *Publications of the American Jewish Historical Society* 50: 202–238.

Gould, Stephen J. 1981. *The Mismeasure of Man*. New York: Norton.

Grant, David M, Melvin L. Oliver, and Angela D. James. 1996. "African Americans: Social and Economic Bifurcation." In *Ethnic Los Angeles*, ed. R. Waldinger and M. Bozorgmehr, 379–413. New York: Russell Sage Foundation.

Grant, Madison. 1916. *The Passing of the Great Race: Or the Racial Basis of European History*. New York: Charles Scribner.

Green, M., and B. Carter. 1988. "'Races' and 'Race-makers': The Politics of Racialization. *Sage Race Relations Abstracts* 13, 2:4–29.

Green, Venus. 1995. "Race and Technology: African American Women in the Bell System, 1945–1980." *Technology and Culture* supplement to 36, 2:S101–S143.

Greer, Scott. 1965. *Urban Renewal and American Cities*. Indianapolis: Bobbs-Merrill.

Gregory, Steven. 1992. "The Changing Significance of Race and Class in an African-American Community." *American Ethnologist* 19, 2:255–274.

————, and Roger Sanjek, eds. 1994. *Race*. New Brunswick, N.J.: Rutgers University Press.

Gutman, Herbert. 1976. *Work, Culture, and Society in Industrializing America*. New York: Vintage.

Guttmann, Allen. 1971. *The Jewish Writer in America: Assimilation and the Crisis of Identity*. New York: Oxford University Press.

Hacker, Sally. 1979. "Sex Stratification, Technology and Organizational Change: A Longitudinal Case Study of AT&T." *Social Problems* 26, 5:539–557.

Hall, Jacqueline D. 1979. *Revolt Against Chivalry: Jessie Daniel Ames and the Women's Campaign Against Lynching*. New York: Columbia University Press.

————. 1987. "Disorderly Women: Gender and Labor Militancy in the Appalachian South." *Journal of American History* 73, 2:354–382.

————, J. Leloudis, R. Korstad, M. Murphy, L. Jones, and C. Daly. 1987. *Like a Family: The Making of a Southern Cotton Mill World*. Chapel Hill: University of North Carolina Press.

Handlin, Oscar. 1952. "Party Maneuvers and Civil Rights Realities." *Commentary* 14, 3:197–205.

Haney Lopez, Ian F. 1996. *White by Law: The Legal Construction of Race*. New York: New York University Press.

Harding, Sandra. 1991. *Whose Science? Whose Knowledge?* Ithaca, N.Y.: Cornell University Press.

———, ed. 1993. *The Racial Economy of Science: Toward a Democratic Future*. Bloomington: Indiana University Press.

Harney, Robert F. 1985. "Italophobia. English-speaking Malady?" *Studi Emigrazione/Etudes Migrations*, 22, 77:6–43.

Harper's Weekly. 1902. "Secretary Hay's Note and the Jewish Question" (11 October), 1447.

Harris, Cheryl I. 1995. "Whiteness as Property." In *Critical Race Theory: The Key Writings That Formed the Movement*, ed. Kimberlé Crenshaw, Neil Gotanda, Gary Peller, and Kendall Thomas. New York: The New Press.

Harrison, Faye V. 1992. "The Du Boisian Legacy in Anthropology." *Critique of Anthropology* 12, 3:239–260.

———. 1995. "The Persistent Power of 'Race' in the Cultural and Political Economy of Racism." *Annual Reviews in Anthropology* 24, 47–74.

———, and Donald Nonini, eds. 1992. "Introduction." Special issue on W.E.B. Du Bois and anthropology. *Critique of Anthropology* 12, 3:229–237.

Harrowitz, Nancy A., and Barbara Hyams. 1995. *Jews and Gender: Responses to Otto Weininger*. Philadelphia: Temple University Press.

Hartman, Chester. 1975. *Housing and Social Policy*. Englewood Cliffs, N.J.: Prentice-Hall.

Havighurst, Robert J., John W. Baughman, Walter H. Eaton, and Ernest W. Burgess. 1951. *The American Veteran Back Home: A Study of Veteran Readjustment*. New York: Longmans, Green and Co.

Herman, Felicia. 1998. "The Way She *Really* Is: Images of Jews and Women in the Films of Barbra Streisand." In Antler 1998, 171–190.

Higginbotham, Evelyn Brooks. 1992. "African-American Women's History and the Metalanguage of Race." *Signs* 17, 2:251–274.

Higham, John. 1955. *Strangers in the Land*. New Brunswick, N.J.: Rutgers University Press.

———. 1975. *Send These to Me: Jews and Other Immigrants in Urban America*. New York: Atheneum.

Hill, Herbert. 1996. "Black-Jewish Conflict in the Labor Context: Race, Jobs and Institutional Power." In Ignatiev and Garvey 1996, 215–246.

Hobsbawm, Eric, and Terence Ranger, eds. 1983. *The Invention of Tradition*. New York: Cambridge University Press.

Hondagneu-Sotelo, Pierrette. 1994. *Gendered Transitions: Mexican Experiences of Immigration*. Berkeley: University of California Press.

———. 1995. "Women and Children First: New Directions in Anti-Immigrant Politics." *Socialist Review* 25, 1:169–190.

hooks, bell. 1989. *Talking Back*. Boston: South End Press.

Horne, Gerald. 1996. "Black, White, and Red: Jewish and African Americans in the Communist Party." In Brettschneider 1996b, 123–135.

Horowitz, Bethamie, and Jeffrey R. Solomon. 1992. "Why Is This City Different From Other Cities? New York and the 1990 National Jewish Population Survey." *Journal of Jewish Communal Service* 68, 4 (summer):312–320.

Horowitz, Daniel. 1996. "Rethinking Betty Friedan and The Feminine Mystique: Labor Union Radicalism and Feminism in Cold War America." *American Quarterly* 48, 1:1–42.

Horowitz, Sara. 1994. "Jewish Studies as Oppositional? or Mighty Lonely Out There." In *Styles of Jewish Activism*, ed. Philip Goldstein, 152–164. Newark: University of Delaware Press.

Howe, Irving. 1980. *World of Our Fathers*. Abridged edition. New York: Bantam.

Hurd, Charles. 1946. *The Veterans' Program: A Complete Guide to Its Benefits, Rights and Options*. New York: McGraw-Hill Book Company.

Hyman, Paula E. 1980. "Immigrant Women and Consumer Protest: The New York City Kosher Meat Boycott of 1902." *American Jewish History* 70, 91–105.

———. 1995. *Gender and Assimilation in Modern Jewish History: The Roles and Representations of Women*. Seattle: University of Washington Press.

Ignatiev, Noel. 1995. *How the Irish Became White*. Cambridge, Mass.: Harvard University Press.

———, and John Garvey, eds. 1996. *Race Traitor*. New York: Routledge.

Jackson, Kenneth T. 1985. *Crabgrass Frontier: The Suburbanization of the United States*. New York: Oxford University Press.

James, C.L.R. 1963. *The Black Jacobins*. New York: Vintage.

Jewell, K. Sue. 1993. *From Mammy to Miss America and Beyond: Cultural Images and the Shaping of U.S. Social Policy*. New York: Routledge.

Jiobu, Robert M. 1988. *Ethnicity and Assimilation*. Albany: SUNY Press.

Joel, Judith. 1984. "Anthropology and the Demystification of Racism." In Berlowitz and Edari 1984, 39–49.

Johnson, Jesse J. 1967. *Ebony Brass: An Autobiography of Negro Frustration Amid Aspiration*. New York: The William Frederick Press.

Jones, Jacqueline. 1985. *Labor of Love, Labor of Sorrow*. New York: Basic Books.

———. 1992. *The Dispossessed*. New York: Basic Books.

Jordan, Winthrop. 1968. *White Over Black: American Attitudes Toward the Negro*. Chapel Hill: University of North Carolina Press.

———. 1974. *The White Man's Burden: Historical Origins of Racism in the U.S.* New York.: Oxford University Press.

Jordanova, Ludmila. 1981. "Natural Facts: A Historical Perspective on Science and Sexuality." In *Nature, Culture, and Gender*, ed. C. MacCormack and M. Strathern, 42–69. Cambridge, U.K. and New York: Cambridge University Press.

Junne, George. 1988. "Black Women on AFDC and the Struggle for Higher Education." *Frontiers* 10, 2:39–44.

Kahan, Arcadius. 1981. "Jewish Life in the United States: Perspectives from Economics." In Gittler 1981, 237–270.

Kallen, Horace M. *Culture and Democracy in the United States*. New York: Boni and Liveright.

Kann, Kenneth. 1993. *Comrades and Chicken Ranchers: The Story of a California Jewish Community*. Ithaca, N.Y.: Cornell University Press.

Kaplan, Temma. 1982. "Female Consciousness and Collective Action: The Case of Barcelona, 1910–1918." *Signs* 7, 3:545–567.

Karabel, Jerome. 1984. "Status-Group Struggle, Organizational Interests, and the Limits of Institutional Autonomy." *Theory and Society* 13, 1–40.

Katznelson, Ira. 1981. *City Trenches: Urban Politics and the Patterning of Class in the United States*. New York: Pantheon Books.

Kauffman, Deborah R. 1991. *Rachel's Daughters: Newly Orthodox Jewish Women*. New Brunswick, N.J.: Rutgers University Press.

Kaye/Kantrowitz, Melanie. 1996. "Stayed on Freedom: Jew in the Civil Rights Movement and After." In Brettschneider 1996b, 105–122. New Brunswick, N.J.: Rutgers University Press.

Keller, John F. 1983. "The Division of Labor in Electronics." In Nash and Fernandez-Kelly 1983, 346–373.

Kelley, Robin D. G. 1990. *Hammer and Hoe*. Chapel Hill: University of North Carolina Press.

———. 1997. *Yo' Mama's disfunktional!: Fighting the Culture Wars in Urban America*. Boston: Beacon Press.

Kerber, Linda K. 1986. *Women of the Republic: Intellectuals and Ideology in Revolutionary America*. New York: W. W. Norton.

———. 1995. "A Constitutional Right to Be Treated Like American Ladies: Women and the Obligations of Citizenship." In *U.S. History as Women's History: New Feminist Essays*, eds. Linda K. Kerber, Alice Kessler-Harris, and Kathryn Kish Sklar. Chapel Hill: University of North Carolina Press.

Kessler-Harris, Alice. 1976. "Organizing the Unorganizable: Three Jewish Women and Their Union." *Labor History* 17, 1:5–23.

———. 1982. *Out to Work*. New York: Oxford University Press.

———. 1990. *A Woman's Wage: Historical Meanings and Social Consequences*. Lexington: University Press of Kentucky.

———. 1995. "Designing Women and Old Fools: The Construction of the Social Security Amendments of 1939." In *U.S. History as Women's History: New Feminist Essays*, ed. Linda K. Kerber, Alice Kessler-Harris, and Kathryn Kish Sklar, 87–106. Chapel Hill: University of North Carolina Press.

———, ed. 1979. *The Open Cage: An Anzia Yezierska Collection*. New York: Persea Books.

Kessner, Carole S., ed. 1994. *The "Other" New York Jewish Intellectuals*. New York: New York University Press.

King, Deborah. 1988. "Multiple Jeopardy, Multiple Consciousness: The Context of a Black Feminist Ideology." *Signs* 14, 1:42–72.

Kingsolver, Barbara. 1989. *Holding the Line: Women in the Great Arizona Mine Strike of 1983*. Ithaca, N.Y.: ILR Press.

Kleeblatt, Norman, ed. 1996. *Too Jewish?: Challenging Traditional Identities*. New Brunswick, N.J.: Rutgers University Press.

Kornblum, William. 1974. *Blue Collar Community*. Chicago: University of Chicago Press.

Kosmin, Barry A., and Jeffrey Scheckner. 1992. "Jewish Population in the United States." *Jewish Yearbook* 92, 261–284.

Krickus, Richard. 1976. *Pursuing the American Dream: White Ethnics and the New Populism*. Garden City, N.Y.: Anchor Press.

Kristol, Irving. 1965. "A Few Kind Words for Uncle Tom." *Harpers* 230, 1377:95–103.

———. 1966. "The Negro Today Is Like the Immigrant Yesterday." *New York Times Magazine* (11 September).

Kugelmass, Jack, ed. 1988. *Between Two Worlds: Ethnographic Essays on American Jewry*. Ithaca, N.Y.: Cornell University Press.

Kunzel, Regina. 1994. "White Neurosis, Black Pathology: Constructing Out-of-Wedlock Pregnancy in the Wartime and Postwar United States." In Meyerowitz 1994, 304–334.

Labor History. 1995. Daniel Leab, managing editor. 36, 1 (winter). Tamiment Institute.

Laclau, Ernesto, and Chantal Mouffe. 1991. "Recasting Marxism: Hegemony and New Political Movements." In *Unfinished Business: Twenty Years of Socialist Review*. London: Verso, 53–68.

Ladd-Taylor, Molly. 1994. *Mother-work: Women, Children, Welfare, and the State, 1890–1930*. Urbana: University of Illinois Press.

Ladner, Joyce. 1970. *Tomorrow's Tomorrow*. New York: Doubleday Anchor.

———. 1973. *The Death of White Sociology*. New York: Random House.

Lamphere, Louise. 1987. *From Working Daughters to Working Mothers: Immigrant Women in a New England Industrial Community*. Ithaca, N.Y.: Cornell University Press.

Lauter, Paul. 1996. "Strange Identities and Jewish Politics." In Rubin-Dorsky and Fishkin 1996, 37–46.

Leinenweber, Charles. 1968. "The Class and Ethnic Basis of New York City Socialism 1904–15." *Labor History* 22, 1 (winter):31–56.

Lerner, Gerda. 1969. "The Lady and the Mill Girl." *American Studies* 10, 1–11.

Lerner, Michael. 1993. "Jews Are Not White." *Village Voice* 38 (18 May):33–34.

Letwin, Daniel. 1995. "Interracial Unionism, Gender, and 'Social Equality' in the Alabama Coalfields, 1878–1908." *Journal of Southern History* 61, 3:519–554.

Levine, Naomi, and Martin Hochbaum, eds. 1974. *Poor Jews: An American Awakening*. New Brunswick, N.J.: Transaction Books.

Levitas, Daniel. 1995. "Sleeping with the Enemy: A.D.L. and the Christian Right." *The Nation* (19 June):882–888.

Levy, Peter B. 1994. *The New Left and Labor in the 1960s*. Urbana: University of Illinois Press.

Lewis, David Levering. 1992. "Parallels and Divergences: Assimilationist Strategies of Afro-American and Jewish Elites from 1910 to the Early 1930s." In Salzman et al. 1992, 17–35.

Lieberman, Rhonda. 1996. "Jewish Barbie." In Kleeblatt 1996, 108–114.

Lieberson, Stanley. 1980. *A Piece of the Pie: Blacks and White Immigrants Since 1880*. Berkeley: University of California Press.

Liebman, Arthur. 1979. *Jews and the Left*. New York: John Wiley & Sons.

Lief, Beth J., and Susan Goering. 1987. "The Implementation of the Federal Mandate for Fair Housing." In Tobin 1987, 227–267.

Liggio, Leonard. 1976. "English Origins of Early American Racism." *Radical History Review* 3, 1:1–36.

Light, Ivan, and Edna Bonacich. 1988. *Immigrant Ethnic Entrepreneurs: Koreans in Los Angeles 1965–1982*. Berkeley: University of California Press.

Lipsitz, George. 1995. "The Possessive Investment in Whiteness: Racialized Social Democracy and the 'White' Problem in American Studies." *American Quarterly* 47, 3:369–387.

Lott, Eric. 1993. *Love and Theft: Blackface Minstrelsy and the American Working Class*. New York: Oxford University Press.

Machung, Anne. 1984. "Word Processing: Forward for Business, Backward for Women." In Sacks and Remy 1984, 124–139.

MacKinnon, Catherine. 1987. *Feminism Unmodified: Discourses on Life and Law*. Cambridge, Mass.: Harvard University Press.

MacLean, Nancy. 1982. *The Culture of Resistance: Female Institution-Building in the Ladies Garment Workers' Union 1905–1925*. Occasional Papers in Women's Studies, University of Michigan.

Marable, Manning. 1995. *Beyond Black and White: Transforming African American Politics*. London and New York: Verso.

Markowitz, Ruth Jacknow. 1993. *My Daughter, the Teacher: Jewish Teachers in the New York City Schools*. New Brunswick, N.J.: Rutgers University Press.

Martin, Emily. 1987. *The Woman in the Body*. Boston: Beacon.

Martyn, Byron Curti. 1979. *Racism in the U.S.: A History of Anti-Miscegenation Legislation and Litigation*. 3 vols. Ph.D. dissertation, University of Southern California.

Marx, Karl. 1978 [1843]. "On the Jewish Question." In *The Marx-Engels Reader*, 2d edition., ed. Robert C. Tucker, 26–52. New York: W. W. Norton.

Massarik, Fred, and Alvin Cherkin. 1973. "United States National Jewish Population Study." In *American Jewish Year Book 1973*, 74:264–316. New York: The American Jewish Committee.

Massey, Douglas S., and Nancy Denton. 1987. "Trends in the Residential Segregation of Blacks, Hispanics and Asians 1970–80." *American Sociological Review* 52 (December):802–825.

———. 1993. *American Apartheid: Segregation and the Making of the Underclass*. Cambridge, Mass.: Harvard University Press.

May, Elaine Tyler. 1989. *Homeward Bound: American Families in the Cold War Era*. New York: Basic Books.

Medina, Laurie Kroshus. 1999. "Ethnic Mobilization among Workers in Belize: A Class 'Politics of Difference.'" *Transforming Anthropology* 8, 1.

Mendelsohn, Ezra. 1976. "The Russian Roots of the American Jewish Labor Movement." *YIVO Annual of Jewish Social Science* 5, 16:150–177.

Meyerowitz, Joanne J. 1988. *Women Adrift: Independent Wage Earners in Chicago, 1880–1930*. Chicago: University of Chicago Press.

———. 1994. *Not June Cleaver: Women and Gender in Postwar America, 1945–1969*. Philadelphia: Temple University Press.

Milkman, Ruth. 1987. *Gender at Work: The Dynamics of Job Segregation by Sex During World War II*. Urbana: University of Illinois Press.

Miller, Marc Scott. 1988. *The Irony of Victory: World War II and Lowell, Massachusetts*. Urbana: University of Illinois Press.

Mink, Gwendolyn. 1995. *The Wages of Motherhood: Inequality in the Welfare State, 1917–1942*. Ithaca, N.Y.: Cornell University Press.

Mintz, Steven, and Susan Kellogg. 1988. *Domestic Revolutions: A Social History of American Family Life*. New York: The Free Press.

Mohanty, Chandra Talpade, Ann Russo, and Lourdes Torres, eds. 1991. *Third World Women and the Politics of Feminism*. Bloomington: Indiana University Press.

Monkkonen, Eric H. 1988. *America Becomes Urban*. Berkeley: University of California Press.

Montgomery, David. 1979. *Workers' Control in America*. Cambridge, U.K., and New York: Cambridge University Press.

———. 1987. *The Fall of the House of Labor: 1865–1925*. Cambridge, U.K., and New York: Cambridge University Press.

———. 1993. *Citizen Worker: The Experience of Workers in the United States with Democracy and the Free Market during the Nineteenth Century*. Cambridge, U.K., and New York: Cambridge University Press.

Moore, Deborah Dash. 1981. *At Home in America: Second Generation New York Jews*. New York: Columbia University Press.

———. 1992. "On the Fringes of the City: Jewish Neighborhoods in Three Boroughs." In *The Landscape of Modernity: Essays on New York City, 1900–1940*, ed. David Ward and Olivier Zunz. New York: Russell Sage Foundation.

Moraga, Cherríe, and Gloria Anzaldúa. 1983. *This Bridge Called My Back: Radical Writings by Women of Color*. New York: Kitchen Table Press.

Morrison, Toni. 1988. "Unspeakable Things Unspoken: The Afro-American Presence in American Literature." *Michigan Quarterly Review* 28, 1:1–34.

———. 1990. *Playing in the Dark: Whiteness and the Literary Imagination*. New York: Vintage.

———. 1993. "On the Backs of Blacks." *Time* 142, 21:57.

Morsy, Soheir A. 1994. "Beyond the Honorary 'White' Classifications of Egyptians: Societal Identity in Historical Context." In Gregory and Sanjek 1994, 175–198.

Mosch, Theodore R. 1975. *The GI Bill: A Breakthrough in Educational and Social Policy in the United States*. Hicksville, N.Y.: Exposition Press.

Moynihan, Daniel P. 1965. *The Negro Family: The Case for National Action*. Washington, D.C.: U.S. Government Printing Office.

Mullings, Leith. 1984. "Ethnicity and Stratification in the Urban United States." In Berlowitz and Edari 1984, 21–38.

———. 1997. *On Our Own Terms: Race, Class and Gender in the Lives of African American Women*. New York: Routledge.

Murphree, Mary C. 1984. "Brave New Office: The Changing World of the Legal Secretary." In Sacks and Remy 1984, 140–159.

Naison, Mark. 1983. *Communists in Harlem During the Depression*. New York: Grove Press.

Nalty, Bernard C., and Morris J. MacGregor, eds. 1981. *Blacks in the Military: Essential Documents*. Wilmington. Del.: Scholarly Resources, Inc.

Naples, Nancy. 1991. "Contradictions in the Gender Subtext of the War on Poverty: The Community Work and Resistance of Women from Low-Income Communities." *Social Problems* 38, 3:316–332.

———. 1994. "Contradictions in Agrarian Ideology: Restructuring Gender, Race-Ethnicity, and Class." *Rural Sociology* 59, 1:110–135.

———. 1997. "The 'New Consensus' on the Gendered 'Social Contract': The 1987–1988 U.S. Congressional Hearings on Welfare Reform." *Signs* 22, 4:907–946.

Nash, Gary B. 1986. *Race, Class and Politics: Essays on American Colonial and Revolutionary Society*. Urbana: University of Illinois Press.

———, Julie Roy Jeffrey, John R. Howe, Allen F. Davis, Peter J. Frederick, and Allen M. Winkler. 1986. *The American People: Creating a Nation and a Society*. New York: Harper and Row.

Nash, June, and Maria Patricia Fernandez-Kelly, eds. 1983. *Women, Men and the International Division of Labor*. Albany, N.Y.: SUNY Press.

Newman, Katherine S. 1988. *Falling from Grace: The Experience of Downward Mobility in the American Middle Class*. New York: The Free Press.

Norwood, Stephen. 1990. *Labor's Flaming Youth: Telephone Operators and Worker Militancy, 1878–1923*. Urbana: University of Illinois Press.

Novick, Paul. 1977. "The Distorted 'World of Our Fathers': A Critique of Irving Howe's Book." New York: Morning Freiheit.

Okonjo, Kamene. 1976. "The Dual Sex Political System in Action." In *Women in Africa*, ed. Nancy Hafkin and Edna Bay. Stanford, Calif.: Stanford University Press, 45–58.

Oliver, Melvin, and Thomas Shapiro. 1995. *Black Wealth/White Wealth: A New Perspective on Racial Inequality*. New York: Routledge.

Omi, Michael, and Howard Winant. 1994. *Racial Formation in the United States from the 1960s to the 1990s*. 2d ed. New York: Routledge and Kegan Paul.

Ong, Paul, and John M. Liu. 1994. "U.S. Immigration Policies and Asian Immigration." In Ong, Bonacich, and Cheng 1994, 45–78.

Ong, Paul, Edna Bonacich, and Lucie Cheng, eds. 1994. *The New Asian Immigration in Los Angeles and Global Restructuring.* Philadelphia: Temple University Press.

Orleck, Annelise. 1995. *Common Sense and a Little Fire: Women and Working-Class Politics in the United States, 1900–1965.* Chapel Hill: University of North Carolina Press.

Page, Helan E. 1997. "The 'Black' Public Sphere in White Public Space: Racialized Information and Hi-Tech Cultural Production in the Global African Diaspora." Paper delivered at the conference on Post-Boasian Studies of Whiteness and Blackness, New York Academy of Sciences (13–14 March).

Palmer, Phyllis. 1989. *Domesticity and Dirt: Housewives and Domestic Servants in the United States, 1920–1945.* Philadelphia: Temple University Press.

Pardo, Mary. 1990. "Mexican-American Women Grassroots Community Activists: 'Mothers of East Los Angeles'." *Frontiers* 11, 1:1–7.

Park, Robert E. 1922. *The Immigrant Press and Its Control.* New York: Harper & Brothers Publishers.

———, and Herbert A. Miller. 1921. *Old World Traits Transplanted.* New York: Harper & Brothers Publishers.

Parr, Joy. 1990. *The Gender of Breadwinners: Women, Men and Change in Two Industrial Towns 1880–1950.* Toronto, Canada: University of Toronto Press.

Patterson, Thomas C. 1997. *Inventing Western Civilization.* New York: Monthly Review Press.

Peiss, Kathy. 1985. *Cheap Amusements: Working Women and Leisure in Turn-of-the-Century New York.* Philadelphia: Temple University Press.

Petchesky, Rosalind P. 1985. *Abortion and Woman's Choice.* Boston: Northeastern University Press.

Podhoretz, Norman. 1992 [1963]. "My Negro Problem—and Ours." In Salzman et al. 1992, 108–117.

Polatnick, M. Rivka. 1996. "Diversity in a Women's Liberation Ideology: How a Black and a White Group of the 1960s Viewed Motherhood." *Signs* 21, 3:679–706.

Pope, Jacqueline. 1989. *Biting the Hand That Feeds Them: Organizing Women on Welfare at the Grass Roots Level.* Westport, Conn.: Greenwood.

Porter, Jack Nusan, and Peter Dreier, eds. 1973. *Jewish Radicalism: A Selected Anthology.* New York: Grove Press.

"Postwar Jobs for Veterans." 1945. *The Annals of the American Academy of Political and Social Science* 238 (March).

Prell, Riv-Ellen. 1990. "Rage and Representation: Jewish Gender Stereotypes in American Culture." In *Uncertain Terms: Negotiating Gender in American Culture*, ed. Faye Ginsburg and Anna Lowenhaupt Tsing. Boston: Beacon, 248–268.

———. 1993. "The Begetting of America's Jews: Seeds of American Jewish Identity in the Representations of American Jewish Women." *Journal of Jewish Communal Service* 699, 2/3 (winter/spring):4–23.

———. 1996. "Why Jewish Princesses Don't Sweat: Desire and Consumption in Postwar American Jewish Culture." In Kleeblatt 1996, 74–92.

———. 1998. "Cinderellas Who (Almost) Never Become Princesses: Subversive Representations of Jewish Women in Postwar Popular Novels." In Antler 1998, 123–138.

Race and Housing: An Interview with Edward P. Eichler, President, Eichler Homes, Inc. 1964. Santa Barbara: Center for the Study of Democratic Institutions.

Rawick, George P. 1972. *From Sundown to Sunup: The Making of the Black Community.* Westport, Conn.: Greenwood.

Reich, Michael. 1981. *Racial Inequality: A Political-Economic Analysis.* Princeton, N.J.: Princeton University Press.

Remy, Dorothy, and Larry Sawers. 1984. "Economic Stagnation and Discrimination." In Sacks and Remy 1984, 95–112.

Rex, John. 1986. *Race and Ethnicity.* Great Britain: Open University Press.

———, and David Rex, eds. 1986. *Theories of Race and Ethnic Relations.* Cambridge, U.K., and New York: Cambridge University Press.

Rich, Adrienne. 1976. *Of Woman Born: Motherhood as Experience and Institution.* New York: Norton.

———. 1983. "Compulsory Heterosexuality and Lesbian Existence." In *Powers of Desire,* edited by Snitow, Stansell, and Thompson. New York: Monthly Review Press, 177–205.

Rieder, Jonathan. 1985. *Canarsie: Jews and Italians of Brooklyn Versus Liberalism.* Cambridge, Mass.: Harvard University Press.

Ripley, William Z. 1923. *The Races of Europe: A Sociological Study.* New York: Appleton.

Rischin, Moses. 1962. *The Promised City: New York's Jews 1870–1914.* Cambridge, Mass.: Harvard University Press.

Rivo, Sharon Pucker. 1998. "Projected Images: Portraits of Jewish Women in Early American Film." In Antler 1998, 30–52.

Robinson, Cedric. 1983. *Black Marxism.* London: Zed.

Robinson, Jo Ann Gibson. 1987. *The Montgomery Bus Boycott and the Women Who Started it: A Memoir of Jo Ann Gibson Robinson.* Edited by David J. Garrow. Knoxville: University of Tennessee Press.

Rodriguez, Sylvia. 1997. "Tourism, Whiteness, and the Vanishing Anglo." Paper presented at the conference "Seeing and Being Seen: Tourism in the American West." Center for the American West, Boulder, Colorado, 2 May.

Roediger, David. 1991. *The Wages of Whiteness: Race and the Making of the American Working Class.* London: Verso.

———. 1994. "Gaining a Hearing for Black-White Unity: Covington Hall and the Complexities of Race, Gender and Class." In *Toward the Abolition of Whiteness: Essays on Race, Politics, and Working Class History,* by D. Roediger, 127–180. London: Verso.

Rogin, Michael. 1996. *Blackface, White Noise: Jewish Immigrants in the Hollywood Melting Pot.* Berkeley: University of California Press.

Rollins, Judith. 1985. *Between Women.* Philadelphia: Temple University Press.

Romero, Mary. 1992. *Maid in the U.S.A.* New York: Routledge.

Rose, Arnold, and Caroline Rose. 1948. *America Divided.* New York: Alfred A. Knopf.

Rose, Arnold M., ed. 1951. *Race Prejudice and Discrimination: Readings in Intergroup Relations in the United States.* New York: Alfred A. Knopf.

Rose, Nancy E. 1993. "Gender, Race and the Welfare State: Government Work Programs from the 1930s to the Present." *Feminist Studies* 19, 2:319–442.

———. 1994. *Put to Work: Relief Programs in the Great Depression.* New York: Monthly Review Press.

———. 1995. *Workfare of Fair Work: Women, Welfare, and Government Work Programs.* New Brunswick, N.J.: Rutgers University Press.

Rose, Peter. 1969. *The Ghetto and Beyond: Essays on Jewish Life in America.* New York: Random House.

Rosenblum, Gerald. 1973. *Immigrant Workers: Their Impact on American Radicalism: Their Impact on American Labor Radicalism.* New York: Basic Books.

Rotundo, Anthony E. 1990. *American Manhood: Transformations in Masculinity from the Revolution to the Modern Era.* New York: Basic Books.

Rubin-Dorsky, Jeffrey, and Shelley Fisher Fishkin, eds. 1996. *People of the Book: Thirty Scholars Reflect on Their Jewish Identity.* Madison: University of Wisconsin Press.

Ruiz, Vicki L. 1987. *Cannery Women Cannery Lives: Mexican Women, Unionization and the California Food Processing Industry, 1930–1950.* Albuquerque: University of New Mexico Press.

Ryan, Joseph A. 1974. *White Ethnics: Their Life in Working Class America.* Englewood Cliffs, N.J.: Prentice-Hall.

Sabel, Charles. 1982. *Work and Politics: The Division of Labor in Industry.* Cambridge, U.K., and New York: Cambridge University Press.

Sacks, Karen Brodkin. 1976: "Class Roots of Feminism." *Monthly Review* 27, 9:28–50.

———. 1978. *Sisters and Wives.* Westport, Conn.: Greenwood Press.

———. 1984. "Generations of Working Class Families." In Sacks and Remy 1984, 15–38.

———. 1988. *Caring by the Hour.* Urbana: University of Illinois Press.

———. 1989. "Toward a Unified Theory of Class, Race and Gender." *American Ethnologist* 16, 3:534–550.

———, and Dorothy Remy, eds. 1984. *My Troubles Are Going to Have Trouble with Me: Everyday Trials and Triumphs of Women Workers.* New Brunswick, N.J.: Rutgers University Press.

Said, Edward. 1979. *Orientalism.* New York: Vintage Books.

Salzman, Jack, with Adina Back and Gretchen Sullivan Sorin, eds. 1992. *Bridges and Boundaries: African Americans and American Jews.* New York: George Braziller.

San Juan, E. Jr. 1992. *Racial Formations/Critical Transformations: Articulations of Power in Ethnic and Racial Studies in the United States.* Atlantic Highlands, N.J.: Humanities Press.

Sanchez, George. 1993. *Becoming Mexican American: Ethnicity, Culture and Identity in Chicano Los Angeles, 1900–1945.* New York: Oxford University Press.

Sanjek, Roger. 1994. "Intermarriage and the Future of Races in the United States." In Gregory and Sanjek 1999, 103–130.

Sansbury, Gail. 1997. "'Dear Senator Capehart:' Letters Sent to the U.S. Senate's 1954 FHA Investigation." *Planning History Studies* 11, 2:19–46.

Sarvasy, Wendy. 1992. "Beyond the Difference versus Equality Debate: Postsuffrage Feminism, Citizenship, and the Quest for a Feminist Welfare State." *Signs* 17, 2:329–362.

Saxton, Alexander. 1971. *The Indispensable Enemy: Labor and the Anti-Chinese Movement in California.* Berkeley: University of California Press.

———. 1977. "Review Essay: Nathan Glazer, Daniel Moynihan and the Cult of Ethnicity." *Amerasia Journal* 4 (summer):141–168.

———. 1990. *The Rise and Fall of the White Republic: Class Politics and Mass Culture in Nineteenth Century America.* London: Verso.

Schappes, Morris. 1973. "Review of Nathan Glazer's *American Judaism.*" *Journal of Ethnic Studies* 1, 95–99.

————. 1978. "Irving Howe's 'World of our Fathers': A Critical Analysis." *Jewish Currents* 32, 1:37 (part 1); 32, 2:31 (part 2).

Schoener, Allon. 1967. *Portal to America: The Lower East Side 1870–1925*. New York: Holt, Rinehart, and Winston.

Segrest, Mab. 1996. "The Souls of White Folks." Paper presented at "The Making and Unmaking of Whiteness: A Conference." University of California at Berkeley, 11–13 (April 1997).

Seligman, Ben B., and Eli E. Cohen. 1950. "The American Jew: Some Demographic Features." and "Economic Status and Occupational Structure." Reprint from the *American Jewish Year Book*, vol. 51.

Seller, Maxine, ed. 1981. *Immigrant Women*. Philadelphia: Temple University Press.

Selznick, Gertrude, and Stephen Steinberg. 1969. *Tenacity of Prejudice: Anti-Semitism in Contemporary America*. New York: Harper & Row.

Showstack, Gerald. 1990. "Perspectives in the Study of American Jewish Ethnicity." *Contemporary Jewry* 11, 1:77–89.

Sifry, Micah. 1993. "Anti-Semitism in America." *The Nation* (25 January), 92–99.

Silberman, Charles E. 1985. *A Certain People: American Jews and Their Lives Today*. New York: Summit Books

Simon, Kate. 1982. *Bronx Primitive: Portraits in a Childhood*. New York: Harper and Row.

Sklare, Marshall. 1971. *America's Jews*. New York: Random House.

————, ed. 1982. *Understanding American Jewry*. New Brunswick, N.J.: Transaction Books.

Sklare, Marshall, and Joseph Greenbaum. 1979. *Jewish Identity on the Suburban Frontier*. 2d edition. Chicago: University of Chicago Press.

Smedley, Audrey. 1993. *Race in North America: Origin and Evolution of a Worldview*. Boulder, Colo.: Westview.

Smith, Dorothy. n.d. "Telling the Truth after Postmodernism." Unpublished paper.

Smith, Judith. 1985. *Family Connections: A History of Italian and Jewish Immigrant Lives in Providence, Rhode Island, 1900–1940*. Albany: SUNY Press.

Smith, M. G. 1982. "Ethnicity and Ethnic Groups in America: The View from Harvard." *Ethnic and Racial Studies* 5, 1–22.

Sochen, June. 1998. "From Sophie Tucker to Barbra Streisand: Jewish Women Entertainers as Reformers." In Antler 1998, 68–84.

Socialist Review. 1990. Special Issue: "Is That All There Is? Reappraising Social Movements." 90, 1:35–150.

Solinger, Rickie. 1992. *Wake Up Little Susie: Single Pregnancy and Race Before Roe v. Wade*. New York: Routledge.

Sorin, Gerald. 1985. *The Prophetic Minority: American Jewish Immigrant Radicals, 1880–1920*. Bloomington: Indiana University Press.

Sowell, Thomas. 1981. *Ethnic America: A History*. New York: Basic Books.

Spencer, Herbert. 1899. *The Principles of Sociology*. 3rd ed. New York: D. Appleton and Company.

Spruill, Julia Cherry. 1938. *Women's Life and Work in the Southern Colonies*. Chapel Hill: University of North Carolina Press.

Squires, Gregory D., ed. 1989. *Unequal Partnerships: The Political Economy of Urban Redevelopment in Postwar America*. New Brunswick, N.J.: Rutgers University Press.

Stansell, Christine. 1986. *City of Women: Sex and Class in New York, 1789–1860*. New York: Alfred A. Knopf.

Steinberg, Stephen. 1974. *The Academic Melting Pot: Catholics and Jews in American Higher Education*. New York: McGraw Hill.

———. 1989. *The Ethnic Myth: Race, Ethnicity and Class in America*. 2d ed. Boston: Beacon Press.

———. 1995. *Turning Back: The Retreat from Racial Justice in American Thought and Policy*. Boston: Beacon Press.

Stoler, Ann. 1989. "Making Empire Respectable." *American Ethnologist* 16, 4:634–652.

Stowe, David. 1996. "Uncolored People: The Rise of Whiteness Studies." *Lingua Franca* 6, 6:68–77.

Strikwerda, Carl, and Camille Guerin-Gonzales. 1993. "Labor, Migration, and Politics." In *The Politics of Immigrant Workers: Labor Activism and Migration in the World Economy since 1830*, edited by Guerin-Gonzales and Strikwerda. New York: Holmes and Meier, 3–48.

Sugrue, Thomas J. 1995. "Crabgrass-Roots Politics: Race, Rights and the Reaction against Liberalism in the Urban North, 1940–1964." *Journal of American History* 82, 2:551–578.

Synott, Marcia Graham. 1986. "Anti-Semitism and American Universities: Did Quotas Follow the Jews?" In *Anti-Semitism in American History*, ed. David A. Gerber. Urbana: University of Illinois Press, 233–274.

Szajkowski, Zosa. 1970. "The Jews and NYC's Mayoralty election of 1917." *Jewish Social Studies* 32, 4:286–306.

Takagi, Paul. 1983. "Asian Communities in the U.S.: A Class Analysis." *Our Socialism* 1 (May):49–55.

Takaki, Ronald. 1989. *Strangers from a Different Shore*. Boston: Little, Brown.

Tax, Meredith. 1980. *The Rising of the Women: Feminist Solidarity and Class Conflict 1880–1917*. New York: Monthly Review Press.

Taylor, Henry Louis Jr. 1995. "The Hidden Face of Racism." *American Quarterly* 47, 3:395–408.

Teres, Harvey M. 1996. *Renewing the Left: Politics, Imagination, and the New York Intellectuals*. New York: Oxford University Press.

Thomas, Laurence Mordekhai. 1996. "The Soul of Identity: Jews and Blacks." In *People of the Book*, ed. S. F. Fishkin and J. Rubin-Dorsky. Madison: University of Wisconsin Press, 169–186.

Thompson, E. P. 1963. *The Making of the English Working Class*. New York: Pantheon Books.

Tobin, Gary A., ed. 1987. *Divided Neighborhoods: Changing Patterns of Racial Segregation*. Beverly Hills, Calif.: Sage Publications.

Tomasky, Michael. 1996. "Reaffirming Our Actions: Maybe It's Time to Shift Affirmative Action into 'Universal Remedy' Programs." *The Nation* 262, 19:21.

Trillin, Calvin. 1969. "Lester Drentluss, A Jewish Boy from Baltimore, Attempts to Make It through the Summer of 1967." In Rose 1969, 495–500.

Trotter, Joe William, ed. 1991. *The Great Migration in Historical Perspective: New Dimensions of Race, Class, and Gender*. Bloomington: Indiana University Press.

Trunk, Isaiah. 1976. "The Cultural Dimension of the American Jewish Labor Movement." *YIVO Annual of Jewish Social Science* 5, 16:342–393.

Twine, France Winddance. 1997. *Racism in a Racial Democracy: The Maintenance of White Supremacy in Brazil*. New Brunswick, N.J.: Rutgers University Press.

U.S. Bureau of the Census. 1930. *Fifteenth Census of the United States*, V.2. Washington, D.C.: U.S. Government Printing Office.

U.S. Bureau of the Census. 1940. *Sixteenth Census of the United States*, V.2. Washington, D.C.: U.S. Government Printing Office.

U.S. Department of Commerce, Bureau of the Census. 1970. Subject Report: *Government Workers*, vol. 2, part 7.

U.S. Immigration Commission. 1911. *Immigrants in Industries*, vol. 8. Washington, D.C.

Urciuoli, Bonnie. 1991. "The Political Topography of Spanish and English: The View from a New York Puerto Rican Neighborhood." *American Ethnologist* 18, 2:295–310.

———. 1994. "Acceptable Difference: The Cultural Evolution of the Model Ethnic American Citizen." *Political and Legal Anthropology Review* 17, 2:19–29.

Vanneman, Reeve, and Lynn Weber Cannon. 1990. *The American Perception of Class*. Philadelphia: Temple University Press.

Vasta, Ellie, and Stephen Castles. 1996. *The Teeth Are Smiling: The Persistence of Racism in Multicultural Australia*. Sydney, Australia: Allen and Unwin.

Vogel, Lise. 1983. *Marxism and the Oppression of Women: Toward a Unitary Theory*. New Brunswick, N.J.: Rutgers University Press.

Walker, Olive. 1970. "The Windsor Hills School Story." *Integrated Education: Race and Schools* 8, 3:4–9.

Ware, Vron. 1992. *Beyond the Pale: White Women, Racism and History*. London and New York: Verso.

Waskow, Arthur I. 1973. "Judaism and Revolution Today." In Porter and Dreier 1973, 11–28.

Weber, Donald. 1998. "The Jewish-American World of Gertrude Berg: *The Goldbergs* on Radio and Television." In Antler 1998, 85–99.

Weinberg, Sydney Stahl. 1988. *The World of Our Mothers: The Lives of Jewish Immigrant Women*. Chapel Hill: University of North Carolina Press.

Weis, Lois. 1990. *Working Class without Work: High School Students in a De-industrializing Economy*. New York: Routledge.

Weiss, Marc A. 1987. *The Rise of the Community Builders: The American Real Estate Industry and Urban Land Planning*. New York: Columbia University Press.

Weisser, Michael R. 1985. *A Brotherhood of Memory: Jewish Landsmanshaftn in the New World*. Ithaca: Cornell University Press.

White, Deborah Gray. 1985. *Ar'n't I a Woman? Female Slaves in the Plantation South*. New York: W. W. Norton.

Willenz, June A. 1983. *Women Veterans: America's Forgotten Heroines*. New York: Continuum.

Williams, Brackette. 1989. "A Class Act: Anthropology and the Race to Nation Across Ethnic Terrian." *Annual Reviews of Anthropology* 18, 401–444.

———. 1996. "Introduction." In *Women Out of Place: The Gender of Agency and the Race of Nationality*, ed. B. F. Williams. New York: Routledge.

Williams, Brett. 1994. "Babies and Banks: The 'Reproductive Underclass' and the Raced, Gendered Masking of Debt." In Gregory and Sanjek 1994, 348–365.

Williams, Eric. 1966. *Capitalism and Slavery*. New York: Capricorn Books.

Williams, Raymond. 1973. *The Country and the City*. London: Chatto and Windus.

Williams, Rhonda M., and Peggie R. Smith. 1990. "What *Else* Do Unions Do?: Race and Gender in Local 35." *Review of Black Political Economy* 18, 3:59–77.

Wilson, William Julius. 1980. *The Declining Significance of Race: Blacks and Changing Institutions*. Chicago: University of Chicago Press.

———. 1987. *The Truly Disadvantaged: The Inner City, the Underclass, and Public Policy*. Chicago: University of Chicago Press.

Wood, Ellen Meiksins. 1986. *The Retreat from Class*. London: Verso.

Wright, Lawrence. 1994. "Annals of Politics: One Drop of Blood." *New Yorker* (25 July), 46–55.

Wynn, Neil A. 1976. *The Afro-American and the Second World War*. London: Paul Elek.

Yezierska, Anzia. 1975. *Bread Givers*. New York: Persea Books.

Zavella, Patricia. 1987. *Women's Work and Chicano Families*. Ithaca, N.Y.: Cornell University Press.

INDEX □

Abel, Emily, 93
abolitionism, 193n.32, 194n.47
abortion, 98
Abrams, Charles, 46
affirmative action
    abolished at University of California, 52
    alumni, children of, admissions preference for, 31, 32
    athletes, college admissions of, 32
    for Euromales, GI Bill as, 27, 38, 42
    of New Deal, 38
    and Bell Telephone, 67
    required for upward mobility, 51
    of 1960s, 38
    vs. meritocracy, 154–55
African Americans
    as agricultural workers, 73, 92, 194–195n.59
    Bell Telephone's policies toward hiring of, 66–67
    and "benign neglect," 200n.18
    and the blues, 126
    media stereotypes, 52. See also stereotypes
    bondsmen as dependents, 80
    double vision, 189n.2
    effect of LA Freeway on, 48
    and ethnic cultures, 153–154
    exclusion of, from industrial jobs, 193n.15
    and Fair Employment Practices Commission, 92
    and forced sterilization, 95
    freedom movement of 1960s, 50
    geographical distribution of, 194n.52
    intermarriage rates, 74–75
    men, stereotypes of, 84
    middle class, 148
    rhythm and blues music, white appropriation of, 170
    romanticizing of, 19
    at Singer Sewing Machine factory, 59
    and Social Security, 92–93
    stereotyping of, alleged feeblemindedness of, 29; in the media, 52. See also stereotypes
    unfavorably compared to Jews, 146
    violence against, 65, 74
    women, 80–81, 87, 149, 150, 171, 183; defeminization of, 80–81
    World War II veterans, 42–44
Afro-Latinos, 74
agribusiness, 72, 91, 92
    in Hawaii, 73, 194n.58
agricultural work See also labor; job segregation
    excluded from Social Security, 93
Aid to Families with Dependent Children (AFDC), 96
Allen, Theodore, 54, 192n.3
Almaguer, Tomas, 72, 194n.54
Amalgamated Clothing Workers Union (ACWU), 110, 111

ambivalence
  Jewish, 139, 160, 161, 162, 164, 172
  of modernity, 180–181
  whiteness as, 182–184, 185
American Federation of Labor, 63
anarchists, 198n.14
Anglos, white, in New Mexico, 151–152
anthropology, 82–83, 195n.13
anticommunism, 144, 192n.6
antimiscegenation laws, 68
anti-Semitism, 3
  American, early 20th-c., 2, 23, 112, 124, 156, 157
  and Jewish identity, 104–108
  post-World War II American, 36, 144
  Russian, and capitalism, 106
  19th-c. American, 55, 192n.1
Arab-Israeli War of 1967, 172
Arendt, Hannah, 143
artisans /craftsmen
  and autonomy, 63
  and skills, 56, 62–63
  and race, 63, 64–66
  and gender, 61–62
Aryans, exaltation of, 77, 182
Asch, Scholem, 127
Asians, 71
  intermarriage rates, 74
  men, stereotypes of, 84
  and segregated California schooling, 72
assembly lines, 62, 64
  paper, 195n.67
assimilation, 105, 140, 201n.36
  as American myth, 36, 178
  in Jewish literature, 201n.37
assimilationism, 108, 124, 150, 156–158, 173
Association of New England Deans, 31
athletes, affirmative-action college admissions for, 32

Baby and Child Care (Spock), 169
Baker, Ella, 19
Bakke decision, 155
balebostes, 117, 124
Banfield, Edward, 147, 200n.18
Barbie dolls, 143, 169, 171
Barker, Belle, 127
Barth, Belle, 127
Bates, Daisy, 19
Bauman, Zygmunt, 180

Beat generation, 170, 183
Bederman, Gail, 81
Bell, Daniel, 143, 148, 152
Bell Telephone, 65–66, 179
Bellow, Saul, 142
Benedict, Ruth, 202n.2
benefit organizations, 120, 136
Bennett, Lerone, 68
Benny, Jack, 141
Berg, Gertrude, 156
Berle, Milton, 141
Berman, Marshall, 48, 181
Beyond the Melting Pot (Glazer and Moynihan), 145–148
bicultural identity, 9
binary thinking, 180–181. *See also* race: black-white binary
blackface, 152
  white women in, 66
blackness, 68, 70, 192n.3
  appropriated by white feminism, 171
  constructed from whiteness, 183
  romanticized, 172, 183
  and servility, 193n.32
Blau, Zena Smith, 146, 162, 168
Blecher, Louise Rose, 166
block busting, 47
"blond people," 10–11, 17, 18, 23, 182
Bloom, Alexander, 143
Blythe, Myrna, 166
boarders, 96, 97, 100, 115, 116
boarding house system, at Lowell mills, 88
Bodnar, John, 59
Bonacich, Edna, 64, 66
Boyarin, Jonathan, 185
Brandeis University, 140–141
Brando, Marlon, 170
"Bread and Roses" strike, Lawrence, Mass., 94
Bread Givers (Yezierska), 124
Breadwinners' College, 110
Brecher, Jeremy, 55
Breines, Wini, 167, 170
Brighton Beach, New York, 35, 132
Brinton, Daniel, 28
Brodkin, Jack, 3, 4–5
Brodkin, Sylvia, 3
Brody, David, 57
Brody, Jennifer Devere, 80
Buhle, Paul, 173, 185, 198n.16

whiteness (*continued*)
  Jewish. *See* Jewishness: as whiteness
  and job segregation, 57. *See also* job
    segregation: racial
  of Mexicans, 190n.20, 194n.56
  and nonwhite Other, 152
  resistance to, 185–187
  and union membership, 63
  and ethnicity, 154
  and ethnoracial identity, 179–182
  of wage, 91
whites, native, of non-native parentage,
  60
wig, 115
Williams, Eric, 68, 69, 194n.47
Williams, Raymond, 181
Williams, Rose, 86
Winant, Howard, 76, 196n.35
womanhood
  of "blonde people," 23
  generational split in ideas of, 11–12
  grandmother's ideas of, 13–14
  Jewish, as political identity, 13
  racial nature of, 176
women, 137
  African American, 19, 80–81, 86,
    171, 183
  autonomous, 183
  and caring as part of work, 199n.49
  of color, as workers, 193n.16
  domesticity of, 16, 21, 78, 80, 86,
    94, 100
  education of, 107
  and evolution, 83
  family management by, 15–16, 125,
    137
  in garment industry, 61
  good *vs.* bad, 97, 100
  home-based enterprises of, 58
  Jewish. *See* Jewish women
  laid off after World War II, 43
  marriage to white men, 80, 91
  minority, replacing men on produc-
    tion line, 40
  political, 137
  racial ideals of, 101
  response to stereotyping, 165–168
  single Jewish, 115
  trophy wives, gentile, 162
  and true (white) motherhood, 77,
    78, 80, 81, 89

  and unions, 61, 129, 132, 193–
    194n.42
  and unwaged work, 116
  as wage earners, 90, 129, 137
  "welfare queen" stereotype, 97, 98,
    102
  white farm daughters, and the mills,
    88
  white femininity of, and work, 87–88
  white manliness and protection of,
    84
  white, nonwhite male lust for, 85
  in workforce, 76, 87–88
Women's Army and Air Force, veterans
  of, 42, 191n.33
Women's Trade Union League, 133
woodworking, 61
work. *See also* labor
  after marriage, Jewish women's, 124
  agricultural, 73, 92, 93, 194–
    195nn.58–59
  caring as part of, 199n.49
  clerical, 195n.67
  construction of, and craft autonomy,
    63
  degradation of. *See* job degradation
  domestic, 17–18, 55, 58, 85, 87, 88,
    93, 116
  and domesticity, 21
  foundry and blast furnace, 58, 59
  gang labor, 86, 100, 195n.59
  as love, 16
  in manufacturing, 56, 58, 59, 87
  in mining, 59
  professional, organization of,
    195n.67
  real if wage paid, 125
  in service industries, 59, 73
  in steel industry. *See* steel industry
  unwaged, women's, 116
Workers' Cooperative Colony, 111
Workers' University, 110
workfare, 99, 102
working class
  agrarian, 194–195n.59
  alienated from means of production,
    202n.8
  and company housing, discrimina-
    tion, 90
  ethnic heritages, 186–187
  hegemonic culture of, 120–123

ABOUT THE AUTHOR ☐

Karen Brodkin is a professor of anthropology and women's studies at the University of California, Los Angeles. She has written many scholarly articles and is author of *Caring by the Hour* and *Sisters and Wives,* and coeditor of *My Troubles Are Going to Have Trouble with Me.*